MODERN VALUE EDUCATION

MODERN
VALUE EDUCATION

[Useful for B.Ed. / M.Ed. Students and Other Competition Aspirants]

By
Mohammad Naqi

ANMOL PUBLICATIONS PVT. LTD.
NEW DELHI - 110 002 (INDIA)

ANMOL PUBLICATIONS PVT. LTD.
4374/4B, Ansari Road, Daryaganj
New Delhi - 110 002
Ph.: 23261597, 23278000
Visit us at: www.anmolpublications.com

Modern Value Education

First Published, 2005

ISBN 81-261-2176-9

PRINTED IN INDIA

Published by J.L. Kumar for Anmol Publications Pvt. Ltd., New Delhi - 110 002 and Printed at Mehra Offset Press, Delhi.

Contents

Preface

Education is a vast discipline and Teachers' Training is a vital part of it. The responsibilities of the educationists and educators are focused on the task of providing better training to the future teachers for their better learning and proper development. Needless to say that this responsibility can only be exercised, if the trainers are equipped with the required knowledge of the subject concerned. That's why it becomes essential for making adequate provisions for each course to the student-teachers or teacher trainees. The present series is designed for providing a solid workable base for all course-papers. It has been prepared strictly according to the syllabus of the B.Ed class, prescribed by the UGC for different universities.

No doubt, there are so many other books on the subject, available in the market, written by worthy authors. However, every writer has his or her own style and way of presentation. The present work also has its own features and characteristics.

In preparation of this series of texts, the editor had to refer to the works of other authors and information sources. The editor feels a deep sense of gratitude for incorporating their ideas in the text. Hopefully, this series would serve as a 'ready to refer' tool for all teachers, teacher-students and others.

—Editor

1

Introduction

One of the aims proposed by the Kothari Commission of 1966 is the "Cultivation of moral values." The National Policy on Education of 1966 states that education should promote the "Development of a sense of right and wrong."

The Ramamurthi Report of 1990 spells out Value Education to include a respect for all forms of life, establishment of linkage between school and community so as to stress the harmony and interdependence between human beings, as well as between nature and human beings.

The Concept

These may be considered by reference to the term "morality", which comes from the Latin word "moralis", which means, "customs, manners or patterns of behaviour that conform to the standards of the group." At every age the individual is judged by how he conforms to the standards of the group. These judgments lead society to label him as "moral" or "immoral", depending on the extent to which he conforms. The expectations of the social group are expressed according to rules, customs and traditions of the social group. If the individual obeys the rules and laws of society, he is considered "moral." Sometimes he may not agree with the rules and laws of the group, but he conforms to them, because that is the only course open to him. Some people choose to do the right thing, because it has the least harmful results to them. If the individual acts according to the laws and rules of society because of controls from within himself, then, he is known as a "morally mature" person. The "immoral" person is one who fails to conform to group expectations, as defined by rules, customs laws. He does so, not because of ignorance of these expectations, but rather because he feels no obligations to the group, neither does he approve of the standards of behaviour expected by the group.

Meaning of Values

There is no evidence to prove the prevailing belief that a person is born good or bad in the sense that he acts or does not act according to the rules of the society to which he belongs. On the other hand there is much psychological evidence that morality is learned. Like all learning morality can be controlled and directed so that the individual will obtain the ability to act according to the expectations of society. The process of becoming a moral person, begun early in childhood, continues through the years of adolescence. Moral behaviour is the true morality rather than from fear of outside. There are six phases in the development of moral behaviour in the young.

(1) Learning control impulses.

(2) Learning moral rules and principles.

(3) Learning motives and attitudes from people, specially the people who are nearest to the individual.

(4) Formation of an ideal self as early as five or six years of age, as a model to imitate. This ideal self may change as the individual grows older—but it is a valuable guide.

(5) Forming a scale of values.

(6) Ability to apply moral principle to new situations.

Attitudes and values which are learned at a young age often change as the adolescent meets people having different attitudes and values. Changes may occur, but the foundations laid earlier, generally persist. This indicates that the most important learning in the cultivation of morality is what is learnt in the home and the social group.

Very often the learning in the home emphasizes the negative aspect of moral behaviour. Thus the children learn what they should not do or how not to behave.

In ancient times, education was the business of the temple, maktabs or church, and moral education was imparted through direct teaching based on religious scriptures. Gradually, both in the west and in the east, religious education has given place to secularism in most state-supported schools, and moral education has been relegated to a very important position.

Moral education consists not only of teaching the individual the moral codes of the group, but also of instilling in him a high regard for these values, so that he may be willing to accept them and direct his behaviour in accordance with them.

It is necessary that the growing pupil learns to control his behaviour himself, so that external controls will not be needed. This will be of benefit to him and also good for the social group. As he becomes an adult he will be responsible for his own actions, and will no longer rely on parents and teachers to tell him what to do and what not to do. He should be able to decide for himself and act according to his own decision, not only for his own benefit but also for the benefit of others.

Meaning of Morality

There are certain moral concepts regarding which the pupil should form a definite attitude and have clear ideas about behaviour situations in relation to them. A few of these may be mentioned. Honesty as opposed to cheating, lying, stealing. Destructiveness, Drinking, Drug habits—Responsibility, Co-operation, Sex offences, Cruelty. The school should provide for situations in which these areas are discussed, and the pupils should express their opinions on them.

Moral Values through Discipline: The term "discipline" comes from the Latin word "disciplina" which means "teaching" or "institution". Today, as in the past the main purpose of discipline is to teach the individual a reasonable amount of social conformity. Besides this, discipline teaches the pupil that the world responds in an orderly way to his actions, and that certain behaviour of his will be praised and other behaviour will be punished. Discipline helps the pupil to gain self-control and to direct himself, so that he may be able to make wise decisions on his own responsibility.

Thus the modern concept of discipline puts an emphasis on learning what the social group expects, self-control, and self-directed activity, both of which lead to becoming sensitive regarding the welfare of others. Through discipline, an attempt is made to correct the behaviour which is opposed to the standards set by society. However, many homes and parents set entirely different standards of discipline and training. Some parents obtain obedience and conformity to their children in the home through beating, nagging, or using harsh language. These are negative attitudes, which cause much harm to the growing child.

Discipline and Philosophies in Education

(1) Naturalists, like Spencer, regard the problem of discipline from a hedonistic viewpoint. According to

them, conduct is based on impulse or instinct or on the experience acquired through the reaction of environment on the physical environment of the individual without the intervention of such factors as will and conscience—Discipline, therefore, should be based on the natural consequences of one's actions. Spencer would wish the child to suffer the unavoidable consequences or their evitable reactions of his conduct. These natural consequences constitute the punishment. Spencer believed that such punishment would be proportionate to the offence. The punishment is to be direct, unhesitating and unavoidable. He advised the parents to see that their children habitually experience the true consequences of their conduct. Rousseau said "Children should never receive punishment as such—it should always come in as the natural consequence of their fault".

Critics of this theory maintain that the consequences of one's action may not be proportionate to the fault. The consequences may do more harm to the offender than he deserves. Often nature does not distribute her penalties in a fair or just manner. Again discipline by natural consequences may be inadequate for moral training, since it is supported by no absolute notion of morality.

(2) The Idealists hold that a pupil cannot realize his spiritual possibilities without submitting himself to a process of discipline. Through order and training, the pupil can appreciate the great values of life and the inherent spiritual goals. As such, the teacher's guidance is necessary. The teacher is to provide the right type of environment consisting of rules and percepts. Free discipline as advocated by the naturalists, is likely to lead the child astray. The idealists are against free discipline as well as that discipline which amounts to external constraint and suppression of spontaneous activity.

(3) The Pragmatists disapprove of the individual or personal concept of discipline. They believe that discipline should be social, and that this is possible through the free, happy, purposive and co-operative activities of the school. The pursuit of such activities will lead to self-discipline which has also the sanction of the group. It will lead to moral and character training. The pragmatists agree in principle with "the discipline of natural consequences." They urge that the individual should learn the difference between right and wrong actions by experiencing for himself their direct results. Then emphasis is on experience in a social set up, however, they caution that natural consequences should not be allowed to get dangerous to the child.

(4) *The Behaviourists*—Their approach is essentially that of interest in the modification of behaviour. Little attention is devoted to the cause of the trouble underlying behaviour. The inner dynamics and motives underlying the phenomena of behaviour exhibited by the child, are given secondary impor-tance. The teacher is primarily concerned with behaviour rather than with its causes: Rewards of approval are given in the performance of a desired task. The approved behaviour is reinforced by some means. There is extinction of undesirable behaviour. Punishment is used in some cases as an intervention technique against undesirable behaviour. The advantages of behaviouristic techniques in modifying children's behaviour has been demonstrated in laboratory settings as well as in natural settings. This approach offers specific and practical methods for use in day to day classroom problems.

Liberal Attitude

Freedom can be discussed in various contexts, political, economic, social or educational. Politically, we speak of individual freedom or liberty as well as collective liberty. Democratic thinkers are concerned with individual liberty rather than with collective liberty, which is regarded as significant by socialistic thinkers. Smith, in The Democratic Way of Life defines liberty: "To do as one pleases, this alone is liberty". Harper's definition is: "Freedom is the condition of where the person may do whatever he desires, according to his wisdom and his conscience". Von Hayek's interpretation is more modest: "Freedom is a condition of men in which the coercion of some by others is reduced as much as possible."

In this chapter, we shall confine our discussion to freedom in its educational context, from the point of view of educational philosophy and practice. Freedom, from this angle, is a function of individuality. Brubacher's opinion is that if pupils have no individual differences, there would be no demand for freedom. Every one would act alike, no one would want to be different, or free. Children, we see around us are so different from one another in many ways, and yet in many ways they are also alike. Thus any system of education will have to deal with heterogeneity as well as homogeneity. The question arises—how much similarity? How much diversity is there in children? What characterizes the individual? Each individual is of necessity partially dependent upon others throughout his life. No one can stand completely apart from his fellows in his adulthood any more than he can in his infancy. Each one of us depends upon others for stimulation, companionship, and the satisfaction of needs. What is the extent of independence or freedom to be achieved and the equation between freedom and dependence? The relation between training in freedom and achievement of self-control is very complex and needs appraisal.

Traditional or Authoritarian School: These thinkers are also called repressionists by some, and they support the notion that the child should learn unquestioning obedience to the authority of the teacher and parent. The child, according to them, is immature, therefore, he does not know as much as the adult.

He therefore, needs to have an implicit trust in the authority of the teacher and the parent. This is the only path to acquiring true knowledge and sound morals. Brubacher commenting on this approach says that "Our forebears were so confident about the pedagogical principle that they claimed it was better for a child be right in chains than wrong in freedom." Severe repressionists insist on absolute quiet and order at all times. They use corporal punishment as their chief instrument for disciplining children. They believe that man is born with original sin in him. There are three characteristics of the authoritarian method: first, little or no attempt is made to explain to the child or adolescent, the reason for the rules he is expected to submit to; second, it is assumed that his breaking of rules is intentional and he is not given an opportunity to explain his reason for doing so; and third, punishment is almost always corporal and of a harsh and sometimes cruel nature. The authoritarian and traditional parent or teacher regards punishment as a reinforcer, consequently the harsher it is, the better it will teach the individual that he must conform to adult commands.

In homes and schools where authoritarian control is used, parents and teachers set high standards for their children and punish them when they tail to live up these standards.

Authoritarian parents and teachers commonly use one of two different typos of control: they either use threats that leave the youth insecure and afraid to engage in any new behaviour, or they set certain limits, at the same time encouraging the adolescent to engage in approved forms of activity. The second type of control produces better results.

The Limitations: Children and adolescent brought up by this method of control receive their morality ready-made from domineering parents. As a result, they are unprepared to meet any future problems that may arise. If they are given more freedom at any time, they are unprepared and unsure about how to handle it. They lack confidence in their ability to make decisions and to carry them out successfully.

Over strictness causes the young to believe that the whole world is hostile. He may, then, become submissive if he does not act in an openly rebellious manner. As a result he may, and often does, become a high achiever in whatever he undertakes. He is not troublesome to his parents, teachers or others in authority. He puts on an attitude of moral superiority, and shows a contempt for those who are troublesome. He is disliked by members of his peer group because of his arrogant attitude.

More often, however, over strictness which leads to feelings that the world is hostile, causes the young person to reject authority and to assert his independence. The stricter the parents, the stronger the revolt for freedom. Many adolescents drop out of school, or leave home when the authoritarian attitude of teachers or parents becomes unreasonable and unbearable.

Emancipationists Educators: They adopt a "laissez faire" attitude towards children. They consider individual differences among children as fixed features, they defend the freedom of the young to assert the unique differences which characterize his individuality. They would like teachers to keep out of nature's way so that it may fulfil itself according to its own inherent laws. The young child, according to them, neither needs nor does he like restraint. He cannot learn when and where there its too much of external control.

Rousseau, Montessori, A.S. Neill advocate this freedom in education. Rousseau's plea is "freedom" and "absence of restraint" for Emile. It is only in an atmosphere of freedom that Emile can develop his innate powers spontaneously. Rousseau believes that the child's nature is essentially good, and any intervention is, therefore, harmful.

The doctrine of liberty or freedom and the principle of individuality reflect the emancipationist's views of Montessori. She believes that freedom is the fundamental right of every human being, and therefore she advocates the spontaneous development of the child through liberty and the absence of restraint. The inborn powers of the child should not be marred or stifled through harsh controls.

A.S. Neill believes that discipline dogmatically imposed and punishments create fear, and fear arouses hostility. Sometimes this hostility is neither conscious nor overt, yet it can paralyse endeavour, effort and honest feelings. He also maintains that the extensive disciplining of children is harmful and thwarts psychic development. But freedom for A.S. Neill does not mean license, it is born out of mutual, individual respect.

Some educators do not base freedom on the inherent goodness of child nature, as Rousseau, Montessori or Neill do. They favour freedom because of the evil consequences of its opposite approach, namely authoritarianism or repression. Vesting absolute authority in the teacher may corrupt the teacher into becoming a tyrant and may make children either too rebellious or too submissive. Children who are rebellious may not recognise any authority while those who are submissive may suffer from a loss of initiative. According to Mortimer J. Adler, constant frustration of the pupil's assertiveness, may make him a bully among younger and weaker children, and encourage tyranny.

Impressionist School: In between the repressionists and the emancipationists, there are educators who may be described as impressionists. They are against punishment and traditional repression, and they believe that desirable modes of behaviour in children can be brought about through the teacher's personality and personal influence. They are in favour of using moral persuasion and of providing children with good conditions so that children may show respect and love rather than fear in the educative process. In the extreme form, the impressionists attitude implics that the teacher's will does prevail over that of the child. The teacher has in mind certain standards of behaviour which he tries to establish, not by appealing to fear, but by appealing to the submissive and imitative tendencies in the child. It is a kind of gentle force if not coercion.

Democratic Control: Family relationships and teacher-pupil relations under this form exist when rules are explained and warnings are given about the consequences of breaking rules. There is a training in self-control brought about. External control becomes internal control, and the pupil develops a super-ego because he becomes a conscious agent in the process of socialization. The individual achieves the super-ego as he thinks and passes on from the impulsive stage to the problem-solving stage, which has many alternatives to choose from and he makes his own choice.

Necessary Components

If the pupil is to learn what society expects of him and if he is to be encouraged to control his behaviour to conform to these expectations, discipline should include three important components: education in moral concepts; rewards for socially approved behaviour; punishment for doing wrong by intention. We should not neglect these if we wish the student to attain the desired objective of self-controlled and self-directed behaviour.

Education in Moral Concepts: Many grown-up people, parents and teachers assume that when a child grows up, he has learnt what is right or wrong, and that no further training is needed. This is incorrect. As the child becomes an adolescent, his social horizons widen, and boys as well as girls should realize what boundaries society places on them. They should know what actions society will tolerate under any new situations. Rules and laws have the function of teaching the individual what these boundaries are, so that he may act in a desirable manner.

The adolescent should know what is expected of him. For example, that he is not permitted to smoke or drink, he should be home by ten o'clock at night, that he is to be polite and considerate to his elders and so on. While he may not entirely agree with these rules and laws and may attempt to break them, he still knows that he must face the consequences if he does. In general, the learning of moral consequences should be completed or almost so, before the adolescent becomes an adult of legal age. After that he will be responsible for his own actions without the supervision of his parents and teachers.

Reward for Socially Approved Behaviour: There are two purposes of giving rewards: firstly, rewards have an educational value, they tell the adolescent that his behaviour is socially approved, and, therefore it is "good" behaviour; secondly, they are ego supporting, and this stimulates and encourages him, so that he can continue to act in that way. Many adults do not approve of giving rewards to adolescents, they consider that they will make an adolescent conceited, he will not have any motivation to do what is expected of him. Some adults say that it is better to use threats of punishment to the adolescent, for wrong doing, rather than to reward him for good behaviour.

However, there is much evidence to show that rewards do not have bad effects; on the contrary, they are strong motivating forces to encourage the growing individual to act according to society's expectations.

Material rewards are always acceptable to children and adolescents, provided these articles have prestige in the opinion of the peer group and can be shown off to friends, for example, clothes, toys, money, a transistor radio, a watch, a book. However, for a child or an adolescent the highest reward is praise and encouragement. Too often, parents and teachers criticise a child for wrong-doing, but never praise him for doing the right thing. A word of praise is a great relief from constant criticism. The pupil realizes that his action was commendable and that it was worthy of praise. However, in order that praise may be a powerful instrument in discipline, it should be used wisely, and not only when the parent or teacher is in a good mood. The strength and the degree of praise should be in proportion to the goodness of the action performed. Lavish praise has no educational value, because the child has no way of judging the relative goodness of the action.

Punishment for Intentional Wrongdoing: Like rewards, punishment is said to serve two major functions in discipline. First, it deters the repetition of socially undesirable acts, and second, it shows the adolescent what the social group considers wrong. Punishment can be physical or corporal or it can be for form of detention, extra assignments, isolation, humiliation, suspension from school, academic failure, or giving students a "talking to" in private. Many teachers are sceptical whether punishment should be resorted to or not. They are also sceptical of the results that are achieved. On the whole, teachers in many countries in the world, have become generally more permissive than they were a generation ago. Psychological experiments on learning in children have demonstrated that some punishment may be unavoidable or may be useful. For example, learning experiments have shown that recognition learning, specially in pre-school age children is facilitated the correct ones. Rewarding or positive reinforcement has been found more effective than punishment of wrong responses.

From the philosophical point of view, punishment has been justified on the basis of the retribution or retaliation theory. According to this theory, punishment is a sort of revenge. Again, some justify punishment on the grounds that it protects society by making an example of the offender, in other words, it acts as a deterrent. In the classroom, antisocial behaviour is punished in order to protect other students.

A third theory of punishment which justifies its use or non-use, is called educative. According to this theory, only that punishment should be administered which can re-educate the offender. The offender, through the punishment, realizes what he has done, how others see his offence, and how he can improve his behaviour. Often, the child is punished by an adult who is angry by what the child has done. The severity of punishment, under such circumstances, reflects the adult's anger more than the seriousness of the misbehaviour. If punishment is to serve the purpose of aiding in self-control and in being educative, it should have the following characteristics:

(1) It should be related in some form to the misbehaviour.

(2) It should be certain and consistent.

(3) It must be fair and just.

(4) It should be impersonal.

(5) It should be constructive and conducive to better self-control.

(6) Punishment should be withheld until the child's motive for the offence is understood.

(7) The punishment should not arouse fear in the child's mind.

(8) It should not involve the assignment of extra work that is unrelated to the act for which the offender is being punished.

Practical Aspects

Discipline is necessary in the classroom in order to carry on instruction. Law and order are as necessary in the classroom as they are essential for other pursuits in life. Before however, we can determine the methods of obtaining discipline in the classroom, we must discover some of the reasons for indiscipline among children in the classroom.

Group Psychological Factors: These are the result of an interaction of individual disturbances. The reasons are:

Dissatisfaction in the Work Process—The curricula and teaching approaches are inconsistent with the child's needs. The assignments are too easy or too difficult, the verbal instruction is too abstract or too distant for the child's social background.

Emotional Unrest in Interpersonal Relations—There is conflict between colleagues, or among friends, or over the distribution of roles.

Disturbances in the Group Climate—For example, if there is a punitive and harsh atmosphere in the classroom, or if the atmosphere is characterized by fear, or vicious competition.

Composition of the Group—If the classroom group consists of a very heterogenous group of pupils, some very bright and some very slow, or of very different backgrounds, and there is no homogeneity among them in any way, this may initially cause problems of discipline. But gradually as homogeneity in certain respects is achieved, and some common relationship established among the pupils, these problems tend to disappear, under a capable teacher.

Summary: From the preceding discussion we may briefly review how discipline resulting in law and order may be maintained in the school and classroom.

Discipline should be a condition preceding instruction. Let there be some codes of behaviour established which the pupil is expected to follow in the classroom, for learning to take place.

Discipline should be made possible through interesting instruction. Classroom teaching and learning should be so appealing and engrossing to the child that his curiosity and eagerness are harnessed, and he gets completely involved in the material of learning. All curricular activity should be meaningful and significant for the child and his needs, as well as for the adolescent, and his interests. Discipline will follow interest and involvement in the learning process: the pupils will cooperate wholeheartedly without creating any behaviour problems.

Discipline can be maintained if the centre of authority is shifted from the teacher to the class as a whole. The rule by one may be replaced by that of the many. Let the teacher and pupils engage themselves in joint activities. Each pupil will, in this way, exercise moral compulsion on every other and in turn will submit to moral compulsion from others. This democratic type of discipline has a very educative value. The teacher and pupils share in planning and purposing classroom activities, thus there is very little command or compulsion, both parties cooperate, and discipline is enforced of itself in a constructive atmosphere. There is self-control and self-government in place of external control or command, and is the highest form of discipline for the growing pupil.

QUESTIONS

1. Explain the word "discipline". Compare and contrast views of the naturalists, idealists, pragmatists and behaviourists on discipline.

2. Discuss Huxley's view that "repression is out of line with democratic ideals." Describe instances of repression that you may have encountered in schools or homes.

3. What do you understand by "freedom" in education? Is there any place for freedom in discipline.

4. Discuss various views on punishment. Can punishment have any educative value?

5. "A continual resort to corporal punishment is a degradation of teacher and taught alike." Explain what you, think it implies in this statement. What are your views on physical punishment?

6. As a teacher how would you obtain discipline in the classroom? Give some suggestions.

7. How would you give a training in democracy to pupils at school through discipline?

8. How is discipline a means of inculcating moral values and vice versa?

9. Show how you would relate discipline to citizenship?

10. Describe methods of introducing moral concepts to children.

11. Write an essay on "Moral Values in the Indian School Curriculum."

2

Moral Education

An important feature of value-education is the ability of the educator and the educatiors skill to to discriminate between right and wrong. What may be nectar for one may be poison for another. We may be clearing forests to build human habitats, which is a laudable objective, but in the process we may be depriving animals of their natural shelter and food and humanity of many environmental benefits. In many Indian communities, a wedlock between a girl and a boy may not be permissible unless the two are removed from each other by a gap of some generations; whereas among some, marriage between cousins may be auspicious. A debate on the subject can go ad infinitum without coming to any precise conculusion; but as pointed out earlier every community has its own written as well as unwritten behavioural norms which it expects its members to observe.

Practical Aspects

In order to decide if the educational institutions should play some part in the dissemination of these accepted norms, the following statement was included in the questionnaire for students:

"Value-education i.e, education regarding discrimination between what is right or wrong, should be impacted in schools and colleges." (S-1)

The reaction of the five categories of students, constituting the total student-population of 267 was as follows:

S.No.	*Category Agreeing*	*Number Undecided*	*Number Disagreed*	*Number persons who expressed no opinion*
(1)	Total no. of student respondents (267)	254 (95.2)	6 (2.2)	61 (2.2)
(2)	School students (Male) (70)	68 (97.2)	1 (1.4)	1 (1.4)
(3)	School Students (Female)	84 (97.6)	1 (1.2)	(86) (1.2)
(4)	College Students (M)* (34)	27 (79.6)	4 (11.8)	3 (8.8)
(5)	African College students (M)* studying in the Delhi Colleges. (7)	7 (100)	3 —	4 —
(6)	Indian College students (F)* (70)	68 (97.2)	— —	11 (1.4)

* (i) Abbreviations M and F stand for Male and Female respectively throughout this work.

* (ii) The following norms has been adopted in this study for categorisation of scores:

Below 26% Poor — 50% Average — 51-74% Above Average

26-49% Below Average — Above 74% High

It is thus observed that every category of students expressed high degree of agreement for making a provision of value education in the educational institutions. Speaking in comparative terms, more of college students (males) expressed their disagreement with the statement or were undecided in this regard.

Therefore, if one were to work for a programme of moral or value-education in our educational institutions, one is likely to come across a receptive rather than an indifferent audience, provided the programme is given due importance in the curricula and the teacher imparting value-education is capable of doing justice to the job.

The following news-item appearing in one of the national dailies in India shows that there is a world-wide demand for imparting moral education to the students.

"The (U.K.) Government is to direct its latest attack on violence, disorder and crime at children as young as seven". In a Cabinet meeting it was felt that 'the roots of criminality' must be tackled early and that "moral dimension will be added to the new national curriculm".

Sometime earlier to it in the economic summit in Toronto (Canada), Mrs. Thatcher, the British Prime Minister had raised her concern on the behavioural problems of the young people. She said that although western nations had gone a long way to bring about a technological change, they had to do much in terms of training people to have respect for the law. The Government (of U.K.) had proposed preparing experimental lessons for the youth with this objective in view. For example, in such lessons the school going youth may be told about a young man who drinks, steals a car, becomes a hit-and-run driver and ultimately one day lands in the custody of the police. The lesson may depict the consequence (jail etc.) to be faced by the delinquent youth, misery of the family whose members had been hit by this criminal and also the misery of the criminal's own family because of his unlawful act. For this purpose parents, teachers and media have to unite. Teachers cannot provide lessons which are the responsibility of the parents.

Resembling the above statement (S-1) in the questionnaire for students, there was a statement (G-13) in the questionnaire for the general public. The statement was as follows:

" Moral education i.e., education regarding what is right or wrong should be imparted

a) In schools

b) In colleges

c) Through mass media such as radio, TV, newspapers etc. (G-13)

Use of Modern Means

Number of persons who agreed, disagreed with the above , three parts of the statement or were Un-decided in this regard was as follows:

S.No.	*Category*	*No. Agreeing*	*No. Un-decided*	*No. Dis-agreeing*	*No. of persons who expressed no opinion*
(a) In schools	Total no. of respondents (881)	717 (81.6)	136 (15.5)	16 (1.8)	10 (1.1)
(b) In colleges	Total no. of respondents (881)	510 (57.9)	315 (35.8)	43 (4.9)	13 (1.4)
(c) Through mass media	-do-	655 (74.4)	194 (22)	16 (18)	16 (1.8)

The above statistics show that the elements of disagreement and indecision are comparatively higher in the case of part (b) of the statement. Also the largest number of the respondents appeared to be of the opinion that moral education should be imparted in schools.

The analysis in the case of the statement 13(a) indicates that in comparison to the remaining age-groups of the respondents, those between 18-25 years of age expressed lesser degree of agreement (of 71.2%) with this statement. The remaining 28.8% of the respondents in this group were undecided.

Analysis of the reactions of the respondents on the basis of their educational qualifications revealed that quite a large number of respondents in every group, sub-group seemed to be undecided on the issue whether moral education programme should be introduced at the college stage. The reasons for this must be as follows:

(a) Higher education is a stage of specialisation in one or the other discipline, therefore general education in morals was not supported by any sub-group as was done in the case of the school stage.

(b) The college students are mature enough to decide for themselves as to what is right and what is wrong.

It would be interesting here to study the attitude of male and female college teachers to the same statement *i.e.* 13(b).

S.No.	*Category of college teachers*	*Number Agreeing*	*Number Undecided*	*Number Disagreed*	*Number of persons who did not express any opinion*
1.	Female (39)	25 (64,1)	11 (28.2)	2 (5.1)	1 (2.6)
2.	Male (50)	37 (74)	10 (20)	1 (2)	2 (4)

Parts (a), (b) and (c) of the statement were further analysed with reference to age, educational qualifications and income of the respondents. Some of the results obtained were as follows:

Analysis with Reference to Ages of the Respondents

S. No.	*Category of Respondents*	*No. Agreeing*	*No. Undecided*	*No. Disagreeing*	*No. of Persons who expressed no opinion*
1.	Below 18 years (11)	9 (81.9)	2 (18.2)	—	—
2.	18-25 years (52)	37 (71.2)	15 (28.8)	— —	— —
3.	25-40 years (234)	191 (81.6)	38 (16.2)	2 (0.9)	3 (1.3)
4.	Above 40 years (574)	474 (82.6)	79 (13.8)	14 (2.4)	7 (1.2)
5.	Those who did not indicate their ages (10)	8 (80)	2 (20)	—	—

Analysis with Reference to Educational Qualifications of the Respondents

S.No.	*Category of Respondents*	*Number Agreeing*	*Number Undecided*	*Number Disagreeing*	*Number of persons who expressed no opinion*
(1)	Below High school	6	7	2	—
	(15)	(40)	(46.7)	(13.3)	—
(2)	High school or equivalent	66	50	5	2
	(123)	(53.7)	(40.6)	(4.1)	(1.6)
(3)	B.A. or equivalent	157	96	13	1
	(267)	(58.8)	(35.9)	(4.9)	(0.4)
(4)	M.A. or above or equivalent	274	157	23	10
	(464)	(59.0)	(33.8)	(5)	(2.2)
(5)	Those who did not indicate their educational qualifications	7	5	—	—
	(12)	(58.3)	(41.7)	—	

Analysis with Reference to Monthly Income of the Respondents

S.No.	*Category of Respondents*	*Number Agreeing*	*Number Undecided*	*Number Disagreeing*	*Number of persons who expressed no opinion*
(1)	Below Rs. 1000	16	11	-	1
	(28)	(57.1)	(39.3)	-	(3.6)
(2)	Rs.1000-1999	68	27	1	2
	(98)	(69.4)	(27.5)	(1)	(2)
(3)	Rs. 2000-3999	246	75	10	3
	(334)	(73.6)	(22.5)	(3)	(0.9)
(4)	Rs. 4000 or above	318	74	5	10
	(407)	(78.1)	(18.2)	(1.2)	(2.5)
(5)	Those who did not	7	7	—	—
	indicate their income	7	7		
	(14)	(50)	(50)	—	—

The degree of support expressed in case of statement that moral education should be imparted in colleges is considerably more both by female and male college-teachers than the overall support given by the general group. College students themselves (of both sexes) also expressed considerable support to the idea of providing moral education in our educational institutions while reacting to statement S-1.

In the case of statement 13(c), maximum agreement was expressed by the income-group having a monthly income of Rs. 4000 and above. Starting with this, as we come to the sub-groups with lower monthly incomes, the degree of agreement to this statement successively decreases. May be that the people with higher incomes have a better appreciation of the role of mass-media on account of their greater exposure to these media.

Behaviour : Conveying Element

It would be desirable to briefly mention here some basic factors which influence our thought and behaviour pattern.

Samskarns or Natural Tendencies: Every person is born with certain propensities, likes and dislikes, potentialities-inherited or otherwise. The ancient thinkers of India called them samskaras or impressions accumulated by an individual spirit in its previous births. All this is called individual's inherent nature which differs from person to person. The nature of an individual plays an important role in determining his or her behaviour.

Education and Environment: It may be difficult to say if an individual's nature or his nurture plays a greater role in shaping the individual's conduct; but it goes without saying that nurture in the form of education and environmental influences have a significant impact in shaping the character of a person.

Free Will: Every individual is endowed with a 'free-will'. By exercising his free-will an individual becomes the architect of his own destiny.

Every individual, when he enters this world, brings with him a set of samskaras—impressions, tendencies, and attitudes. As he goes through his life, by the process of education and interaction with various situations in the social milieu, he acquires new samskaras and his old samaskaras get modified. With the judicious application of one's free-will, every individual raises the behavioural edifice of one's life and becomes the architect of his own future.

Past Experience

History of education reveals that in ancient times, say upto the 6th century A.D., many countries laid considerable emphasis on character-training of the young children. In India, religion emphasised ethical conduct, art, literature, jurisprudence, etc. In Rome, cultivating respect for traditions, austerity and frugality was an important function of education. Character-training was a salient feature of the Mauryan education. Chinese regarded moulding of character a prime concern of education. Zoroastrians, in ancient Persia, attached considerable importance to training the young in practices of good thoughts, good words and good actions. Byzantine system of education went even to the extent of mostly confining itself to religious instruction to students and encouraging among them ascetic practices and thus developing in them an attitude of indifference towards secular subjects. Athens, the cultural centre of ancient Greece, was known for the stress it laid on moral training of the youth and cultivating good conduct and grace in them. Sparta in Greece, besides training the youth (from the age of seven) in physical culture, taught them the art of lying and theft etc., as these were some of the values with the Spartans. Spartan morality, however, demanded that this kind of Machiavallianism was to be practised only while dealing with the foreigners.

During the medieval India, when there was Islamic rule in the country, maktabs, i.e. institutions of early education taught the students to say their daily prayers as indicated in the Holy Quran. In the institutions of higher learning i.e. madrassas, Hadit was taught. A number of denominational schools in India still teach students religious practices of their respective faiths. Bible discourse is still compulsory in the schools of England. In Russia after the great Revolution character was attempted to be moulded through the teachings of communism:

Role of Institutions

Educational institutions constitute the biggest organised sector for imparting various kinds of training, including moral training, to the growing youths. As regards the stage at which moral education programme should begin in the educational institutions, Meriel Downey says :

"It (moral development) is an area to which no pupil owes 'cold', since moral learning, the development of values and attitudes begins at birth and is fed from many sources. For this reason, it is not something that can be delayed, like, say, the learning of Latin, until we feel that pupils have readied an appropriate stage of mental development to cope with the demands which it will make upon their intellectual abilities".

A number of people are of the view that moral education, in the school system, should begin from the pre-primary stage so that students develop proper samskaras and attitudes from the early years of their lives.

It would be relevant to study the views of various commissions and committees on the subject of moral education.

Pre-independence Period

(i) The Education Commission of 1882 had recommended that, based upon the fundamental principles of natural religion, an attempt be made to prepare a text book on moral education. This book should be taught in all Government and non-Government colleges. The principal or one of the professors in each Government and aided colleges should deliver a series of lectures to all the classes on the duties of a man and a citizen.

The Government, however, rejected the proposal by its Resolution No.10/309 of October 2, 1884.

(ii) Thereafter a significant recommendation in this regard was made in the Memorandum of the Post-War Educational Development (1944). The recommen-dation runs as follows:

"Religion in the widest sense, should inspire all education and that a curriculum devoid of an ethical basis will prove barren in the end".

(iii) The Religious Education Committee of the Central Advisory Board of Education (CABE) recommended in 1945, "Spiritual and moral teachings common to all religions should be an integral part of the curriculum and provision/facilities for instructions therein should be the responsibility of the State."

Post-independence Period

(i) The 42nd Constitutional Amendment of 1976, inserted as Article 51A in Part IVA of the Indian Constitution lays down ten Fundamental Duties (or values) for each citizen. This amendment was inspired by the idea of arresting the falling moral standards in the country and that of ensuring higher level of moral conduct from the citizens.

(ii) The University Education Commission (1948-49) recommended that:"unless morality is taken in a larger sense, it is not enough. If we exclude spiritual training in our institutions we would be untrue to our whole historical development".

(iii) The Secondary Education Commission (1952-53) asserted that 'religious and moral instruction played an important role in the growth of individual's character.

(iv) Sri Prakasha Committee on Religious and Moral Instruction (1959) held the view that :

"Many ills that our world of education and our society as a whole is suffering from, resulting in widespread disturbance and dislocation of life, are mainly due to gradual disappearance of the hold of basic principles of religion on the hearts of the people— The only cure, it seems to us, is in deliberate inculcation of moral and spiritual values from the earliest years of our lives."

(v) The subject was also dealt with by the Indian Education Commission (1964-66), which recommended that:

"Conscious and organised attempts be made for imparting education in social, moral and spiritual values with the help, wherever possible, of ethical teachings of great religions".

(vi) Challenge of Education (1985), published by the Union Ministry of Education, summed up the position in this regard as follows:

"Thoughtful people in all walks of life are greatly disturbed by a progressive erosion of values and the resultant pollution of public life. The fact that this crisis of values is as pervasive in schools, colleges and universities, amongst teachers as well as students as in other walks of life, is seen as a highly dangerous development. It is, therefore, being urged that the process of education should be reoriented and young people should be made to realise that exploitation, insecurity and violence cannot be contained nor can an organised society be sustained without adhering to and enforcing some norms of social, political and economic behaviour. Learning from past experience, it is expected that a coherent and an operationally viable value-system would be inculcated through educational process, based upon rational and scientific and moral approach to life".

(vii) The Document on Approach to the Seventh Five Year Plan (1985-90) published in July 1984, states, " Value-orientation in education should constitute a special thrust in the Seventh Plan, teacher-education in particular-being reoriented for this purpose".

Various Approaches

(1) At the boy-hood stage, individual's physical propensities have a full play; during manhood and old-age intellectual and spiritual values start dominating the corporeal values. Therefore, while imparting moral education, educators must keep this fact in view and no attempt be made to burden the students with intellectual exercises in moral education during early years of their lives.

(2) Value-perspective may be two-dimensional or three dimensional. A two-dimensional view is caring for oneself as well as forthe other because both need each other and any transgression of values may harm both sides. USA and USSR had been very unfriendly till the eighties of this century; but both have respected each other's sovereignty because either of these countries could destroy the other with the pile of destructive weapons it possessed. This kind of need and reciprocity-based value-system would be followed by many people. When the value system is ideal-based as well, it becomes a three-dimensional value system. The three dimensional value-system can be followed over a long period of time by a few persons only.

(3) The Education Commission (1964-66) suggested that social, moral and spiritual values should be imparted both through indirect and direct methods. The Commission remarked, "We attach great importance to the role of indirect influence in building up good character. The school atmosphere, the personality and behaviour of the teachers, the facilities provided in the

school, will have a large say in developing a sense of values. We would like to emphasise that the consciousness of values must permeate the whole curriculm and programme of activities in the school. It is not only the teachers incharge of moral instruction who are responsible for building character. Every teacher, whatever be the subject he teaches, must necessarily accept this responsibility.—The school assembly, the curricular and co-curricular activities, the celebration of religious festivals of all religions, work-experience, team games and sports,, subject clubs, social service programmes—all these can help in inculcating the values of cooperation and mutual regard, honesty and integrity, discipline and social responsibility. These values have a special significance in Indian society today, when young men and women are passing through a crisis of character,"

In regard to direct moral instruction, agreeing with the recommendations of the Sri Prakasha Committee, the Commission stated that " one or two periods a week should be set aside in the school time-table for instruction in moral and spiritual values".

At the early school-stages, moral instruction can be imparted through parables or stones which have an appeal to the emotions of the children. At the secondary stage, there can be discussions between the teacher and the taught on the values to be imparted, thus resorting to an intellectual approach to the subject. According to V.K.R.V. Rao, one time Union Education Minister, "Ethics should be taught only through parables, stories, religion, and sayings of great people and their lives. Right from the start, children should be taught about the founders of great religions of India. Films should be shown to them depicting temples, mosques, gurudwaras etc."

(4) In ancient times, some states imparted moral education through edicts or some other forms of permanent writings. For example, the Romans expected the children to learn by heart the Twelve Tables of laws. The Japanese

employed the imperial edicts for this purpose. One example of the edict is given below.

"Our imperial ancestors have founded our Empire on a basis broad and everlasting and have deeply and firmly implanted virtue; our subjects, ever united in loyalty and filial piety, have from generation to generation illustrated the beauty thereof. This is the glory and the fundamental character of our Empire, and herein also lies the source of our education. Ye, our subjects, be filial to your parents, affectionate to your brothers and sisters; as husbands and wives be harmonious; as friends true; bear yourselves in modesty and moderation; extend your benevolence to all; pursue learning and cultivate arts, and thereby develop intellectual faculties and perfect moral powers; furthermore, advance public good and promote common interests; always respect the Constitution and observe the laws; should emergency arise, offer yourselves courageously to the state; and thus guard and maintain the prosperity of our imperial throne. So shall ye not only be our good and faithful subjects, but render illustrious the best traditions of your forefathers."

(5) In the teaching of moral practices, both theory and practice are of equal significance, because cognition, feelings and action are interdependent. The quality and depth of information and its sources-all play an important role in influencing our attitudes. Without a proper conceptual background, all action may be reduced to a blind ritual only. However, translation of information into proper action is of great importance, because simple parroting of Ten Commandments cannot make a Moses of an individual. Emphasising the superiority of example over precept, N.K. Dutt says:

"Albert Camus once experimented with inculcation of moral values through teaching. He encouraged students to write an essay on 'Truthfulness'. The best essay was written by the biggest liar of the class. He further said that if the purpose of education is merely to impart information and skills, then thanks to the present day teaching technology, perhaps an idiot can teach another idiot calculus."

The same remarks apply to speech-making also. A person may play a big hoax on the people by play of words and thus claim to be a big preacher of values whereas his own actions may be just the opposite of what he might say.

N.K. Dutt adds that according to Mao-Tse-Tung, "The thoughts of intellectuals are like arrows in a quiver which scratch the back but never fly".

(6) Value orientation is a continuous process. As man evolves intellectually and otherwise, his expectations also get modified. This is true in regard to values also. Society's expectations rise in respect of moral values also, therefore imparting of value-education and adjustment to values should be a continuous process.

Apart from the educational institutions mass media, i.e. media which has the potential to transmit messages to the masses at large, can play a fareaching role in any scheme of imparting value education-formal, nonformal or informal. Some of these media are privately owned and independent of the government whereas others are directly under the government machinery. Although some government departments bring out various kinds of journals, etc., but by and large press and publications in India are free of government control. Some of the mass media under the Union Government are television, radio, Department of Field Publicity, Publication Division, Department of Advertising and Visual Publicity and Song and Drama Division. Though there is a Films Division under the Union Ministry of Information and Broadcasting, it produces documentaries only. Feature-films production is totally in the private sector and this medium is very powerful in influencing the attitudes of the people.

One may, of course, argue that in India mass-media has not been the mass media in the real sense—some of the reasons for this being as follows:

According to 1981 census, India had nearly 140 million families and only 25 million radios and one million TV sets. If TV sets are possessed by the same 25 million who own the radio sets, the reach of these two media is only to 17.9 per cent population and if the TV sets are considered to have been owned by some who own the radio sets and some who do not own the radio set, even then the reach of these two media is to a maximum population of 18.6 per cent of the country's population.-the total circulation of newspapers and journals in India is around ten million which comes to less than 1.5 for every hundred people. As nearly half the population in the country is still illiterate, the newspapers and journals have a limited impact on the education of the masses. One may agree that the mass media are not able to reach the vast masses of India inhabiting the length and breadth of the country, yet they have, admittedly a great potential of wielding a considerable influence on human minds, therefore these media can be gainfully employed in the moral education programme.

It is, thus, observed that there is a general consensus that moral education should be imparted in our educational institutions as well as through the mass-media. Various commissions and committees on education have been stressing the need for social, moral and spiritual education programme being introduced in our educational institutions. Any programme of value-education must take into account the age and other factors of the target population. The programme, in order to be useful, should lay equal emphasis on precept and practice. The character of the teacher or any other person imparting moral education is of greater significance than his precepts as actions always speak louder than the words and the totality of the educator's personality is far more important than his utterances, howsoever loud and pious these might be. Mass media, which have a deep and powerful influence on human minds, should also devise a well-planned programme in respect of moral education and thus contribute to resolving the present crisis of character in the society.

3

Significant Features

Axiology the third branch of philosophy deals with values. Ethics (moral behaviour) and aesthetics (appreciation of beauty) are two sub-branches of axiology in philosophy. Philosophy, education and values are intimately related to the branches of knowledge. Further, education and values seem to be the reciprocal planes of each other. To be more specific and precise in this regard, it is said that "Education is Value Enterprise." Since education is a means of value development, the end product is development of moral character, personality and good human being. The whole thrust of education is the development of values in human behaviour.

Before discussing the conceptual framework of values and value oriented education from philosophical stand point, it will be pertinent to list certain questions. It will help to have a vivid understanding about values.

(i) What is the concept of value?

(ii) What is value system?

(iii) Can values be taught?

(iv) Are values contextual in nature?

(v) Are values relative or absolute?

(vi) What is the conceptual framework of values and value education?

(vii) What are the methods for inculcating values?

(viii) In what manner values can be integrated in curriculum at different stages of education?

Various Orientations

Value has been defined in diverse ways. The philosopher, the educationist, the administrator, the psychologist, the sociologist all have different perspective while explaining a value. It depends upon one's mindset or orientation as per the discipline, one has studied. Different view points have been expressed with regard to concept of a value :

(i) According to N.T. Ram, "A value is what is desired or what is sought. Values may be operationally, conceived as those guiding principles of life which are conducive to one's physical and mental health as well as to social welfare and adjustment and which are in tune with one's culture."

(ii) According to Clyde Kluckhohn, "value is a conception, explicit or implicit, distinctive of an individual or characteristic of group, of the desirable which influences the selection from available means and ends."

(iii) R.K. Mukherjee says, "values are socially approved drives and goals that are internalised through the process of conditioning, learning or socialization and that becomes subjective preferences, standards and aspirations."

(iv) Allport observes, "The term value means the relative prominence of the subject's interest or the dominant interest in personality."

(v) D.H. Parker says, "values belong wholly to the inner world of mind. The satisfaction of desire is the real value, the thing that serves is only an instrument. A value is always an experience never a thing or an object."

(vi) Edger Brighman observes, "In the most elementary sense, value means whatever is actually liked, prized, esteemed, desired, approved or enjoyed at any time. It is the actual experience of enjoying a desired object or activity."

(vii) Dr. Prem Kripal says, "values may be defined as—

— What we believe-professed values

— What we practice—operational value and

— What we learn from experience in order to adopt and renew traditions received from the past traditional values."

Important Elements

(i) A value has its worth and importance.

(ii) A value is subject, community and national oriented.

(iii) Value is the result of interaction between personal and impersonal elements.

(iv) Value is means as well as an end.

(v) Value is a desired preference.

(vi) Value is a cherished idea.

(vii) Value is a strong belief put to action.

(viii) Value is an internalised idea or thought.

(ix) Value gives direction to human action.

(x) Value is an abstract idea which is cherished, expressed, demonstrated in behaviour and affirmed publicly.

Fundamental Aspects

A value has three pronged structure which covers all the possible aspects/dimensions of human personality.

— *Cognitive Aspect (Thought)*—A value is an idea abstract in nature. More is the idea clear, strong will be the value. Therefore it is to be assumed that a value is related to mental activity and cognitive development about an idea, thought or an object.

— *Affective Aspect (Emotion/Feeling)*—A value possesses a strong emotional bound with idea, thought or material object. Happy association is the secret of a value. Feelings, sentiments and attitudes are involved in one's value structure. In fact, values are the cherished goals, preferences or desired things. Involvement of emotion and feeling is the secret for one's action which is pleasure giving in the long run.

— *Cognitive/Psychomotor Aspect (Action/Behaviour)*—A value results into an action or behaviour. This aspect is the final stage or culmination of a value. The first two aspects i.e. cognitive (idea) and affective (emotion/ feeling) pave the way for action. Therefore 'action' is the acidic test of one's value in life.

The Discipline

Values exist or function in a system. A system is a network of certain components. In this regard, a value system is a collection of certain values or a set of values which functions as a significant or meaningful whole to realise a goal. Therefore, existence of values may be described as a system of personality traits which are in harmony with the inner nature of an individual and which are also in harmony with the values approved by the society.

The process of valuing is what we go through when we make judgement about things, events and people that we encounter in our day to day life.

Values and process of valuing go hand in hand. One supports the other. Process of valuing is determined by one's internal make up of the mind and state of body and the external factors which occur in natural setting. The end product of the process is culmination of a value or new form of a value.

A value system is accepted as a system which is always in the process of change with regard to its stability and change in values. Some values can be more or less fixed whereas some values may be under the process of change in a value system.

Every human being forms his own value system having 5/6 values in which one/two values work as master values which determine his total behaviour towards others. It will be very interesting and contributive in one's life one may understand one's value system and master value(s).

The Categorisation

Values are of various shades and variety. They are classified differently depending upon the criteria fixed for these. Some of the workable classifications have been made by some thinkers and institutions. They are as under:

(a) Walter G. Everelt in his book 'Moral Values' classifies human values in the following groups:

(i) *Economic Values*—These are indicated by market price. Economic values are instrumental (means) to realise other values.

(ii) *Bodily Values*—These values relate to the health efficiency and beauty of the body and happiness in physical life.

(iii) *Recreational Values*—These values are related to play, leisure and creative activities which enrich life and bring happiness.

(iv) *Values of Association*—These values are related to human relations. They include numerous forms of human associations such as family life, friendship and community.

(v) *Character Values*—Here we may include personal values, social virtues including justice, truthfulness, self-control, benevolence, etc.

(vi) *Aesthetic Values*—Beauty of nature, works of art, manners, etiquettes are the aesthetic values.

(vii) *Intellectual Values*—Values related to knowledge and quest for an attainment of truth are included in this category.

(viii) *Religious Values*—There values relate to God, self and purpose of life. They include faith in God, devotion to higher reality, compassion, love for all type of life.

(b) ***Parker's Classification:*** Parker has classified values according to the interest. He has classified as under:

(i) Biological values

(ii) Economic values

(iii) Affective values

(iv) Social values

(v) Intellectual values

(vi) Aesthetic values

(vii) Moral values

(viii) Religious values

(c) ***Plato:*** Plato has classified values according to ultimate realities. They are:

(i) Goodness

(ii) Beauty

(iii) Truth

There are some other criteria on which values can be classified. Some illustrations to this effect are:

Instrumental Values—These values refer to means in order to achieve the end point or goal.

Immediate Values—These values refer to time. Those values which help to complete the task or adjust to new situations are named as immediate values. They can be material in nature.

Ultimate/Terminal Values—These values relate to time or stage of life. There are certain values which are achieved after long time or at the end of a period.

Competent Values—These values relate to one's ability, capability and competency. Values required to complete a particular task/work are known as competent values. While learning subjects like Mathematics, Science, Language and Social

Sciences, learner develops certain powers, competencies, abilities. They are known as competent values.

Indeginous Angle

Since vedic times, Indian philosophers and rishis have developed Sanatana (eternal) values. They have been evolved while having a close interaction with society and nature having spiritual perspective in mind. The source of all values are four stages of life, four sections of society (work based) and four purusharthas (aims of life). Four pursharuthas are the fountain heads of Indian values. Four pursharthas are:

(i) Dharma (duty based morals) (ii) Artha (material development based values) (iii) Karma (aesthetics related values-Creative faculties expressed in fine arts and, performing arts) (iv) Moksha (Spiritual and divinity related values-God, self, purpose. Idealistic approach towards values in Indian setting of iife is—Satyam (Truth), Shivam (Goodness) and Sundaram (Beauty).

There are certain institutions which have classified values based on their institutional philosophy or rationalistic basis. They are:

Sri Sathya Sai Institute of Higher Learning—Based on huma-nistic parameters, five values have been identified. They are:

— Truth

— Righteousness

— Non-violence

— Love

— Peace

National Council of Educational, Research and Training (NCERT)-NCERT has worked out 84 values. These values have been identified after having discussions at the National level. These values are related to all categories of human experience at three planes—Body, Mind and Spirit.

Evolution and Growth

Like education, valuing is well defined process which takes into view different aspects of it such as stages of learner's growth, processes of valuing, models of value development. A brief description of these aspects is made here for better understanding:

Stages of Growth for Moral Development: Jean Piaget and later Lawrence Kohlberg studied as how children make moral judgements and found that there are distinct sequential stages of moral development. Piaget has classified them into four whereas Kohlberg classified them into three levels with two stages at each level. Kohlberg's stages of moral development are as follows:

Pre-conventional Level

Stage 1 : Punishment and obedience orientation (avoidance of punishment and deference to power)

Stage 2 : Instrumental relativistic orientation (right action instrumentally satisfies one's own needs and sometimes of others)

Conventional Level

Stage 3 : Interpersonal concordance orientation (good behaviour pleases or helps others and is approved by them)

Stage 4 : Law and order orientation

(Orientation towards authority, fixed rules and maintenance of social order).

Post-conventional or Autonomous Level

Stage 5 : Social contract legalistic orientation (right actions defined in terms of individual right and standards).

Stage 6 : Universal ethical principles orientation (right action is defined by decision of conscience—principles are ethical and abstract).

Kohlberg found that these stages are quite sequential in order. Therefore, educational programmes for valuing need to be designed accordingly.

Processes of Valuing: There are seven steps/processes/criteria involved in the development of values. They are stated as:

(i) Choosing freely.

(ii) Choosing from among alternatives.

(iii) Choosing from thoughtful consideration of the consequences of each alternative.

(iv) Prizing and Cherishing.

(v) Affirming publicly.

(vi) Acting upon choice.

(vii) Repeating.

These seven processes/or criteria involve cognitive affective and conative elements. They have selective and directional quality. Educational programmes need to be designed in the background of seven criteria or processes of value development.

Rohidekar (1995) in the background of his experiences and research came out with a pyramidical structure as:

Spontaneous

↓

Action with Effect

↓

Discrimination

↓

Appreciation

↓

Knowledge

(Sequential Stages of Valuing)

Model of Values Development: There are certain models which can be used for developing values. Some suitable and effective models are:

(i) Value Discussion Model

(ii) Inquiry Model

(iii) Discovery Model

Here we shall discuss one model as an illustration. It will pave the way for designing instruction for the development of values in classroom.

Value Discussion Model: This model is conceptualised under certain steps/captions like—Effects, Requirements of Value Discussion Model (VDM), Syntax, Social System, Principle of Reaction and Support System.

Effect: VDM can give rise to two effects namely, instructional effects and nurturant effects.

The instructional effects are the direct effects of value Discussion Model while the nuturant effects are the indirect effects of VDM.

Instructional Effects of VDM

— Improving value clarification

— Improving value judgement

Nurturant Effects of VDM

— Improving learning skills

— Improving self-esteem

— Improving attitude towards school/college.

— Improving adjustment

— Improving classroom climate

— Nourishment of personal power

Requirement of VDM

— Dilemma—issues in conflict (dilemmas should be simple, open ended, choice of actions)

— Discussion—free discussion and non-judgemental statements are the main requirements of VDM.

— Syntax:

It has five phases such as:

Phase 1 : Presenting the dilemma/issue

Phase 2 : Dividing on Action

Phase 3 : Organizing small group discussion

Phase 4 : Conducting a class discussion

Phase 5 : Closing the discussion.

Strategies of Value Development : The following can be profitably employed as educational strategies to inculcate, perpetuate or to modify values among children especially at the elementary and secondary stages:

Value Development Strategies

Level	*Strategy*	*Stage of Development*
Level-I (For Initiation)	1. Precept—Ideal Method	Mainly for initiation and introduction to value acquisition
	2. Intense Identification	
	3. Profitable Association	
	4. Ventilation	
	5. Porable or Allegory attempts	
Level-II (For stability)	6. Introjection	Value conceptualization and substance of value
	7. Conscientization	
Level-III (For Modification)	8. Role Play (Socio-drama) 9. Modelling	Value change and modification
	10. Sensitization and desensitization	
	11. Shaping	
	12. Token Task Technique	

Social System : A non-judgemental classroom is to be established that reflects trust, informality and tolerance. Students can sit in a large circle so as everyone can face and clearly hear each other.

Principle of Research : The teacher plays different roles like leader, mediator. Teacher handles responses of students very carefully and in balanced way.

Support System : To make system functional teacher needs to be trained in the application of the model. The literature in the form of dilemma, lesson planning, need to be made available. Besides, availability of Video recording of a live session, flexibility in the time-table, formation of groups, seating arrangements are other considerations under a support system.

Principles of Valuing : In the context of value development and education, John Wilson author of 'Introduction to Moral Education' has advocated 5 clear cut principles to be followed. They are:

(i) A consideration for others.

(ii) Awareness of feeling of one's own and of others.

(iii) Ability to take a decision in a conflicting or problematic situation demanding a moral choice.

(iv) Ability to collect valid data regarding situations involving questions of moral choice.

(v) A will to act on the decision taken on the basis of convincing logical thinking.

Level-I

Precept—Ideal Method—Imitation is the basis of this strategy. Quality of value development depends upon the environment created by parents, teachers and community. Overall environment stimulates the process of value development through conscious and unconscious imitation.

Intense—Identification Method—In this method, the child identifies with a person who becomes his 'ideal' or 'hero'. The child imbibes the value and attitudes as evinced by his 'hero' or the 'significant other'. He may even dedicate to propagate the values cherished by his teacher, parent, leader who has influenced his life. Story of Ekalavya, Dhruv, John or Arc, etc. are some of the examples.

Profitable Association Method—Useful association and condition serve as the basis of this method. Child can be exposed to a group situation. These situations provide satisfaction and enjoyment. In the process of group interaction the values are translated to the child which he accepts and propagates in life. Nature study group, environmental protection forum, mercy to annuals, worker's groups, science clubs, etc. are some of the examples in this regard.

Ventilation Method—The pupils are given opportunities to express their feelings and view points. Teacher or the parents should form a rapport to facilitate conversation for the free flow of opinions. They should be sympathetic, analytical and objective while giving response. A healthy communication and objective evaluation can lead to form the basis of value—formation among the students.

Parable or Allegory Method—Citing instances, episodes and even the story telling can profitably be used for inculcating values among children. The parable will form the basis and shall contain the moral lessons.

Level-II

Introjection—It is the process of internalising the values and making it a part of our psyche through evolving ego ideals. In the process there should be a healthy interaction between the 'ego' and the environment in evolving the value—ideals. The processes of imitation, identification, internalization, sublimation, and projection may involve in the formation and substance of values through introjection.

Conscientization—Paulo Fremire in his book "Pedagogy of the oppressed." suggests the steps of 'proxis' when there is 'prick' or disturbance to one's consciousness with an issue such as child labour, ragging, etc. One enters into the problem, collecting facts, analysing the causal factors related to the issue. With this, one can enter into meaningful dialogue with his peers, express and arrive at suitable solutions.

Level-III

Role Play—Role play is a process—oriented group technique. The group can take up an aspect and can be acquainted with role play technique. Students need coaching in three aspects for the role play:

(a) Briefing (the cognitive phase)

(b) The drama (the performance phase)

(c) The follow-up (discussion and constructive evaluation)

Role play can be employed in any situation or related to any subject. It does portray the situation and related values.

Modelling—Refer to the chapter on Techniques of Behaviour Modification.

Sensitization and Desensitization—Refer to the chapter on Techniques of Behaviour Modification.

Shaping—'Shaping' is more of a psychological art than a scientific technique. It is based on B.F. Skinner's principle of reinforcement. For shaping child's behaviour related to value development, reward and punishment act as reinforcers in this technique.

Token Task Method—Students are involved in some kind of planned work or activity in which each member can make significant contribution. There shall be task assigned to each and 'token' reward is expected.

The prerequisite of token task is to specify clearly the tasks to the group and state the goals. The group can be divided into sub-groups or committees and can be assigned with activities relating to values to be developed. In this case, appropriate goal setting, motivation and constant monitoring are very much required.

Conclusion: Values are the pillars of life. They are part of education. Values differ from place to place, culture to culture and time to time. Indian view with regard to values is different because of difference in perspectives of life. Here in this chapter we have discussed conceptual framework of values, process of valuing, model of value development, principles and strategies of value development.

QUESTIONS

1. Discuss the concept of 'values' and role of education in developing values among school children.
2. Critically bring out the nature of values. Explain specific stages of value development.
3. Differentiate between value and valuing. Discuss in detail the criteria/sub-processes of valuing.
4. What do we mean by model of value development? Describe steps of one model for development of values.
5. Briefly discuss some of the strategies of value development.

4

Basic Issues

Man is valuing animal or a valuing creature i.e. he is always interested in the relative importance of or worthwhileness of thing, of courses of actions, of principles, of conduct, of ideas etc. Value of a thing means its worth for us-its worthwhileness in the context of our living. Value is a conception of the desirable and it is in terms of this conception that we make our choices between means and between ends.

Value means a thing which we appreciate.

Each value is uniquely expressible-both by individuals and by groups. All values are cultural products i.e. we get our values from our culture. More specifically speaking, we get our values from our experience with the elements of our culture.

Values are not always expressed in very clear cut terms. Many values continue to exist in a potential form or term and these are rarely expressed or verbalised. The development of values involve both conjunctive and affective processes.

We cherish certain values in life. All human beings do. They live and die to uphold those values.

The Perception

Kluckhohn: "Value is the conception, explicit or implicit, distinctive of an individual or characteristic of a group of the desirable which influences the selection from available modes, means and ends of action."

G.W. Bridger: "Value is a quality of things having intrinsic worth. It is the basis of the principles by which we lead our lives."

H.N. Johnson: defines Values as a conception or standard, cultural or merely personal by which things are compared and approved or disapproved, relative to one another, held to be relatively desirable or undesirable, more meritorious or less, more or less correct.

Objects and Purposes

1. Values are the by-products of pursuit of aims e.g. if our aim is social service and we pursue this aim diligently and persistently, sincerely, we will automatically realise several values such as the need of co-operation among people, the awareness of their problems and difficulties, knowledge of the means that should be adopted to help them in overcoming their difficulties. Further our own sympathies will grow rich in all their dimensions and we will come to know the attitudes, the beliefs, the convictions that people have developed under the influence of culture to which they are exposed.

2. Since values are the by-product of the realisation of aims, the aims are something bigger than values.

3. The worth of an aim also depends upon the number and quality of values that its attainment helps us to realise. It is quite possible that when we are pursuing

any two goals, one of the two goals may help us realise values that are higher than the values that we may succeed in realising from the pursuit of other aim.

4. While setting up or fixing aims of education, it is only natural and right that we should think of relative values and ultimately our choice falls on those aims of education which, on the whole, are of higher or greater worth. Thus the consideration of value is perhaps the most important principle in establishing various aims of education.

5. Other aspects of education such as its contents, its methods, the system of evaluating the achievements of students are also virtually influenced by the consideration of their possible and relative values. Attempt is made to have a curriculum which carries maximum values and from this angle, the curriculum will be defined as a set of values to be conveyed to the new generation.

It may be concluded that the problem of values is the problem of utmost concern for teachers and educators.

Different Aspects

Values are of several kinds, such as biological and physical, economic or material, social, ethical, utilitarian, religious, intellectual, aesthetic, recreational, instrumental, intrinsic, relative and absolute. The kinds are simply several. We shall examine a few of these:

Physical Values: Physical values are found in those objects or activities which are conducive to physical health and racial continuation e.g. Green vegetables have physical value for us because it helps us to keep sound health.

Mating is considered to be valuable biologically because it helps in the continuity of human race.

The point is that things which give us physical and biological satisfaction have physical and biological values.

Physical education enhances physical values. This aspect should not be ignored in our schools.

Economic Values: The price of commodity in terms of money is its value. Different material objects carrying different amounts of value. The more scarce the thing is the more valuable it is. Many human activities in relation to different jobs, occupations or professions carry economic value.

Social Values: Social activities and social assembly groupings which give us social satisfaction possess social value. Friendship has social value for us. Co-operation, respect for each other, marriage have social values.

Ethical Values: The principles of conduct that give us moral satisfaction are deemed to have ethical value e.g. honesty, integrity, truth, sense of justice carry ethical values being gets satisfaction by acting morally.

Religious Values: Activities which give us religious satisfaction are religious values e.g. going to a temple, praying to God, singing bhajans-all these have religious values for us.

Intellectual Values: They are possessed by certain activities which lead to our intellectual development have intellectual value. Acquiring of knowledge has intellectual value. The habit of independent thinking, reading books, free discussion have intellectual values.

Aesthetic Values: Those activities which lead to the appreciation of beauty so that we may enhance the beauty have aesthetic values. These lead to the development of aesthetic sensibility. Dancing, Painting, Poetry have all aesthetic values.

Recreational Values: Those activities which break our monotony, tedium, boredom, possess recreational value-e.g. films, listening to music, watching an interesting game etc. all these have recreational value.

Instrumental or Extrinsic Values: Objects which are a means of achieving some goal, some end, possess instrumental or extrinsic value e.g. pen, copy.

Intrinsic Value: It refers to that value which is within the activity itself e.g. we may acquire knowledge for the sake of knowledge.

Relative Value: These values are those values which are relative to particular time and circumstances. These values continue to exist so long as those times and circumstances persist e.g. Singing war songs and sacrificing our times when our country is at war with some other country.

Absolute Values: Values which are held good for all places, for all times and for all circumstances are known as absolute values e.g. Love for truth and knowledge is good for all times under all circumstances and at all places.

Decisional Impact

Objectivity: The values which are objective are considered higher than those which are subjective. Objective values are those which are recognised by the public.

Universality: By universality we mean values which hold good everywhere or which are accepted by the whole world. The universal values are higher than particular values i.e. which are recognised by particular society.

Frequency: The values which we need more frequently are higher than those values which occur less frequently-all other things being equal e.g. Co-operation occurs more frequently than sympathy or co-operation carries more importance in social field.

Productivity: Values which are more productive are higher than those values which are less productive e.g. free competition (in economics) is more productive than restricted competition. Love is more productive than hatered. Divergent thinking is more productive than convergent thinking.

Absolute Values: They are higher than relative values. Absoluteness is thus the criteria.

Intrinsic Values: They are higher than extrinsic or instrumental values. Intrinsic values are ends in themselves but extrinsic value is a means to that end.

Rareness: Rare things are more valuable than other things— Gold is rare!

Harmony: Values that are in tune with one another are higher than those values which are in conflict or clash with each other e.g. There is an individual who loves only members of his community-on the other hand there is an individual who loves the entire mankind. The second man is thus a better man.

Different Views

There are two theories of values :

1. Subjective
2. Objective

Particular Ideas

According to Subjective theory of value, value is something personal, biological, psychological, in other words, it is a function of our own needs, our own desires. This means that things do not possess values in themselves. They happen to possess values only if they satisfy our needs and fulfil our desires. Let us in brief have a look at the Education implications.

Aims of Education. Pupils will have the liberty etc. to choose their own aims and objectives. You can't prescribe aims. Pupils will love to have those aims which they love to have. Aims can't be permanent either. Aims will differ from pupil to pupil-there will not be any universality.

Content of Education. Content depends upon aims. As aims are not universal, content cannot be prescribed. Simple suggestions about the course can be given. It is for the pupils to pick and choose. No imposition can be there. It depends upon pupils to select and reject. You cannot even suggest the number of courses. In co-curricular activities, the pupils will go in accordance with their liking.

Methods of Teaching. The teaching will have to go by the wishes of the pupils. The method of teaching cannot be imposed either.

Role of the Teacher. The teacher will have to perform those functions in the school which are liked by the pupils. Teachers will have to conduct themselves inside the classroom or outside the classroom in terms of the likes and dislikes of the pupils. Even in the matters of discipline, nothing can be done in the area too which is against the wishes of the pupils.

The Merits: The problem of motivation will stand solve. The students will feel automatically motivated because they will pursue the goals which they like and also because they will be studying such courses which command their liking. They will feel happy.

The Demerits: Everything is uncertain—aims, courses, methods. Aims can clash also. There is hardly any stability. Regarding discipline, you can expect chaos in the school if you are to go by subjective theory. The contribution of subjective theory of values is limited.

According to objective theory of values, value is not exclusively a psychological or biological phenomena. It is rather property of the things in themselves. Objects have certain attributes which make them valuable for us. If these attributes are universally recognised, the values become objective and public.

Obvious Effects

Aims and Objectives. In terms of this theory of values, the aims of education should be such which command favour with the most of people. Thus the aims of education can be prescribed and pupils can be made to achieve them. It is not necessary that we consider the liking of the pupils.

Contents. This makes us to the fact that when aims can be prescribed, contents can be prescribed also. This may or may not be liked by the pupils.

Methods of Teaching. Such methods of teaching have to be employed which teachers universally consider better. Personal preference of students hardly matters. The relative merits and demerits of methods of teaching can be empirically and objectively determined.

Role of Teacher. In terms of objective theory of values, teachers can follow those principles in their dealing with their pupils which most of them consider appropriate. It is not necessary to go after the subjective wishes of pupils. Teachers are at liberty to perform those functions which they consider are in the best interest of pupils.

Discipline. The rules of discipline will be such which are favoured by all or by majority. Individual liking thus will not count in setting up rules of discipline.

Our Education System lacks formal orientation in values. Result is chaos in society. Education has to be value oriented. In Teacher Education Colleges, at the B.Ed., level, a lecture or two on values should be a must. At the M.Ed, level, this topic is there but not considered very important. Result-Majority of the teachers do not know as to what is meant by a value. If we want that pupils should pick up right values, then we have to live values. Teachers have set examples. It is minimum that is expected of them.

Values in Force

Remember, when a value breaks, it becomes a "Jinn" far. 'It will destroy society. Therefore it is time that we develop values. Remember, we are to develop values and not teach about values. How do we do it? Some suggestions are as under

1. Start developing values only when the intellectual life of the child begins to dominate him or her. And as such, the right age is that of adolescence. It is during adolescence that a style of life develops. And during this age, the idea of values can be given.

2. Values are inculcated from the environment. If the environment is full of rapes, murders, bomb blasts, then forget about values. Thus our environment must be exceptionally good. The politicians, cinema, radio and finally now the T.V . have a great role to play in creating congenial environment. Values are caught from the environment.

3. There should be definite programmes for values or value development. In communism the value of "Weness" starts from the beginning. The value of "I" is discouraged.

4. Value must be identified and defined.

5. Values which are easily understood by a common man should be developed first-like casteism, corrup-tion etc. we are to banish these.

6. Lessons on values must be included in language text books. Short story must lead to inculcation of values.

7. Indian culture must be taught to students. Let there be a foundation course in it.

8. Religious discourses on all religions can be given.

9. Extra-curricular activity must lead to development of values.

10. Stress should be given on the development of love and affection.

11. Excellence in human beings should be stressed.

We should teach values to our children because it is most significant and effective thing we can do for their happiness as educationists and parents.

Values inculcate many qualities in children.

Education has main goals of social justice, of national cohesion, of scientific temper, independence and spirit of socialism. These goals are useless if there are no values. Good education is always value oriented but somehow we are neglecting values in recent times. Our personality is undermined. There is value erosion. Violence has increased in all walks of life.

Our outlook has to be changed, hence value education. We should be sensitive to values and we should have the ability to choose right values.

We have already listed eleven points in this connection as above. We shall like to add more:

Prayer should be sung. Gandhiji said. " Begin, therefore your day with prayer and make it so soulful that it may remain with you till evening."

Story telling can be there. The stories should be a mixture of fiction, biography, life experiences.

Thought for the day should be written on the BB. It inspires one and all.

Taking up special projects-organisation of sports and games, social activities and self-reliance programmes, attitude development and role plays are some of the important activities which are commanded as they have great potential for physical, emotional and psychic development. Depending upon the size of the institution, these programmes can be further elaborated.

Group Singing. Singing and music have their own importance.

Through Attitude test and role play techniques it has been found that students can be helped to develop values.

Mass Media can be exploited.

And remember, in all this, teacher is the king pin. The role of this teacher is most important.

What is the method of inculcation of values among the students? The best method is by setting examples himself/herself by the teacher. The child automatically imbibes the behaviour pattern of the teacher. The teaching and the behaviour should be full of values which we wish to develop amongst children. The negative side of behaviour is not to be reinforced. To be specific, the methods are Presentation of examples of self (Teacher) Discussion Dramatization Value Clarification Exposure to incidents full of values Films shows.

A question is asked about sources of value and value education. An educationist has tried to answer it this way:

The sources of values and value education are:

1. *Curriculum.* Science tells us about truth and the spirit of free inquiry.

2. Co-curricular activities-like clubs, associations, N.C.C. etc. These will teach us about democratic living, secularism.

3. Teacher Already pointed out.

4. Atmosphere of school—It is sum total of all influences.

5. Parents

6. Books

These are all sources from where values can be picked up. Maths teaches us about logical thinking and precision. History tells us about self-sacrifice. Appreciation can come from literature.

So curriculum is a rich source of values and value education. The only thing is that teaching should be correct.

The Assessment

Cleanliness

1. Understands the need for personal and environmental cleanliness.

2. Keep his body, belongings and surroundings clean for promoting personal health and public health.

3. Eats clean food moderately at regular timings

Purity

1. Understands that mental purity refers to the dominance of positive thoughts like those of compassion, kindness, brotherliness, service and sympathy towards others.

2. Is keen to keep his mind pure.

3. Prays to have mental purity.

4. Entertains pure thoughts of brotherliness towards members of other.
5. Entertains positive thoughts.
6. Reads edifying books.

Courtesy

1. Shows respect towards his parents.
2. Shows respect towards teachers and others.
3. Appreciates even the smallest help rendered to him.
4. Shows consideration for the views of fellow pupils.
5. Greets fellow pupils.
6. Speaks politely.
7. Does not talk unnecessarily using abusive terms.

Peace

1. Believes that "the world is a family of independent countries and that other countries are as independent as ours and should be respected as such."
2. Believes that we should all live in peace.
3. Believes that differences among countries, states, language groups, communities, etc., should be resolved through peaceful means.
4. Believes that it is inhuman differences between parents and children should be resolved through loving understanding.
5. Believes that the school should not resort to the punishment of the pupils in any circumstance.

6. Seeks information regarding organizations and personalities striving to establish world peace.

7. Is not related by success or discouraged by a failure.

8. Does not lose temper during difficult situations.

9. Tries to maintain the equanimity of mind in the face of pleasant and unpleasant situations and experiences.

Joy

1. Is cheerful in different situations.

2. Has a sense of humour.

3. Laughs in pleasant situations.

4. Smiles in unpleasant situations.

5. Enjoys group activities.

6. Enjoys creative activities.

7. Takes pleasure in outings in the midst of nature.

QUESTIONS

1. What is Value ?

2. Write about three aims ?

3. How many kinds of values are there ?

5

Part of Philosophy

The epistemology is a branch of Philosophy, which deals with knowledge. The problems with which epistemology grapples are mainly concerned with the process of knowledge, nature of knowledge, its limits and the relation of knower with the known. It provides the basic foundation of knowledge. It critically examines different methods to achieve different types of knowledge. It discusses philosophically the truth and falsehood, validity of knowledge, limits of knowledge, nature of knowledge, knower and the known, etc. Some of the questions that are answered by epistemology are: What is the relation between the knower and the known? Is the content of knowledge identical with the external object or is it different from it? How can we know that our knowledge is a real knowledge of the object? What are the limits of knowledge? What are the sources of knowledge? and so on. Besides, the epistemologists raise certain other questions also such as (1) What is knowledge? (2) Is the knowledge of the knower possible? if not, then, what is known? (3) If the known is an object, then what is this object? (4) Is the knowledge of the existence of an object possible without its being known? (5) How can we distinguish between true and false knowledge? (6) What is ignorance? (7) Is ignorance a form of knowledge or different from it? (8) What is the process of knowledge? (9) Do we know something which was already existent before our knowledge of it? (10) What is forgetting of knowledge? (11) What is the basis of validity of knowledge? (12) What are the errors possible in the process of knowledge? (13) Is our knowledge definite or is the definiteness based purely on our feelings and faith? (14) How is it that some beliefs are considered to be more valid than others? (iv) What are the distinctions between different types of knowledge? (15) What are the relations of knowledge with science and philosophy?.

There are different views presented by different philosophical schools about different aspects of knowledge. Empiricist school of philosophy discussed the methods and value of knowledge. Its opposite rationalists school pointed out how some of the knowledge is innate. Scepticism shows that the limits of knowledge and its certainty are not possible in the field of sciences. Agnosticism shows the relativity of human knowledge. Criticism shows that our knowledge is neither a-priori nor a-posteriori emphasizing that it is synthetic requiring sensibility, understanding, and reasoning. Intuitionism shows that intellect and intuition are complementary. Mysticism shows the value of spiritual experiences in the field of religion. Pragmatism holds that the value of knowledge is in its use. Instrumentalism points out that reason is an instrument for the satisfaction of human needs. Humanism shows that the criterion of all knowledge is man himself and there is no ultimate knowledge. Experimentalism and relativism point out that knowledge is experimental and relative.

Thus, the various aspects of knowledge have been variously described in philosophy.

To the idealists only knowledge one has of his environment is his idea of it. The environment can never be known directly. It can be known only through the intermediary ideas of a human knower. Hence, the kind of knowledge one can have is determined by the way it is apprehended by the human knower. It is supplied by the human mind. It is the sum total of a-priori categories of thought. To them knowledge is universal. For that reason Plato asserted that knowledge of true realities comes not through senses but through understanding, through reason.

To the idealists the universe is knowable. They believe that the universe can be comprehended through the mind only, because both the mind and the universe are constituted of the same elements, intellect and spiritual essence. Hegel has gone so far as to identify nature and mind by saying that the various categories of knowledge or mind are the different stages of the universe's development.

For pragmatists knowledge is what is learnt through experience. As they embrace the method of science knowledge so gained is less certain than that of idealists' or realists' view. They speculate about things. These speculations are tested empirically and in the light of purposes. Ross (1947) said, true knowledge, according to the pragmatists, is not the acquiring of a dead culture, particularly from books; it is rather the power to do the right thing in a given situation. They accept the nurture view of knowledge emphasizing that knowledge is the food of the mind. Knowledge of the environment and of everyday life are useful knowledge. Valid knowledge, to them, is useful knowledge. They say that should be known which is of some utility. True knowledge is something more than acquisition of facts. True knowledge, desirable knowledge is. that which is capable of functioning, which is potentially a power to do. True knowledge is the material out of which a resourceful mind is made, which enables one to understand the world. To the pragmatists knowledge is something which is wrought out in action. Before it is used it is merely information. Information becomes knowledge when it is judged to be relevant to the solution of a particular problem.

According to realism objects have an existence independent of any knowledge of them. The objects have their own qualities independent of the mind. They are known directly and are universal. The realists maintain that objects are precisely what they appear to be. Some realists like Montaigne said that knowledge to be gained should be practical. Inductive method of gaining knowledge was emphasized by some realists like Francis Bacon. Direct experience and experimentation were considered important by Ratke, a supporter of empirical realism.

The existentialists considered subjective knowledge more important than objective knowledge. Truth, to them, is subjectivity. It may be remembered that there is no consensus among existentialists as to what is the essential nature of existentialism. Some of them are theist while others are atheist. So there are different views of existentialists about knowledge too.

Truth and only Truth

Metaphysics, ontology, cosmology and theology are the specific branches of philosophy that deal with the problems of reality or existence. Metaphysics is the science of existence or reality. Its main problems are what is reality?, Is the world one or many?, What are the fundamental characteristics of creation?, What is space?, What is matter?, What is relation?, What is the purpose of creation?, Is there God?, Metaphysics discusses the three aspects of Reality: (i) the universe, (ii) the self, (iii) the God. It is the main branch of philosophy. Cosmogony (study of creation), cosmology (is the world one or many), ontology (study of ultimate reality), and philosophy of self are all branches of metaphysics. Various schools of philosophy such as Idealism, Naturalism, Pragmatism, Realism and Existentialism discuss these problems of existence or Reality in different ways.

A school of thought referred to as idealism accepts a dual concept of reality consisting of (1) the perfect world of ideas and (2) the imperfect world of everyday existence. The real and true knowledge, according to them is in the perfect world of ideas which can only be grasped by the mind. The material existence is an imperfect manifestation of the real world of ideas. True knowledge is a deductive process of mind and is a non-material idea. Immanuel Kant did not, however, accept the concept of "other worlds" of ancient idealism. Instead he invented the concept of pure reason which according to some philosophers meant "knowledge that does not come through our senses, but is independent of all sense experiences, knowledge which comes through the inherent nature and structure of the mind.

Realism had a straightforward concept of reality and the nature of knowledge. To them the everyday physical world is reality and exists independently of pure reason, Truth exists in the material world and we deal with it everyday in our existence. This true knowledge can be discovered in this real, rationalistic world through the use of scientific method, they said. Three basic tenets of realistic philosophy are: (i) there is a world of real existence which men have not made or constructed, (ii) this real existence can be known by the human mind, and (iii) such knowledge is the only reliable guide to human conduct, individual and social. Both the idealists and the realists believe in universal truths. The realists discover these laws of nature through scientific research and are, thus, materialistic. Breed (1939) wrote, "The realist observes that a stubbornly objective world, one's physical and social environment has veto power on human interests. Man proposes, but it, like God, disposes. Man projects an idea, but the constitution of the external world finally determines its validity." (p.55).

Experimentalists (or pragmatists) also reject the fixed and final world of realists and the dualism of idealists. To them the world is precarious, changing, incomplete, indeterminate. The world of things is real; however, there is constant evolution.

This view of reality vitally influences the nature of knowledge. It makes truth relative and changing. Experimentalists view persons as purposeful and in interaction with the environment, thus creating knowledge not absorbing passively from outside world like the realists, Reality to them is the outcome of person's interaction with his environment. Because the person and the environment both have no fixed, inherent nature and the precarious environment is constantly evolving today's truths may not be those of tomorrow. According to pragmatists there are known realities, known laws to govern human activities.

Existentialism fathered by Kierkegaard championed the realities of the inner person. It said that reality is what man says it is. "Except as man exists, reality is nothing". It says man exists first; then he creates his own essence. It is a gloomy reality that existentialists present, as the existentialists focus upon the realities of human despair, dread, loneliness anguish and the meaninglessness of life enclosed by materialistic axioms. So they reflect upon future reality and emphasize that reality is human freedom to make choices on the basis of human ethics, human making decisions in the interest of humans rather than in the interest of gross national product, etc.

Idealism and Reality: Idealism or sometimes called spiritualism takes many and varied formes but the postulate underlying all is that mind or spirit is the essential world's stuff and that the true reality is of a mental character. It asserts that mind itself is the fundamentally real thing. Reality is to be found in man's mind rather than in external nature. It assumes that the universe is rational. But this orderly working of the universe is not due to mechanical principles; it is due to the existence of universal mind. The universe itself is said to have a body and a mind. The external physical aspect of the universe is "the living visible garment of God, the universal mind". The universe, as was asserted by Hegel, is a great thought process as if God is thinking and the physical universe is the thought externalized and made visible. Subjective idealism presents a view that things do exist, but they are real only when they are perceived. They have no existence apart from the mind. Immanuel Kant said in his *Critique* of *Pure Reason* that the world is just a phenomena or appearance to the mind; it can be studied as that.

According to idealism knowledge of the true reality comes not through the senses but through man's understanding. As said by Plato men can obtain true knowledge through their reason. Idealism of Plato is objective. He asserted that universal forms, ideas, patterns or essences constitute the inner reality of the universe, and not the phenomena which only imperfectly represent them. These ideas and patterns are everlasting. Plato maintained that beyond this world and the life there is another world and another life more true, more beautiful and more real. He further believed that it is this external world that gives us the moral standards which can be known and understood only by reason.

Pragmatism and Reality: Pragmatism is essentially a humanistic philosophy. It says that reality (as held by James) is still in the making and awaits part of its complexion from the future. To the pragmatists "truths are man-made products (James, p. 242). Satisfactory working and utility are held to be the criteria of the true reality. It is the experience that proves what is the true reality. Truth is tested by the way it works in life's situations. So it is not fixed. It is variable. What is true in one situation may not be true in another situation. So the reality is always in the making. Reality or truth is something which happens to man's judgement, which becomes true if it is found to be working well in life's situation. If a judgement or a belief works satisfactorily it may be adopted. This may, then, take the form of reality. To the pragmatists truth is to be conceived dynamically. Truth-making is the process of verification.

Pragmatists are reluctant to enumerate a system of metaphysics but there are views on the nature of reality implicit in it. When they assert that change and process are fundamental, that real being has continuity, that change is evolutionary and purposive, they indirectly express metaphysical ideas, Reality, to pragmatists, is always in the making.

Naturalism and Reality: The naturalists do not involve themselves in the controversy of Metaphysics. They do not discuss what is truth, what is reality. For them the major concerns for all considerations are the environment (nature) and the individual. They have a profound reverence for nature and the child. They unflinchingly believe that the nature of the child (the human being) is basically good and also that human nature develops according to certain well defined laws. If there can be inferred any mataphysical ingredient in their thought about reality, it is that "what is, is right" (Brubacher, 1962). If a question is asked 'what is reality', the naturalists will say "the human being is the reality", "what he does is the reality", "where he does is the reality". Beyond that it is needless to search for any reality.

Values in Discipline

In numerous situations of life man is faced with the problems like, 'what should he do, which is better to do, which is the right thing to do, which ought to be done, which should not be done. All such questions are value questions directly concerned with individual's judgement and values. Almost all decisions in life directly or indirectly involve "valuing". But, what is a value philosphically has always been controversial. Not all philosophies have the same view of value. Each of them views value differently as follows:

Idealism and Values: Idealism is identified with absolute and external values. Their vision of values emanates from their vision of reality. Plato said that beyond this world and this life there is another world and another life more true, more beautiful and more real which give us the moral standards to be followed as recognized by our reason. The fundamental proposition of idealism is that mental or spiritual is more real and, hence, more important than the material. Reality of idealism is of spiritual rather than of material nature: Idealists who accept the doctrine of evolution assert that the whole process of evolution may consist in getting nearer to a realization of the ultimate values that lie at the heart of the universe. Then, the man comes to posses a spiritual nature and becomes a moral being. The idealists stress man's sense of moral values, his ability and determination to follow good and eschew evil. To them the whole universe seems to be working towards a perfect state of rationality. Idealists take value as given maintaining that they are real and give an adequate account of man. They are an essential and outstanding element of human nature. They advocate a threefold analysis of spiritual values truth, beauty and goodness corresponding to threefold classification of spiritual activities such as intellectual, aesthetic and moral activities. They hold a view that spirit desires these values for their own sake and not for any further aim beyond them. Truth, beauty and goodness are seen to be absolutes each existing in its own right and entirely desirable in itself.

Thus, values for idealists are intrinsic (i.e. good in and of themselves), spiritual, predetermined or given, rational and absolute. They are inherent and self-contained.

Pragmatism and Values: The pragmatists believe in instrumental values. i.e., values which are judged to be good or desirable because they are good for something. Their value depends on their consequences when used to achieve some other value. They are instrumental values. They are subjective being dependent on people and situations. They are measured by their efficacy in gaining ends. The pragmatists hold that there are no fixed values in advance. On the other hand values emerge from life's experiences. The law of expedience determines what values must be learned and followed. Values to them are man-made not pre-existing and eternal. Pragmatism is essentially a humanistic philosophy maintaining that man creates his own value in the course of activity. Satisfactory working and utility are held to be the criteria of value.

Ross (1947, p. 81) says since pragmatists deny the existence of value in advance there can for them be no clear vision of a goal. But, when American pragmatists talk of education as the force which creates a finer and better civilization, one is entitled to ask by what criteria they measure the success of their efforts; for it would seem to the ordinary person that some sort of standard is implied. Surely, values and standards, however vaguely realized, are needed to direct efforts, and must exist beforehand. Thus, there is an implied acceptance of a scheme of values among the American pragmatists.

Naturalism and Values: Naturalism is basically concerned with "What it is" and not with "what ought to be" which is the fundamental aspect of value. Hence, it may not be very wrong to say that consideration of value was never an aspect of the philosophy of naturalism. It was never deliberated and discussed by naturalists. However, inference about it may be drawn from what the naturalists said about human nature. Rousseau stated that the object of education is not to make a soldier, magistrate or priest but to make man. It may be concluded from this that there are no fixed or existing values which education should aim at to be developed in pupils; it is value-less development of the child. The naturalists did not emphasize that education should direct the child to grow in any designed way. But, Rousseau also said that if education of the child results in his becoming a better citizen or worker such an outcome should be considered a by-product of aiming at the improvement of his inner worth as an end in itself (Brubacher, p. 114). Thus, value as pre-existing has no value for the naturalists. However, if value is defined as something which one considers important, it may be considered that the child and his environment carry all-important value for them. The romantic naturalists said that 'What is, is right". This may be the only value for naturalists which means child's nature is important and that becomes the norm. The unique as well as the universal in human nature should be respected and given high priority. Beyond child's nature, his interests need and potentialities there is no other value on the earth. Values are set by the nature of the child. The naturalists are interested in the child as he is rather than as he will be. Adult standards of conduct are discarded by them. What is valuable is child's development into an enjoyable, rational, harmoniously balanced, useful and, hence; natural life. Moral training is useless. In naturalism everything intrinsically valuable disappears from the world. That which promotes the interests of living beings in the struggle for existence becomes the all-dominating value. The naturalists are primarily concerned with the world as it is here and now.

Existentialism and Values: This philosophy also puts emphasis on the individual like the pragmatists and the naturalists.

The ultimate concern for the existentialist is with the meaning of existence. For the existentialist also values emerge only when the individual interacts with his environment. They are not pre-existent and to be discovered. Rather. they emerge when the individual faces the harsh reality of life. Hence, it is the individual himself. who creates values out of life-situations. But. values to them are subjective; they are not facts. Reduction of values to facts leads to widespread loss of faith in values. They say most of the ills of the modern man are due to over-objective attitude. This requires a subjectivist correction in the light of existentialist ideas.

The existentialists perception of existence is that it is full of tensions, contradictions, loneliness and anxiety. Life is seen by them as a battle for existence. For this battle the individual needs strength, not goodness, pride not humility, intelligence not altruism; and these, then, become values for the individual. The origin of values to them lies not in the social situation, but in the personal thought.

Realism and Values: The realist or positivist concepts also challenged the views of the idealists about values, like the existentialists. They emphasized that the real world is one wherein people pursue their self-interests. Happiness, however, comes from fulfilment of human responsibilities and obligations. Complete living (to be realized through activities like self-preservation, earning a living, fullfilling duties, etc.) and character development were considered important by some realists.

6

Values in System

Article 51A of the Constitution (Fortysecond Amendment) Act, 1976, lays down the following Fundamental Duties. These may be termed as a value-system which the government expects every citizen of India to observe faithfully.

"Article 51A: It shall be the duty of every citizen of India—

(a) to abide by the Constitution and respect its ideals and institutions, the National Flag and the National Anthem;

(b) to cherish and follow the noble ideals which inspired our national struggle for freedom;

(c) to uphold and protect the sovereignity, unity and integrity of India;

(d) to defend the country and render national service when called upon to do so;

(e) to promote the spirit of common brotherhood amongst all the people of India transcending religious, linguistic and regional or sectional diversities; to renounce practices derogatory to the dignity of women;

(f) to value and preserve the rich heritage of our composite culture;

(g) to protect and improve the natural environment including forests, lakes, rivers and wild life, and to have compassion for living creatures;

(h) to develop the scientic temper, humanism, and the spirit of inquiry and reform;

(i) to safeguard public property and to abjure violence;

(j) to strive towards excellence in all spheres of individual and collective activity so that the nation constantly rises to higher levels of endeavour and achievement.

Based on the study of the Gandhian literature and reports given by committees and commissions on social, moral and spiritual values in education, the National Council of Educational Research and Training, New Delhi compiled an exhaustive list of 84 values. given in the Appendix to the questionnaire.

It is difficult to make comparison of the moral standards between societies. Laws, rules, customs, opinions vary from society to society, from individual to individual and from time to time. Moral relativism is an eternal phenomenon.

Relative Elements

According to ardent Indian scriptures, there are seven seminal concepts of values. These are rta (cosmic order); Verna (class); asrama dharma (duties for different stages of life); law of karma (moral causation); samsara (transmigration); shames (harmlessness); and moksha (liberation).

Indians have the unique distinction of producing and practising philosophical and ethical thought from very early days. "Unlike ethical teachings of ancient Egypt and Babylon, Indian ethics was philosophical in the start. In the oldest Indian writings, the Vedas, ethics is an integral part of philosophical and religious speculation about the nature of reality. These writings date from about 1500 B.C.*. They have been described as the oldest philosophical literature in the world, and what they say about how people ought to live may therefore be the first philosophical ethics." Ancient Chinese regarded filial piety, reverence for the superiors, love of the past and exercising moderation as cardinal virtues. The ethical ideals of ardent Greeks were not influenced by theological considerations. They were more concerned with the duties of an individual as a member of the city-state. Christian-values like humility, meekness, gentleness, compassion and renunciation of the world were held in dewesteem by the Greeks as well as the Romans who were more inclined towards materialistic ideals.

Moral Forces at Work

Anthromorphic man today presents a picture of a mechanomorphic man. There is a general feeling that the industrial man has gone far ahead of the moral man, hence, the present crisis in all our walks of, life. On the contrary, people like Myers hold. In no domain has progress been greater, the gains larger or more precious, than in the moral domain. From clan morality, based on physical kinship, mankind has advanced or is advancing to world morality, based on ethical kinship of man. There appears not only a new physical but also a new moral man. 88 per cent of the respondents to statement G-1 of the questionnaire felt that moral values among Indians have declined over the past 5-10 years. To a simiiar statement (S-4) that "Majority of Indians are selfish and lack dedication of ideals", students reacted as follows:

Sl. No.	*Category of Respondents*	*Number Agreeing*	*No. Undecided*	*Number Disagreed*
1.	Total Population of students	140	42	85
	(267)	(52.5)	(15.7)	(31.8)
2.	School students (M)	38	13	19
	(7)	(54.3)	(18.6)	(27.1)
3.	School students (F)	51	15	20
	(86)	(59.3)	(17.4)	(23.3)
4.	College students (M)	16	5	13
	(34)	(47.1)	(14.7)	(38.2)
5.	African College students (M)	3	1	3
	(7)	(42.9)	(14.2)	(42.9)
6.	College students (F)	32	8	30
	(70)	(45.7)	(11.4)	(42.9)

Diversity of views on the subject notwithstanding, the nation, in general, feels that there is urgent need for elevation of moral standards in the country.

Behavioural Judgement

For planning any programme of moral uplift, it is necessary to delineate the factors which influence human behaviour. Broadly speaking, some of the important determinants of man's behaviour are as follows:

Religion and Science: According to religious people, most of our ills arise from inside ourselves; from desire, pride, lust, etc. For others, the ills come from external agents like poverty and natural disasters, etc., and that we can overcome these external forces through technology and industrialisation. There is no denying the fact that both mora health and material-progress are necessary for mankind's balanced progress.

Science seemed to hold that religion was irrelevant and it was a creation of man's childish ignorance. Having achieved considerable success in science and technology, Europe, today, seems to be turning to East for discovering its spirit. And, surprisingly, Orient is getting lured by material progress of the west.

Nature, Nurture and Free Will: In cold regions, where struggle for existence is hard, life is lived more at the physical plane. That is why cultural growth is comparatively slower there and faster in warm, temperate and fertile regions. This also explains why the story of all conquests is the story of more civilised nations getting conquered by less civilised nations and thereafter the victorious being absorbed by their victims .

The biological or the social environment is also important. Man has considerable influence on another man. The cultural influence of India over East and South East-Asia and that of

Egypt on the West are testimony to this fact. The art of coining money and building temples in India is considered to have Greek influence. Conversely, Buddhism influenced the Gnostic Greek sects. "Numerous drugs of Indian origin are noticed by the Greeks—A variety of treatises on medical science were translated from Sanskrit into Arabic and Persian—The Saracens introduced the Indian method of Arithmetic and the Indian Algebra and Geometry into Europe."

It does not carry conviction that human beings perform their role in this world only at the bidding of fate or some providential force. The inherited genes, and according to Hinduism, the Samaskaras of previous life-cycle, no doubt influence our behaviour pattern, but the claim of nurture in human development cannot be undermined. The environmentalist, J.B. Watson, said in 1920, "Give me a dozen healthy infants, well formed, and my own specified world to bring them up in, and I will guarantee to take any one at random and train him to become any kind of specialist. I might select doctor, lawyer, artist, merchant; and, yes, even beggarman and thief-regardless of talent, penchant, tendencies, abilities, location, and race of his ancestors."

According to Toynbee heredity and environment alone can not explain all behaviour patterns. He says, "I part company with the behaviourists over their belief that behaviour is wholly and exclusively determined by heredity and environment. According to him, self-determination (or free-will as the Hindu scripture Gita puts it), has a good claim to be considered as one of the important determinants of human behaviour.

Materialism: Economic pulls, today, seem to be exercising a great influence on human kind. We seem to be drifting towards Machiavellian philosophy that the end of human existence is profit alone. When a man is dedicated to economics to the exclusion of laws of life, virtue no longer remains his prime concern.

Importance of Conduct

Man's behaviour can be modified in two ways:

(a) By use of behavioural science and technology.

(b) Through the process of education.

Further Dimensions

Scientists have been doing considerable research on the modification of human behaviour in order to find ways and means to remove behavioural pollution.

Drugs: It is learnt that leading nations are secretly engaged in what is known as chemical factors or behavioural drugs; for example drugs which can be sprayed over large population centres and which can make them docile in a manner so as to make the work of the invading armies easier.

Foods: It may be possible to achieve similar results (as by drugs) by proper kinds of foods. The type of food, its quantity as well as quality—all influence the physiology and psychology of living organisms. Therefore, by appropriate kinds of foods it may be possible to shape the desired type of individuals.

Electronics: Electronics provide another measure of behaviour control. Electrodes are implanted in the human brain so as to stimulate certain behaviour centres. The stimulation can be achieved by remote control also.

Genetic Engineering: This has made it possible to remove congenital defects and, in course of time, to engineer a human being of one's choice (good as well as bad).

Reinforcement and Aversive Stimuli: Reinforcement is negative as well as positive—i.e., removing certain things from the environment or adding certain things to it. One can escape from the consequence of fire either by fleeing it or removing the fire from the environment.

Punishment for undesirable behaviour is an aversive stimulus. It may have side effects also. For example, a prisoner may become more intrepid in the jail in the company of other prisoners and pick up more techniques of committing crimes. Motivating a person to do something by offering awards is a positive reinforcement. It has fewer side effects.

Experimental Psychology: Considerable theoretical and experimental work has been done in the field of psychology—a science which deals with the functioning of human mind. This is becoming available to modern man for modifying individual's behaviour.

Some of the technologies described above are still a distant possibility and may not be available to mankind at least for immediate and large-scale application. Therefore one has, at the present juncture, to rely more on the educational process.

Educational Process

Role : Education is a major instrument in modifying human behaviour. In addition to the family, educational institutions have considerable influence on how individuals behave and function. It is, therefore, important that education—defined both in narrow and broader sense-concerned itself with educating the future generation in desirable values. Comenius and Locke described value-education as the hub of educational activity. "Indeed the term 'Humanities', as used to designate a very large section of the curriculum (for a long time, in fact, the whole of the curriculum) indicates by its derivation that relations between man and man were seen as the central, or even the only, concern of education in the full sense. Moral upbringing, or character training, therefore, was far long the central feature of what education itself was understood to be by the great theorists and, indeed, by great practitioners.-It was probably with the development of education for all and the concomitant introduction of a vocational component into the curriculum that moral education lost, in part, this central role."

Moral education programme can be accomplished through educational institutions, religious institutions and the mass media. Whereas schools and colleges will impart moral education to students, religious institutions can be more usefully employed for inspiring the general public and mass media for both these groups to develop in the individuals propensity for higher standards of conduct.

Personal Example : Formal teaching can promote moral values only when children see that teachers themselves practise the code of conduct which they want their students to follow. In the case of moral education, it is necessary to have the marriage of thought and action. Action without thought is blind and is likely to degenerate into superstition; whereas thought without action is of no consequence. Teachers' training-programme should educate the individuals, both, in content and methodology of moral education.

Proper Syllabus: National Council of Educational Research and Training, New Delhi has worked out a syllabus on moral education. Some broad outlines in regard to syllabi on social justice, sex-education, smoking, drinking and protection of environment have been given in the foregoing chapters also. Certain schools in the country have made some ad-hoc provisions for imparting moral education to their students.

Inter-disciplinaryApproach : Values concern all life-forms, birds, plants and even non life such as use of natural resources, etc. Therefore value-education calls for an inter-disciplinary approach. The following episode would explain the usefulness of such an approach.

Once the residents of a housing complex complained to the owner of the housing complex that they had to wait for a long time for the lift. The owner called engineers to find a solution to the situation. One suggested fixing of an additional lift; the second replacement of the old lift by a new one; but the owner turned down these suggestions as costly. A psychologist happened to pass that way. He advised fixing of two mirrors in the waiting lounge, hoping that ladies would keep looking into the mirrors and arranging their hair, etc., and men would keep looking at the ladies in these mirrors and thus waiting will become easy. The suggestion worked wonderfully well with a nominal expense.

Production of Literature : Another important work to be done in this area is the writing of suitable books suiting various age-groups of students. These books as text books or supplementary readers should emphasise the proud record of India's cultural heritage and lives of those who dedicated themselves to the service of mankind. A good deal of published material exists already also and can be used judiciously for this purpose. Besides, import of foreign literature beaming with sex, violence and other unhealthy trends should be stopped. Educational institutions and mass media have, no doubt, an important part to play in restructuring the moral fibre of the society, but it should be remembered that they are surrounded by a system which negates the promotion of moral values and makes their work difficult. Unless their difficulties are resolved, success would remain a distant goal. Further, it should be ensured that no dominant religious, caste, political or any other pressure group is allowed to promote values which serve its particular vested interests. The work is obviously not easy. The example of Vidur, the moral teacher in the *Mahabharata* Epic, is a proof of this statement. However, if adequate steps are not taken to implement the programme of value-education in right earnest, mankind may have to face serious consequences. In the end, it may be added that in India—there is no dearth of ideas and philosophical thought, but unfortunately, most of the reports of research studies, workshops and committees or commissions find their place on the shelves of cold storage only. Preparation of such reports can, in a way be likened to marriages of elephants where everything takes place at high level; there is lot of trumpeting but nothing happens for (two) years. We need to be more realistic as well as practical. The world is moving fast. Our survival depends on our capacity to keep pace with the changing times.

7

Impact on Education

The dynamic side of philosophy has been described as education is a significant discipline. Philosophy gives ideas and education tries to put them into practice. But, there are several philosophies and so there are several different sets of ideas too. These differences, then, result into different theories and practices of education. Different philosophies view the specific aspects of education differently. Not all philosophies, for example, advocate similar goals and objectives of education. Same is the case with regard to the curriculum, the method, the values of education. In this chapter educational implications of four Indian Philosophies (Vedanta, Jainism, Buddhism and Islam) are discussed focusing, particularly, on such aspects of education as (i) the aims of education, (ii) curriculum, (iii) method, (iv) the teacher, (v) the student.

Vedic View

Vedanta is an idealistic philosophy. Hence, education and its functions as perceived by the Vedantists are very much similar to the Western philosophy of Idealism. This section describes how the Vedanta philosophy interprets educational aims, curriculum, methods, the role of the teacher and the role of the students.

Objectives of Education: The aims of education according to Vedanta philosophy may be described as follows

1. Knowledge aim
2. Moral and Spiritual Development aim
3. Cultural aim
4. Character Development aim

To acquire knowledge was one of the most emphasized goal of Vedanta philosophy. In *Mundaka Upnishad* a two-fold concept of knowledge is presented-(a) Para supreme knowledge and Apara, the ordinary knowledge. The aim of acquiring supreme knowledge is said to be the ultimate goal to be achieved by the man. The supreme knowledge is said to be that which helps to destroy spiritual blindness and reveals the ever present spiritual reality behind man and nature, the basis of all forms of knowledge; the knowledge of that by which all else is known. It is not just knowing and learning meaning of words; rather it is knowledge of the Truth, "Meaning of Meanings", Supreme Truth of Being. All the knowledge of science, literature, and arts including even the knowledge of Vedas was regarded by the Upanishadas just ordinary knowledge, Acquisition of supreme knowledge was the highest aim of life. Education, therefore would mean helping the individual to acquire supreme knowledge. It is said to be that knowledge "by knowing which all else becomes known." It transcends all other worldly knowledge. It is Wisdom that goes beyond worldly knowledge. It is spiritual awareness that transforms all knowledge into wisdom.

The knowledge aim of the Vedanta philosophy also emphasized acquisition of knowledge of one's own self i.e., knowing "who am I". (who am I? what are my powers? What is my duty?). This kind of knowledge about the self was the cherished goal of Vedanta philosophy. This knowledge was a kind of realization that man is divine. This was the aim of education that was informally and formally imparted to pupils sitting at the feet of the Guru in the Ashramas and Gurukulas.

Moral and Spiritual Aim: It follows from the foregoing discussion that the aim of education according to Vedanta was pupils' moral and spiritual development. Spirituality was considered a dynamic force, the only basis of continuous advancement towards the only human goal, God realization through varied activities on the social and other planes. The Vedanta said that the Ultimate Principle (Brahman) can be known only by direct intuition and never by logical inquiry and analysis. It was emphasized that study and association with those who had achieved perfection and exalted heights and were capable of leading a searching mind was necessary. A fourfold discipline consisting of Vivek, Vairagva, Satsampat i.e. right conduct including control of thought, self-restraint, Uparati i.e., tolerance, Titiksha i.e. endurance, Sraddha i.e. faith, Sandhan i.e. balanced mental equipoise and Muntuksutva i.e., right desire for attaining liberation by dedicating life to the single goal (The Ultimate Truth) was prescribed.

Character Development: As spiritual development could not be possible without a certain disposition and bent of character, living a pious life according to a definite code of conduct was emphasized. The disciple in the Gurukula was required to follow certain specific rules of conduct strictly. In a way Vedantic education may be considered as the "manifestation of the perfection already within man, the manifestation of the divine already within man". It aimed at human excellence to be achieved through the instrument of education.

In the modern context these aims and objectives may not he literally followed. But the aim of human excellence defined in terms of spiritual living, good moral character based on moral values can not be ignored even by modern education, Education for human excellence, human values backed by Vedantic philosophy should be emphasized by modern education also. Acquisition of Real knowledge. Right thinking and development of Dynamic character in the students should be the aim of modern education also. This seems to be the most desirable implication of Vedantic philosophy. The spiritual growth of the students, i.e., moving from individuality to personality meaning, thereby, development of excellence which is already within him, should form the basis of modern education too. Ultimately, it strongly favours value-based education which is being emphasized today also.

Role of Teacher: Another important aspect of Vedanta philosophy is the source of disciples growth. Who should help the student acquire knowledge and grow spiritually? In this context the teacher (the Guru) was assigned the central place. As the main aim of Vedanta teaching was acquisition of knowledge contained in the Vedas and concerned with the Ultimate Principle, only a person who had himself achieved illumination of the mind and exalted heights could help the student. Only this person had to be the Real teacher. Such teachers were known widely for their knowledge and spiritual exaltation .They occupied very high position of regard and respect due to their knowledge of Vedas and Upanishads and high level of their spiritual growth. Their supreme knowledge (Brahaman Gyan) and Supreme moral living (Adhyatmic Jeevan) were a great source of inspiration for the students. The Vedantic teacher was absorbed in search of the Ultimate Truth and Continuous perfection of life. The implication of this for modern education is that the teacher should acquire mental and moral qualities and live by them in order to inspire his students. He should be a scholar himself if it is desired that the student should develop a passion for knowledge. He should have a good moral character and manifest virtues and human excellence, if the students are desired to be so. The whole philosophy of Vedanta is teacher-centered; and so is the whole of Vedantic education. And, hence the implication of this for modern education is that teacher's position needs to be strengthened. He should be intellectually, socially, morally empowered. He should be an enlightened person, excellent humanity and self-disciplined. Only then, modern education can be an instrument of desirable social change. For this an unbiased, fair and impartial selection and placement of teachers is unavoidable which is possible only when the national governments have a strong will to do so and stop unduly interfering with the system of education.

The Curriculum: As the ultimate aim of the Vedanta teaching was only the spiritual growth of the man, i.e, realization of the Infinite behind his finite organic individuality, it was considered essential to understand this truth and to try to manifest this in himself as well as to help others to manifest it. This was a kind of science of human growth, development and fulfilment. For this purpose the whole of knowledge was divided into two parts, Supreme Knowledge and ordinary knowledge. The supreme knowledge dealt with the concept of soul, the Ultimate Principle and the concept of Maya, the Universal Matter, material cause of the Universe. The Ordinary Knowledge was the study of subjects such as Vedas, Vedang, religion, astronomy, history, puranas, ethics and military science, etc.

The only implication of this may be that there should be provision in the curriculum of the modern education to impart education of moral and spiritual values. This was emphasized in our National Policy on Education-1986 also. It said that erosion of essential values in the society had brought to the focus the need for readjustments in the curriculum in order to make education a forceful tool for the cultivation of social and moral values; education should foster universal and eternal values. An awareness of this need increases with the study of Vedanta philosophy. Hence, in some form, study of Vedanta, its fundamental tenets may be included in the curriculum of, at least, higher education.

The Student: Implications of Vedanta philosophy for the student are of great importance, particularly when the student of today seems to be highly restless, overambitious, defiant and alienated.

The student-teacher relationship as found in Vedas and the Upanishadas was highly cordial. The student was treated as one of the members of the teacher's family. He was very obedient and would serve the teacher in all sincerity. He was required to live a highly religious and moral life. The conditions necessary in him were purity, a real thirst for knowledge and perseverance. The two important conditions of effective learning are that the teacher must have the power to transmit knowledge and values while the student must be fit to receive it. It is, necessary, by implication that the student of today must be fit to acquire knowledge and learn values, the conditions which are seriously lacking in our modern system of education. The students neither have requisite entering behaviour to receive desired knowledge nor they have willingness to learn moral values. The implication of Vedanta philosophy is that, at least, the student must have a desire to acquire knowledge, not the degree or diploma or certificate alone. He should have regard for eternal and spiritual values. The fund of idealism must be there, strong and steady, in our youths; and they must try to keep it alive throughout life. A good student must have good education endowed with an alert mind and strong will, physically vigorous and fit.

The Discipline: The basis of discipline, according to Vedanta philosophy, is the moral and ethical behaviour, not the external control enforced by codes and regulations. The more desirable form of discipline depends upon inner sanctions rather than on external sanctions. It finds an expression into self-restrained individual. It begins with the awakening of the moral law within. Thus, it is self-discipline which is emphasized. This should be the goal of all educational institutions. Through the effective implementation of value-education programmes, efforts should be made to help students learn self-control. Through curricular and extracurricular programmes of education the student must be made to realise the importance of good behaviour. They must be made to learn how to control their passions, their destructive urges and negative emotions. A spiritual orientation of the student's mind is of supreme significance today, if discipline in them is to be fostered on permanent basis.

Buddhist View

The major characteristics of Buddhism are :

1. The fact of four supreme Truths-(i) This world and life of man are full of miseries, (ii) This has a cause which is said to be the ignorance, (iii) This cause (ignorance) can be eliminated, and (iv) the ways and means (path) of eliminating this cause are suggested in Buddha's Ashtangik Marg, the middle course.

2. The Ashtangik Marg is a series of rules of conduct including (i) Right Insight (ii) Right Will Power; (iii) Right Deeds, (iv) Right Vocation, (v) Right Exercise, (vi) Right Memory, (vii) Right Speech, and (viii) Right Meditation

3. One's own desires, greed, aspirations are the main cause of the cycle of birth and death, of world's misery and man's degradation. Man is his own master; he alone can get rid of this cycle and misery (can achieve salvation) by following the Ashtangik Marg.

4. All things originate from some cause and they are momentary. Nothing is permanent on this earth. Everything is perishable (Buddha's Kshanikvad).

5. Existence is purposive. Everything exists for some purpose. Existence is transitory and changeable.

6. The Karma Theory implied that man's sufferings and world's miseries are not providential. They are the results of the bad deeds of the people themselves. 'The man dies but the unperishable impressions of his good-

bad deeds get attached to his newborn body after rebirth, They, then, influence the course of life in this body also.

7. Karma (action) follows a three-state process, mental verbal and physical i.e., thought giving rise to verbalization and finally to action.

Human Excellence: Buddhism may be considered a philosophy of human excellence signifying man's emancipation from worldly pain and miseries which is a harsh reality of life on this earth. Realization of this fact and knowledge of ways and means of escaping this may go a long way in the adjustment of the human being to life's situations. It has a therapeutic value inherent in it. This should, therefore, constitute an aim, a function of modern education to impart this knowledge to the students. A knowledge of all these principles of Buddhism may contribute to students moral and spiritual development.

Realization of the fact that one's own desires and aspirations are a cause of his tensions, pain and miseries, he may try to control his desires, at least the asocial and conflicting desires which may lessen his miseries. This kind of awareness must form a part of man's education.

The knowledge of Kshanikvad and Karma theory may lead to insight into man's sufferings and world's tensions.

The Ashtangik Marg suggests various rules of conduct and human excellence. They should be interpreted in terms of the present reality of social and institutional environment. The teachers and the students along with all those who are associated with the process of education should be made to understand and follow them. They constitute a set of extremely important values. They may constitute foundation stones of student discipline and good life.

The greatest message of Buddhism is observing Self Control and Righteousness which should constitute essential values to be taught and developed in students through education.

Jain Views

The most significant principles and characteristics of Jainism are:

1. It is a non-theistic religion of moral purity and excellence. It aimed at liberating man out of the degradation and sufferings, but not by worshipping gods and going through rituals. The path of pure ethical conduct was considered enough good for this purpose.

2. Jainism denies any Reality beyond this objective world. It asserts that man himself can attain godhood by following the path of moral and spiritual discipline.

3. Man is the true Reality for Jainism. He himself is capable of attaining infinite power, infinite knowledge, infinite faith and infinite bliss.

4. Good and bad actions of man leave an impression upon his soul which go on accumulating and constitute karman body. After death it goes with the soul. Godhood or man's goodliness or excellence is the most developed state of the soul, a stage where man's actions done with passion and past karmas influences are totally exhausted.

5. According to Jainism knowledge is supreme means of salvation which is said to be of two kinds-relative and absolute. Knowledge, however, does not mean mere intellectual or scriptural knowledge; it means inner realization. It means true understanding of man and his environment leading, gradually, to self-enlightenment.

6. Right faith, right knowledge, and right conduct, three-fold discipline called three jewels of Jainism are the means of getting rid of ignorance and bondage and attain liberation. Right conduct means living a detached life and observing five vows such as— (i) non-violence, (ii) satya (iii) asteya, (iv) braham-charya, and (v) aparigraha (non-possession).

7. Besides, a number of practices are recommended to be followed which were considered important as they provide strength to traverse the path of perfection.

Relevance in Modern Times: Some of these principles and characteristics of Jaina philosophy do have implications for modern education. The most significant point of Jainism is moral purity and excellence of man. Modern education must aim at the moral development and excellence of students. The aim of modern education is, no doubt, described to be the spiritual and moral development of students. This is supported by Jainism also. Man is the true Reality for Jainism. This seems to be justified as one of the major considerations of modern education, is the individual aim of education.

When Jainism says knowledge does not mean mere intellectual or scriptural knowledge, it means inner realization, it implies that knowledge should result into Wisdom, into under-standing, into truthful thinking. Modern education also should-emphasize this. Mere cramming or acquisition of knowledge without understanding meaning and implications is of no use. This is what should be avoided. Knowledge which is imparted should result into Wisdom, into enlightenment.

Right faith, right knowledge and right conduct, the jewels of Jainism interpreted in the context of the present society and its conditions must be considered more meaningful. This three-dimensional development of the students may result into a more powerful nation.

Non-violence is a well-accepted principle of human conduct. It was advocated by Mahatma Gandhi also. Interpreted in a very general and broad way it may mean not to do any harm to any living being. This may go a long way in establishing a peaceful and progressive social order.

The principle of penance of Jain philosophy implies that for achieving excellence incessant hard work is essential. The students and the teachers must realize the importance of sustained intense efforts. In the absence of hard work and continuous efforts, success of high order and excellence can not be achieved.

The karma theory also implies that one should do good deeds. A belief in karma theory stimulates men to be good to others, to help others, to be pious and truthful, to be unselfish. Belief in karma theory motivates men to avoid ignoble thoughts and actions. These ideas may appeal to the students also and may cater to their moral and social development.

Islamic View

Major characteristics of Islam are:

1. In Islam Allah(God) is the Ultimate Reality. The whole of the universe is the creation of God. Allah is present everywhere, in everything. There is only one God and He is all powerful. His will is supreme, absolute and perfectly arbitrary.

2. Man in Islam has a duty to serve God in humble submission having no right, no power or will of his own.

3. After death the body is destroyed, but soul rests for a period of time in AI-Berzahk. On the Day of Judgement all the dead rise from their graves and are sent to Heaven or Hell depending upon the deeds either good or bad.

4. The ultimate destiny of man lies in eternal membership, either of heaven or hell.

5. The true knowledge, according to Islam, is the knowledge about Allah contained in the Quran. This knowledge also contains man's duties towards God, man's destiny and life after death. This whole knowledge is the God's word.

6. Islam is a legalistic religion laying down rules to be followed. It teaches people specific ways of sincere devotion and prayer to God, ways and means of self-purification and religious ethics.

7. Islam prescribes disciplinary rules to be strictly followed by all believers in Islam. The five values constituting "Five Pillars of Islam" are—(1) daily prayer (2) absolute oneness with Allah (3) Alms-giving (4) fasting and (5) Pilgrimage to Mecca.

A Way of Life: Islam is more a way of life than a philosophy of life. Its teachings, particularly relate to human conduct and ethics of life. Hence, the values reflected in the Quran are in the form of rules and ideals which should be followed by those who have faith in Islam. These values, at least some of them, can be considered important from the point of view of education of all children.

The aim of self-purification by praying and through full devotion can be considered important. Daily prayer, absolute oneness with God, alms-giving and several other rules of conduct have their importance if human excellence and perfection are desired. No system of education can deny their utility. Taken together all of these constitute man's education.

The teaching of Islam emphasize man's freedom and unity of all people. This is a much needed value which may go a long way in establishing peace and harmony in the society. And this is the fundamental aim of education all over the world. Emphasis on human brotherhood is, no doubt an islamic virtue which should be stressed as part of education of all people.

The teachings of Islam have a bearing only on the aims of education. Being a legalistic religion it influences the concept of discipline and values of life.

QUESTIONS

Explain in brief the Educational implications under :

(a) Hinduism

(b) Buddhism

(c) Jainism

(d) Islam

8

Values of Morality

Value-system and Morality are amorphous concepts. Time, place and social milieu are the chief determinants of all moral codes in the world. Morality, therefore, does not lend itself to any precise interpretation. A few examples would illustrate how man's attitude to moral values tends to change or develop along these variables.

Modern science holds that 'matter' is governed by the theory of 'cause and effect'. Ancient philosophers had looked upon the phenomenon of cause and effect in a wider as well as different context. Indians extended the 'cause and effect' concept to human life-cycle and the world of spirit; and they called it the 'Principle of karma'. According to this theory, the present state of every creature is the *summun bonum* of his or her past actions in the past and the present life. The Buddhists also subscribe to this view. *Zend Avesta* of the Zoroastrians (Parsees) holds that after death, the soul of a good person is met by a beautiful maiden, who says to him, "I am thy own conscience: I was lovely and thou madest me still lovelier; I was fair and thou madest me still fairer through thy good thought, thy good speech, and thy good deeds". And then the soul is led into the paradise of endless light. On the contrary, the soul of a wicked person is met by a hideous old woman, "uglier than the ugliest thing", who is his own conscience. She says to him, "I am thy bad actions. O youth of evil thoughts, of evil words, of evil deeds, of evil religion, it is on account of thy will and actions that I am hedious and vile". Thereafter, the soul is led down into the hell of endless darkness."

It is obvious that convictions of this nature will have a farreaching effect on our thoughts,, words and moral behaviour. However, there are many materialists who believe in cause and effect theory but who have no faith in a life after death. According to them, the five elements of air, earth, fire, sky and water, of which every creature on this earth is made up of, merge into the respective five elements of nature after death and this heralds the end of the lifecycle. Actions of such people are, obviously not conditioned by thoughts of 'life to come' and mans soul facing the consequences of his actions. Let us next consider some more specific examples in relation to varying social milieus.

The Zoroastrians declare 'truthfulness' as the highest virtue. The ancient Persians had a great veneration for truth and a strong punishment, was provided for false swearing. Truthfulness, as a virtue, does not have that high place in Japan. This could also be due to the fact that the Japanese, in view of their great veneration for their superiors, could not say unpleasant things to them even if these were true. The Greeks, prior to Socrates, were reputed for their disregard for promises and truthfulness. They could practise fraud freely to achieve their end. It goes to the credit of Socrates to have tried to reverse this trend among the Greeks and finally Raving laid down his life for the ideal of truth.

The 'caste-system' among the Hindus, which was evolved as a division of labour and was nurtured by them for promoting specialisation in trade, industry and various professions among its adherents, stands condemned today by the Hindus themselves. With the cruelties perpetrated by the high-castes on the low-castes in the past, any discrimination based on caste is now a legal offence in India.

Worse than the caste-system was the custom of slavery which was commonly accepted by the Babylonians, the Romans, the Muslims and the Greeks. In fact, slavery is considered by the historians as an important contributory factor for the fall of the Roman civilisation. The master had an unquestioned authority over his slave; he gloatcd over the agony of his slave till the latter died. This kind of insensitivity to morality would, today, make anyone shiver to the marrow of his bone. According to Hothouse, "the recognition of the slave traffic by Mohammedanism has been, and is to this day, a curse to Africa and a source of disturbance to the world's politics".

Aristotle taught to hunt barbarians (all non-Greeks) for purposes of getting slaves and he considered it as right and proper as to hunt animals for food and sacrifice.

Filial loyalty was at great premium in ancient China. A father, with the consent of the son's maternal uncle, could require a magistrate to whip to death his unofilial son. "A patricide is beheaded, his body cut in pieces, his house torn down, his neighbours are punished, his chief teacher is put to death, and the magistrates of the district in which he lived are degraded or deposed" a Filial piety and duty towards the emperor are the two cornerstones of the Japanese ethics. The latter would invite outright rejection by most modern nations today.

Roman Catholics, among Christians, regard celibacy as a virtue; but among the Zoroastrians celibacy and fasting and self-mor-have no place, Islam goes to the extent of accepting and even justifying polygamy.

For all followers of Christ compassion is a laudable quality. The edifice of Jainism would crumble if the elements of comparison and non-violence are excluded from it. In contrast, the Hellas' motto for justice was 'Do no wrong, and suffer no wrong to self or others', with emphasis on the latter. The Hellas considered revenge a virtue if a person had been wronged. Forgiveness was a onsidaed trait of a timid mind. Hammurabi's code of ethics in Babylon, which is considered to be one of the oldest in the world, recommended "eye for eye and tooth for tooth". If a person killed someone's daughter, the killer's daughter was butchered in retaliation and the society accepted it; It is a matter of conjecture what happened if the killer had no daughter!

The Chinese moralist Mencius called the war marshals as great criminals though are may find the present-day Communist China far removed from this thinking.

The war ethics of today is shrouded with hypocrisy. Today, every war is claimed to have been fought for peace and nuclear weapons are said to have been manufactured for self-defence only The war ethics of our ancestors was, however, more straightforward. In India war was assigned to chiefs. The king could keep an army and it was his duty to protect his people. Manu's laws of war forbade use of poisonous weapons, striking an enemy without armour or an onlooker civilian, or one who was asleep or unconscious, etc. War prisoners could be made to work; but they were to be given proper food. Special care was to be taken of children, women and the old people, and so on. Militarism, in any form has no place in Buddusm. Contrary to this the Assyrians and the Babylonians exulted over the cruelties perpetrated by them in wars. One such account is given below:

" The nobles, as many as had revolted, I flayed; with their skins I covered the pyramid. Some of these I immured in the midst of the pyramid; others above the pyramid I impaled on stakes-three thousand of their captives I burned with fire. I left no one alive among them to become a hostage-I cut off the hands (and) feet of some; I cut off the noses, the ears (and) the fingers of others; the eyes of numerous soldiers I put out. In the middle (of them) I suspended their heads on vine stemp in the neighbourhood of their city. Their young men (and) maidens I burned as a holocaust".

The brief picture indicates the wide variations in the value-systems of different societies living at different times in the same or different geographical regions.

Teaching Morality

Transformation of values takes place due to several factors—political, economic and social. In the political sphere, constitutionally and democratically elected governments have replaced the rule of the colonisers, the maharajas and the nawabs. The valuebased politics of the days of yore de-facto stands condemned today by the political opportunists all over the world. In India too, the principled politics of Mahatma Gandhi, Jawahar Lal Nehru and Jaya Prakash Narain stands abandoned by most of the politicians.

In the sphere of economics, the mercantile industry has been replaced by modern industries bringing a new class of entrepreneurs with new values. The pursuit of heavy industries has led to heavy investments, higher production, consumerism, and so on. It has also led to the concentration of capital in fewer hands. The gap between the rich and the poor in all countries as well as at the international levels has widened, leading to conflicts in several new forms between the rich and the poor. The urge to gain political supremacy in the world has led to the cold-war situation which is altogether a new concept.

In the social sphere, though casteism has been legally banned in India, it gets considerable weightage in the selection of candidates and vote-casting during elections. With India declaring itself a welfare state, formal accountability of public servants has increased manifold compared to what it was during the colonial days of India.

The above scenario keeps on undergoing a continuous process of change. Therefore, the outlook of the people and their values are bound to change so as to adjust to the realities of the new situations created by science, technology, political and other factors.

The Comprehension

Value-system is the fusion of moral and spiritual values. The Report on the Religious and Moral Education, prepared by the, Committee headed by Shri Sri Prakash defined moral behaviour as the conduct of man towards man in various situations in which human beings come together in home, social and economic fields and in the life of outside world generally.— Anything that helps us to behave properly towards others is of moral value.

Spiritual values are also moral values; but in this case there is emphasis on the inner-self of the individual and his relation with the Supreme Being. Anything that takes the individual out of one-self and inspires one to sacrifice for a great cause for the good of others is spiritual.

It may be conceded here that there is no universally accepted definition of 'good' or 'bad. As pointed out earlier, these terms are related to time, place and persons. Good may, by some persons, be equated with the will of God and evil as an inducement of Satan. Good is also identified with pleasure and evil with suffering. There is hardly any defined frontier between licit and illicit. Such a definition is only possible on the basis of certain socially accepted norms or governmental laws. It is easier to discriminate the lawful from the unlawful.

Morality is concerned, both, with beliefs and actions which are in conformity with the social norms shaped, modified and chiselled over a length of time. In ancient Greece, there was emphasis on 'beliefs' whereas in ancient India, the stress was on 'action'. However, action had to be in conformity with Dharma. Thus action itself had moral spiritual base. Manu, the great Indian codifier, on the strength of the Vedas and the Smritis, says that doing noble actions is the highest duty (dharma) of man.

The belief about what is right and what is wrong; what ought to be done and what ought not to be done is generally defined as moral belief. It is a matter of common observance that the beliefs of the people in any group are not always in consonance with their actions. The fact that adultery maybe regarded immoral by many people in a country, yet some people may by involved in this practice and no law may exist against adultery in the country, can be cited as an example in this regard. Numerous religious customs may not stand the test of a rational debate, yet many people believe in them and adhere to them. One cannot categorise such beliefs as 'right beliefs'. There is, therefore, an inherent problem in identifying beliefs', and 'right actions'.

Further, sometimes an action may appear to be moral, yet it may not be so. Reduction in prices of consumer goods would be moral if it is intended to help .the poor and the general public but not so if its motive is to boost up the sales. Therefore, the 'will' and the 'motive' behind the action is very important. An action becomes moral only if the doer acts in 'desirable way' of his own free-will for the good of others.

At times, an act may not be in consonance with the social mores, yet it may not be immoral. For example, the wide spread students demonstrations and marches in Beijing (capital of China) spread over several days in May, 1989 and in violation of the martial law imposed by the Chinese Government could not be termed immoral, because basically the slogan of the students was "We want Mr. Science and Mr. Democracy"

Therefore, notwithstanding the fact that it is difficult to precisely define the philosophical and abstract concept 'morality' one may attempt to understand this term in the following ways:

(a) The basis of morality is right belief and right action.

(b) The element of free-will of the doer is fundamental to any moral act. The doer must adhere to the moral act in spite of a temptation to deviate from it.

(c) Moral act extends both over physiological and psychological domains.

Different Kinds

(i) Moral and spiritual values may be classified in several ways. In terms of importance, values maybe divided into the following three groups.

(a) Trivial values, such as the kind of clothes one should wear while going to a restaurant. Today, even the dress that one wears at a funeral or while attending a marriage party has come to occupy a trivial significance, particularly in the urban context.

(b) More substantial beliefs, such as the ones which also effect people other than the belief-holder himself. These include punctuality, cleanliness, etc.

(c) Fundamental or perennial and emphemeral beliefs, such as practice of truthfulness, spirit of patriotism, kindness towards all life etc.

(ii) The great Indian sage Vatsyayana relates virtues and vices to human faculties and gives the following classification.

(a) Virtues of body: charity, helping the needy, social service.

(b) Virtues of speech: truthfulness, benevolence, gentleness, recitation of scriptures,

(c) Virtues of mind: kindness, unworldliness, piety.

(d) Vices of body: cruelty, theft; sexual indulgence.

(e) Vices of speech: falsehood, harshness, scandal.

(f) Vices of mind: hatred, covetousness, disbelief,

(iii) In terms of social order, values may be classified as political, economic, social, cultural, spiritual, aesthetic and individual values. Thus, values encompass the entire gamut of life. According to the Indian philosophy, individual interest may be sacrificed for that of the family, the interest of the family for that of the don and all interests for that of the soul. According to Indian spiritual philosophers, individual soul is a part and parcel of the universal soul.

(iv) There has been no time in the history of man, when he had no moral values. The values, therefore, can also be grouped as ancient, medieval and modern values. Some people hold that there is nothing modern in the value-system of the present age, for example, according to them the so-called modern concept of egalitarianism existed in olden days in the form of tolerance; and scientific temper in the shape of indepth analysis of the phenomenon of life and forces of nature. It maybe relevant to point out here that when under pressure coal gets transformed into diamond, it is not called coal. It is given a new name, which everyone accepts. The same argument can be applicable in case of ancient and modern values also.

Evolution and Growth

All morality, according to one belief is deemed to have originated from God, His son, His Messengers and His Avtars. Revealed scriptures and great works are other important sources of dissemination of moral values. It is believed that the sun god presented code of laws to Hammurabi; God gave commandments to Moses; Zeus gave moral sense to humans so that they could cooperate with each other and match the beasts who are stranger and speedier than man. Myths such as the one relating to the dual between the gods and the demons (virtue and vice), where gods are shown victorious in the end help in promoting moral values among the people. These may be lies but they are 'noble lies' which originate and disseminate moral values.

Genetic affinity is considered to be an important factor in parental altruism. Anthropologists and historians believe that when homosapiens started living in families, its members developed a sense of obligation to each other. Man may have, as well, imbibed moral behaviour from his animal ancestors. Many animals abide by the norms of mutual cooperation and help. Strikingly, wolves bring the meat of the kill to the members of their group who are not present at the kill; dolphins support their sick to come up to the water surface and breathe. The famous story of the persevering spider which inspired the disappointed king Robert Bruce, to fight once again is included in the school text-books to instil this quality of the spider among students.

The ancient seers of India, perhaps, gave a very highly rational explanation in this context when they said that cosmic order (rta) was the foundation of human ethics. They felt that the beauty in earth, sky and nature, as a whole, emerged from this cosmic law (rta). "Gradually, the cosmic sense of rta as Natural Law developed into the social sense of rta as Moral Law". In other words, morality was as essential to bring about beauty and harmony in life as the cosmic order in nature. Punishment is not based on whims; but it is the result of wrong actions only. One could enjoy life if one could ensure order in one's activities. Rta, in a way, was the basis of the ancient Indian moral laws.

Great men, or for that matter any group of dominant persons, greatly influence the value-system of the society. The Bhaktas and the Sufis, during the medieval period of Indian history, inspired people towards chastity, renunciation, desirelessness and other similar values. Material aspirations came to be looked upon as undivine. The feudal system and dynastic rules of this age, whipped up sex urge among some classes of people and also produced a class of flatterers and courtiers. In the modern era, Raja Ram Mohun Roy, Swami Vivekananda, Sir Syed Ahmed Khan, Badrudin Tyabji, Madan Mohan Malviya, Lala Lajpat Rai, Swami Dayanand Saraswati, Mahatama Gandhi (1869-1948) and a galaxy of other reformers worked for the independence of the country, better deal for women, social justice for the backward classes and many other values which are enshrined in the Indian Constitution.

The Constitution of India, with its 64 amendments (till 1989), is an important source of the present-day Indian value-system. It lists ten Fundamental Duties for each citizen. The Preamble of the Constitution emphasises certain important values. These may be called national values. Cessation of cold war between countries may be categorised as an international value. Preservation of environment is a national-as well as an international value.

The governments try to uphold and promote these values through laws, penal codes and other measures. Parmatha Nath Bose divides the evolution of human values chronologically in three stages.

(a) During the early stages, the predatory man, like animals, sought comfort in material and emotional gratification. Emotional expression in humans found expression through arts, such as' poetry, painting, sculpture etc. Thus, this is the first level of achieve-ment of the value-system in human society.

(b) During the intermediate stage, intellectual development separates him from the animals. He begins to examine physical and psychical processes. It is at this juncture that science and philosophy are born and scientific and philosophical values take shape.

(c) At the advanced stage of his development, man's spiritual faculty has developed and he begins to seek happiness from within rather than from without. Two faculties develop at this stage:

(i) spiritual which inspires belief in supernatural beings; and

(ii) moral faculty which enables a person to perceive moral good or evil independent of expediency, consideration of utility or physical welfare or suffering.

Incidentally this analysis would give students of ethics some idea about the level of cultural heights that India had attained thousands of years ago with her highly developed spiritual culture which remains, even today, unrivalled in the world.

Fundamental Needs

All human values are shaped by our wants. Man has material as well as spiritual wants. These may be termed as wants of the outer and inner life respectively. The former promote qualities of industry, order, perseverence etc., which have a survival value. The wants of inner life promote cultural values like humility, mercy, self-sacrifice etc. Neither of these wants should be considered inferior to the other.

A moral code would have a greater appeal for the people in general if it is simple and not complicated. The Buddhism was able to make a mass appeal because its teachings were simple as compared to Brahmanism which in the days of Buddha had become highly complicated. No moral code would be acceptable in the modern scientific age unless it has a rational basis and can appeal to one's reason.

Socrates, the great Greek philosopher, emphasised right knowledge as the true basis for moral actions. Goethe, on the other hand, observed that man comes to know himself not through reflection but through action or conduct only. He said, "Do thy dutyand thou wilt know what thou art". According to the ancient Indian thought it is the conduct (Aadiaram) which determines the moral standards of an individual or a group. It is said you are judged not by what you say; but what you are in totality.

Important Elements

Is the primary aim of moral education to have more scientists, better cricketers, large number of tennis-stars or athletes who can win more gold medals for the country? Perhaps, not. The chief aim of value education is to achieve maximum human resource development so as to improve our total life. One can not do better than to quote here Edwin Markhani in order to bring out the great importance of value-education. He said:

"We are blind until we see that in the human plan, nothing is worth the making if it does not make the man. Why build these cities glorious if man unbuiled goes? In vain we build the world, unless the builder also grows".

The Other Side

There is hardly any issue on which one may find complete unanimity of views in the society. The situation is no different in the case of the value-system. Many people feel that there is, at presents a state of total chaos in the society so far as moral values are concerned. However, a number of people do not share deep concern over the so-called deterioration of moral values. The great scientist Darwin had remarked that mankind is continuously progressing on a course of evolution. Undoubtedly, he must have been alluding to the biological factors only. The great spiritual leader Aurobindo Ghosh had said that the homosapien would steadily attain super-manhood and that there is no returning for him to the lower forms of life. Some people hold that the psychological man has, in modern times, been left much behind the physiological man and the cultural march of human race has failed to match its technological progress. On the contrary, there is a class of people who feel that from the predatory man to the present-day civilised homosapien, man's cultural advancement excels his achievement in any other field.

The data collected for the study indicated a convergence of views. Bulk of respondents feel that there has been a decline in moral values. To the statement that "over the past 5-10 years, moral values among Indians have declined", (G-I), the 881 respondents expressed their opinions as follows :

S.No.	Category	Number Agreeing	No. undecided	No. disagreed	No. of persons who expressed no opinion
(1)	Total no. of Respondents (881)	775	61	44	1
(2)	Respondents in the age-group 25-40 years (233)	208 (89.3)	10 (4.3)	15 (6.4)	— (0)
(3)	Respondents above 40 years of age (573)	507 (88.5)	39 (6.8)	26 (45)	1 (0.2)
(4)	High School or equivalent (98)	84 (85.7)	6 (6.1)	8 (8.2)	— (0)
(5)	MA and above or equivalent (405)	359 (88.6)	27 (6.7)	18 (4.4)	1 (03)
(6)	Educationists (21)	21 (95.5)	0 (0)	1 (4.5)	0 (0)
(7)	Advocates (10)	7 (70)	1 (10)	2 (20)	0 (0)

Note: (i) Figures in brackets below the columns c to f indicate per centages, whereas such figures below column b give the number of respondents in the corresponding category. (ii) Though this kind of analysis was done in the case of several categories of respondents, but the entire bunch of statistics has not been given here in order to avoid confusion. (iii) The above system has been followed all through in this work.

Of the total 881 non-student general category respondents, 88 per cent concurred with the above (G-I)** statement, 5 per cent of them expressed their disagreement to it and the remaining 7 per cent were undecided on this issue. The moral crisis has, perhaps, became so obvious that the level of education did not make any significant difference in their view-point on this statement. The highest degree of agreement was expressed by the educationists and the least by the advocates. Reasons for this are, perhaps, obvious! Even in the case of the latter, there is a high degree of agreement about the decline in moral values.

Perhaps people of every generation always feel that the values have declined in their time as compared to what they were in the 'golden past'. Even when the Greek civilization had reached its heights, Plato (427-347B.C.) stated more than two millennia ago;

"What is happening to our young people. They disrespect their elders, they disobey their parents. They ignore the laws. They riot in the street, inflamed with wild notions. Their morals are decaying. What is to become of them?"

There may be valid reasons to lament over the loss of values in a society; but sometimes it may be difficult to pin-point whether a value-system is undergoing a metamorphosis or whether it is declining.

For example, during the Indian freedom struggle of 1930's and 40s, many young men and women left their studies, jobs and families to work for their country against the colonial rule. Many in the older generation had then opposed the action of the youths; but later on it was these youths that were acclaimed as national heroes. In 1967, when the students of the Wisconsin University (U.S.A.) staged a massive demonstration against the napalming of North Vietnam by America, they did not receive the requisite general public support in their, struggle; but subsequent events proved that the young students were right.

According to the Ṙishis of ancient India, gods and demons; creation and destruction; good and evil are the products of the same Cosmic Energy. They have coexisted from the inception of this universe. No Age or society ever had good without evil or evil without good and decline in moral values only means absence of a proper balance between the two. It is the domination of demonic destructive, evil and such like tendencies over the godly, constructive and noble tendencies which amounts to the decline in values.

Moral values have an ideological and a philosophical basis. It would not be wrong to say that during the feudal as well as colonial past, these bases were greatly weakened. The struggle for country's independence did, to some extent, restore the ideological basis, but within a couple of decades after independence the hand of the clock again started reversing. Today, we are at a stage where it is difficult to state categorically if any organised section of the society is seriously and consistently working for upholding moral values.

There are various causes for the decline of values in a society. One can concede that the fall in the Indian value-system is a part of world-wide apathy to moral values.

Further, moral values are generally nourished by the middle class. The rich are generally indifferent to the value-system of the society; and the poor, because of inherent economic and other constraints cannot live up to it. Today, the aspirations of the neo-middle class have increased greatly and the value-system has been subordinated to these aspirations. This has subscribed to the lowering of moral values.

Operative Elements

Science and material progress has also greatly contributed to the fall of social and spiritual values. Science has led to industrialisation; industrialisation to capitalism; capitalism to overproduction and concentration of wealth in the hands of the few; and all this to the political and economic exploitation of the many by a few.

The statement contained in the questionnaire in regard to the causes of the fall of moral values in the society read as follows:

The following are the causes for the fall in values in the society:-

(a) Absence of proper religious teaching.

(b) Fall in moral values of our political leaders.

(c) Mass media adopting no proper policy to build moral standards in the society. (G-16)

The scores for these statements are given below:

Statement	*Number of persons who allotted first, second or third positions to the statement*			*Number who left the statement blank*	*Weighted of score*
	I Position	*II Position*	*III Position*		
(a)	224	233	301	123	54.5%
(b)	328	260	170	123	63.3%
(c)	212	269	277	123	54.9%

Thus, among the reasons which were given in the questionnaire, the fall in moral values of our political leaders was considered by the respondents to have contributed significantly to a greater extent than the other two values to the decline of values in the society. It confirms the view-point held by many people that the value-system emerges from the seat of power. Absence of proper religious teaching was given the third place in this regard. Nearly 14 per cent of the respondents did not express any opinion on this statement.

In this respect, Caudwell says, "And the unparalleled increase in the productive power has given birth, not to peace, plenty, and happiness, but to war, famine and misery. Anarchy is the keynote of crisis in all spheres.Why then have not all the psycho-analysis, Eddingtons, Keynes, Spengiers, and Bishops who have surveyed the scene, been able to locate a source of infection common to all modern cultures. For answer, these people must take to themselves, the words of Herzen: 'We are not the doctors, we are the disease".

The Measurement

Leadership in all fields tends to influence the value-system of the common man also. This hypothesis is truer when viewed in the context of the politicians, the teachers and the parents. The impact of the politicians, is on a wide cross-section of the society, whereas the impact of the teachers and parents is deeper on the childern as among other things, it starts working during the early and impressionable years of the individuals. Therefore, an attempt was made through the questionnaire meant for the general public and the one meant for the students to rate politicians, teachers and parents on the basis of some of the statements that follow.

The Assessment

"Keeping in view the conduct of majority of Indian political leaders, one concludes that their quality is

(a) Of the desired level

or

(b) Average

or

(c) Below the desired level." (G-8)

Of the 881 respondents in the G group*, 848 i.e., 96.2 per cent opted for one of the above three options. 3 per cent were undecided and the remaining 0.8 per cent recorded disagreement to these options.

Option	***Number of Persons Agreeing***	
(a)	45	(5.%)
(b)	154	(17.5%)
(c)	649	(73.6%)
Total (881)	**848**	**(96.2%)**

The general public have given a clear verdict that the majority of the Indian political leaders are below the desired level.

In this context, one should not forget that the class of politicians during and immediately after the country's independence struggle were highly respected by the public. Leaders like Mahatama Gandhi, Jawahar lal Nehru, Sardar Patel, Rafi Ahmad Kidwai, Khan Abdul Ghaffar Khan, are revered even today. They made great sacrifices for the national good. The profiles of the politicians who made up the country's Constituent Assembly also fall in the same category. However, while talking of the majority of the present-day politicians, the picture draws a blank.

The Bofors, and the Oil and Natural Gas Commission deals bring a lot of disrepute to the politicians.

No doubt, the charges of nepotism, accumulation of undeclared black-money, etc., are not confined to the politicians alone, but this does not exonerate the politicians from being responsible for malpractices and setting an unworthy example of leadership before their people.

Commenting on the criminalisation of politics with muscle and money power and multitude of corrupt practices, one of the English dailies of national standing had once remarked as follows:

"Every passing day reveals disturbing evidence of growing criminalisation of Indian politics. The results of Sunday's (16.10.88) elections for the pramukhs (chiefs) of block development committees in U.P are latest manifestations. In several districts in east U.P criminals or candidates supported by them, won elections convincingly at the expense of the candidates backed by political parties. Most remarkable was the victory of a known bandit chief of Banda district. Not only did he win, four of his candidates also won. A well-known mafia don won, unopposed, from Sitapur block, which is right near to Lucknow-the State Capital. All this should come as no surprise. The link between criminals and politicians has assumed alarming proportions in the Hindi belt since 1967, when booth-capturing first occurred on a massive scale in Bihar.—But this phenomenon is not confined to the Congress; the links between Janta big wigs and mafia dons of Dhanbad are not even sought to be overt."

The following remark by a scholar-poet-politician, a former Minister in the country's Union Cabinet, and later on Ambassador, is highly significant.

"Of course the present-day politician is rated differently from the luminaries of the freedom struggle, but then he is only elected by the people. Perhaps, no people can rise much above their moral and cultural ethos in elections also."

Teachers:

Statement S-la read as follows:*

(i) "Keeping in view the conduct of majority of Indian teachers, one concludes that their quality is—

(a) Of the desired level

Or

(b) Average

Or

(c) Below the desired level." (S-10)

(ii) "The following factors are responsible for lowering the status of teachers

(a) Lack of scholarship in teachers;

(b) Teachers' lust for money;

(c) Absence of sacrifice among teachers for their students."

In the second statement, the respondents were asked to grade the various reasons in descending order of importance. (S-14)

The guru or the acharya, as the teacher was known in this country in ancient times, had a place of reverence in India. He was the repository of knowledge and a person of exemplary high character. During the period of education of the student, the guru assumed the responsibility of acting as the parent of his students and the students were part and parcel of his family. The mother and the father gave physical birth to the child; and the teacher gave the second, i.e. the intellectual birth to him. Being a religious as well as an intellectual leader of the society, the teacher enjoyed great respect, even in the court of the kings. The Indian teacher basked in the sunshine of this glory (though somewhat to a lesser degree with the passage of time) till the advent of the British rule. During the British rule, education became procurable and saleable for money. Its past sanctity started vanishing. Any assessment of the present day Indian teachers, must obviously take the above historical background into account. However, the Indian ethos demand a certain level of accomplishment from the teachers. Once they enter the teaching profession, they must come up to the expectations of the society. In order to come up to the expected level of accomplishment, the teachers need to have some idea of their image which they now have in the public eyes.

Rating the Teachers

Option	*No. of Persons Agreeing*	*Per centage*
(a) Of the desired level	32	12
Or		
(b) Average	182	682
Or		
(c) Below the desired level.	46	172
Total	**261**	**97.4%**

Six, i.e. 2.2 per cent respondents were undecided and one (0.496) of the school students (male) expressed disagreement with the statement that the teacher's quality was below the desired level. Thus, by and large, teachers have been rated as mediocres by the students. Students' rating of teachers may give teachers some pseudosatisfaction when compared with the following assessment of the politicians by the general public.

	Politicians	*Teachers*
(a) Of the desired level 5.1 P.c.	12.0 P.c.	
Or		
(b) Average	175 P.c.	682 P.c.
Or		
(c) Below the desired level	73.6 p.c.	172 p.c.

It goes without saying that the academic and behavioural excellence of teachers will tend to make their students also likewise. Similarly, the mediocrity of teachers is likely to produce the products of an average quality only.

Teachers have, thus, to accept their share of the existing social malaise, especially in respect of their students. It has been aptly remarked, "Teachers can escape from their influence over the moral and spiritual development of their pupils by closing their schools." Teaches are charged with an important responsibility of guiding their students. By entering the teaching profession they, ipso-*facto*, accept this responsibility. In order to fulfil this obligation, they must raise their own level of conduct in their own eyes as well as in the estimation of the public. The Urdu poet was not wrong when he said—

"Rahbar-e-gum gashta ko lazim hai apni ahtiat, Rah pe bane se pahle rah pe ana bhi hai."

'A guide has to be very careful about himself. He has to be on the right track himself, before he can bring others onto it.'

It would be appropriate to diagnose here a couple of causes responsible for lowering the status of teachers.

Causes Responsible for Lowering Teachers Status

Statement	*Number of persons who alloted first, second or third positions to this statement*			*Number of persons who left the statement blank*	*Weighted score*
	I	*II*	*III*		
(a)	42	80	142	3	53.4%
(b)	116	82	66	3	72.1%
(c)	106	102	55	4	72%

Thus in the opinion of the college as well as school students it is not so much the lack of scholarship as the other two factors which are responsible for bringing down the status of teachers. Their lust for money and absence of the element of sacrifice among teachers have been considered almost equally important factors for lowering the status of teachers. In this regard a respondent (a colonel in the Defence Services) had remarked very appropriately: "The ethos of the teachers needs to change from those of the merchants to those of the gurus."

In this connection, the students were to react to the following statement.

"Yonger generation will show more respect to their parents, if:

(a) Parents give greater freedom to their children as children grow in age:

(b) Parents spend more time with their children;

(c) Parents themselves keep adjusting to changing social values". (S-15)

Students were required to rank the above statements.

Parents Assessed by Children

	Overall score as given by all respondents	*Scores given by male students in*		*Scores given by female students in*	
		schools	*colleges*	*Schools*	*colleges*
(a)	45.8%	46.6%	51%	42.6%	44.3%
(b)	66.9%	64.8%	66.6%	69.4%	68.1%
(c)	83.1%	88.6%	79.4%	88%	81%

It is interesting to observe that the order assigned , to various statements by the total group and different sub-groups-of students is identical.

All students, whether in schools or colleges, also want their parents to spend more time with them, for this greatly contributes to establishing emotional rapport between the parents and their children. Such a rapport is necessary so as to ward off psychological problems among children. In some cases where the parents are educated, dialogues and meetings between parents and children are also a source of education for the latter.

However, these meetings can be fruitful only if parents with the changing times keep on adjusting to the changing social values. Present day parents are not what their parents were and their children cannot be what they are. This is a fast changing world where scientific discoveries, mass-media, and international influences are revolutionising the thought-processes which were so far circumscribed when these factors were absent or had a limited impact. In case where the parents refuse to adjust to the transforming social values, the rift between parents and their children is bound to ensue sooner than later. It is worth noting that the young students have not accorded high priority to have greater freedom.

It is difficult to say that the moral values have totally declined. For every treacherous traitor, there has always been a courageous fighter in the world. If there are terrorists, there are Vinoba's and Mother Teresa's also to heal the wounds of the oppressed. Of course, the cases of moral decline are sensationally highlighted through the mass media whereas hundreds of people leading a pious life do not catch the attention of the mass media because they do not create sensation. Notwithstanding all this, a fairly large section of the society feels that the moral values in the present-day Indian society have declined. Other important causes, besides the ones stated above, for the fall in the value-system, maybe summed up as follows.

(i) The gap between the material and the spiritual progress is an important cause of the present moral crisis. Nuclear capability is a great (material) achieve-ment, but our failure to coordinate it with moral values poses serious dangers to the human race. We have, somehow, forgotten that there is a psychological man behind the physical man. Stating this idea philosophically, the ancient Indian had declared that the cosmic matter (prakriti) coupled with cosmic spirit (Pursha) alone gives meaning to life. The import of this great thought seems to have been lost somewhere.

(ii) The fall in values in modern times is attributable to overemphasis on wealth power, and consumerism.

(iii) The present social milieu, as some people believe, is such that it takes us to the moral downfall. While criticising the social environs, we should remember that the individual is a block as well as a builder of the social system. The social ethos depend on the ethos of the individuals constituting the group, therefore, why not to start the process of moral regeneration of the society with ourselves?

(iv) When India became free, the West was highly affluent and was immersed in the consumer-goods civilisation.

It had a glamour for every developing country. Indians also wanted to reach the same stage of affluence. The short-cut approach to it lay through the sacrifice of values. Our weak spiritual and educational background, which was the result of the colonial rule, contributed to our undermining the higher values of life.

(v) Western literature introduced some new trends in the Indian literature, some of which were unhealthy. These trends brimmed with sex, crime and violence. This had an adverse impact on the social ethos. What is true of literature, is true of films also, which is literature on a silvery-screen.

(vi) There has been a sea-change in the political, economic and social structure of the human society during the last about 150 years. Princely states have given way to democratic systems. Altruism has been replaced by self-centredness, acquisition and consumerism. Galloping urbanisation has ushered in the apartment-culture and pushed off the rural life values, including socialisation. With the ever-increasing speed in life and both the parents racing from one appointment to another, there is limited socialisation even at home. All this has brought about changs in our outlook to the existing value-system. The trend needs to be rectified.

(vii) Democracy has made a great contribution to alleviating the lot of the common man, particularly the downtrodden and the backward. However, one cannot be oblivious to its negative role in regard to nurturing of higher moral values. Winston Churchil once described democracy as the worst form of government till a better alternative was available. Pramatha Bose said:

"There is, perhaps, no tyranny more incompatible with higher culture than the tyranny of an ignorant democracy. The leaders of Greek thought, from Pythagoras to Aristotle, were mostly persecuted some of them sent into exile and some condemned to death."

In a democracy, the lower strata are elevated at the expense of the higher strata. Under democratic process the influence of the 'higher strata', spheres of art, literature etc., included, gets weakened. Knowledge extends over wider surface but loses in depth. Authors have to adapt to the capabilities of the 'common' man. There is a trend towards writing light rather than thoughtful literature.

All this highlights the need for an enlightened and a fresh approach to the important question of value-education.

9

Retrospect on Idealism

Since idealism has its roots in ancient philosophies of the east and the west, it would be worthwhile examining some of the contributions of leading thinkers and of the treatises on the subject.

One of the longest and most exhaustive enquiries into idealism may be found in the Upanishads. The Upanishads speak of the highest knowledge as "Pravidya" which is distinct from all other knowledge "Apara." "Pravidya" is that knowledge through which ultimate reality is known, and this forms the subject matter of the Upanishads. The seers and philosophers of the Upanishads, sought the source of all life and knowledge. The world was young, and factual knowledge was limited, so they withdrew and looked inwards, away from the material world, to discover true knowledge. The chief aim of the Upanishads is to educate the mind itself as the creative principle in man. Its primary concern is the mind, and the principle of knowing, the roots from which knowledge springs and grows and leads to the complete realization of the Atman. The supreme knowledge cannot be gained by mere speculation, but comes by revelation, as a result of self-growth. The acquisition of such knowledge is a lifelong process.

According to the Upanishads, education is a process of the control of the mind, which directs it to its deeper layers. The technique of spiritual discipline is Yoga or unit, and refers to the method of concentration and sublimation in order to grasp reality by intuition. Self-control and meditation, essential in Yoga destroy ignorance and lead one to the truth. The assumption underlying the Upanishadic philosophy is that mental life is not dependent on the world of objects, it seeks to open up the avenues of knowledge to teach the life of the spirit. Hence, we see that idealism permeates the philosophy of the Upanishads.

According to the Bhagawad Gita, the problem facing man is "the integration of his personality and the development of a divine existence in which the spiritual principle has the mastery over all the powers of soul and body.... the whole teaching of the Gita requires man to choose the good and to realize it by conscious effort." The Gita urges the exercise of intelligence, faith and action. The message of the Bhagawad Gita is that the highest duty of every human being is to acquire supreme knowledge both of the Self and of Brahma. Plato and the Buddha are in the agreement with the view that meditation brings the soul into contact with ethereal regions. Contemplation helps to compose the mind and to concentrate upon the object in view. The Hindu-Buddhist philosophies attach supreme importance to the place of the Guru in their scheme of education. The basic upward urge for fulfilment is aspiration, and this acquires a living force largely from the concrete example of the Guru's life. His example reinforces and strengthens the aspirations of his pupils. An inspired Guru, who has discovered himself, is capable of helping and directing his pupils and of evoking their receptivity. St. Thomas Aquinas refers to such a reciprocal relationship between pupil and teacher in his De Majistro. Education, according to the ancient Hindus, is a man's rebirth in the world of matter and spirit. He becomes, according to Dr. Radhakrishnan, "his own masterpiece". The learner is a finite person, growing when properly guided, by his Guru, into the image of the infinite.

Bishop Berkeley, a great Irish philosopher in the early eighteenth century, believed that there is only one substance underlying both the mental and objective world; this substance is Spirit or God. By Spirit, Berkeley meant a single active being whose two chief activities are: creating and perceiving. Reality is what we experience it to be within ourselves. Since the world appears to be a meaningful world of ideas, it must be the creative expression of an Infinite Mind or God.

Immanuel Kant, an eighteenth century German philosopher, made important and outstanding contributions to idealistic philosophy, some of which are briefly stated below:

(1) Kant believed that there are certain universal moral laws in the Universe.

(2) That man has an obligation to obey there moral laws. This sense of duty is not a result of experience, but is rooted in reason, just as perception and conception are.

(3) Kant believes in freedom. An individual can act in a certain way out of an intention to do good, or to fulfil the moral laws.

(4) Kant believes in the immortality of the soul, and also in the existence of God.

Fichte, another German philosopher of the idealist school, was a disciple of Kant. He was profoundly interested in the ethical side of life. He thought of reality as a morally purposeful will, and regarded the world as designed to develop the will of man and bring his character into being.

Hegel (1770-1831) was one of the foremost philosophers in the idealistic movement in the nineteenth century. According to him, if you want to find the value of any single fact or experience, you can never do so by dealing with the fact in isolation. You must relate it to the whole. Similarly, if you wish to discover yourself, and if you want to become the real self, which is in you to become, then you must relate yourself to the totality of the cosmos and all existence. According to Hegel, Reality, in its ultimate, final and absolute essence is Mind or Spirit. This reality is not just the basis of the physical world; it is the final goal to which all creation moves. The phenomenal world, with all of its manifold inter-relationships is a manifestation of Infinite Mind, realizing itself in finite and temporal processes.

Among the twentieth century Indian Philosophers may be mentioned:

Rabindranath Tagore, who believed that "Education is an all-round growth and development of the individual in harmony with the Universal Supreme Person. This Universal Man holds within himself all that is and will be in future." In Tagore's philosophy, there is a love for truth, goodness and beauty. A subtle blending of idealistic principles with some naturalistic practices is evident in Shantiniketan.

Aurobindo Ghosh, seer of Pondicherry, believes in the evolution not only of forms, but of consciousness. Education, according to him, should aim at the recovery of the old spiritual knowledge and experience in all its splendour, depth and fullness. His philosophy represents a synthesis of Hegelian idealism with Vedantic philosophy. Philosophy, according to Aurobindo is a quest for the truth of things by the human intellect. The endeavour to realize the truth in the inner self as well as in outer life is DHARMA.

The philosophy held by Annie Besant, a Theosophist, is idealistic. According to her, the object of education is to train the body in health, vigour and grace, so that it may express the emotions in beauty, and the mind with accuracy and strength. Education should train the emotions to express the emotions to love all that is noble and beautiful to sympathise with the joys and sorrows of others. Education should inspire to service ever widening in its areas until we love our elders as our parents, our equals as our brothers and sisters, and youngsters as our children. Education should enable us to find joy in sacrifices for our great causes and for the helpless; to feel reverence for all who are worthy of it. Education should enable and discipline the mind in right thinking, right judgement and right memory.

Education, in short, should make man a good citizen of a free and spiritual commonwealth of humanity.

Mahatma Gandhi's philosophy was idealistic. He stressed the dignity of man and the significance of values. He emphasises repeatedly, in his speeches and writings, the ultimate aim of self-realization, the ideal of service of humanity, preservation of moral values, and development of the harmonious personality. The Ashrams at Wardha and at Sevagram were the outcomes of Gandhiji's idealistic philosophy. However, in his Basic scheme of education, while based on idealistic principles, yet has elements of naturalism and pragmatism in it, and is a remarkable combination of the three philosophies in education.

Historical Backdrop

Idealism in Education is Based on Two Principles

Intellectual Training—The world is an absolute order of physical objects and is based on natural laws that are eternal and unchanging. Idealism emphasizes the study of these laws. The world is a logical consequence of an absolute order. Reason is above everything else in the universe, hence in education, physical laws based on reason must be taught, because Nature is simply the outer expression of an inner, logical order.

The Unique Nature of Man—(i) Man is different from all other creatures, because he alone can understand logic and order in existence. Through the power of his mind, he is a rational being, unlike animals, (ii) While other creatures are slaves of their instincts and immediate circumstances, man is a free being, because he alone has the power to recall the past and foresee the future. He can shape himself in line with his own powers. Man overcomes his animal nature through self-discipline and reason. (iii) Man can change, due to upbringing and the discipline provided by the family and the school. This process is called education, and acquires an effort of the mind and will, (iv) Man also changes by historical evolution; social habits help the process of rational development. The family, the school, the church and the State encourage the formation of such habits.

Objectives and Aims

The idealists believe that the greatest work of God is the human personality; their aims in education are based on this assumption.

Exaltation of the Human Personality—The highest potentialities of the self must be realised in a social and cultural environment provided by the school and the home. This should be the goal of all educative effort. Education should lead to perfection in the individual. There should be an unfolding of the divine in man.

Development of Rationality—The universe is a thought-process in which there is a perfect order. Certain inevitable laws govern the universe/Education should aim at helping the pupil to direct his effects towards understanding these laws. Intellectual development requires a training in logical understanding and perception.

Transmission of Culture—The spiritual and cultural inheritance of mankind must be preserved and imparted to students in the school. Education should aim at providing the means of acquainting the student with great achievements in literature, art, mathematics, sciences. He should not merely learn culture, but should be able to invent, create and produce new and beautiful ideas and objects for community and society. Education should emphasize and encourage invention and creation, as a part of culture.

Education for All—Idealists hold that every human being must receive a chance to be educated, and their goal is Universal education. However, as outlined in Plato's Republic, education should be imparted according to needs of the individuals being educated: (a) Slow learners have to be educated and trained for the job market or for manual work, (b) The average student may be educated for a specialist's job, (c) The very bright student may be given an extensive education in many general truths and the nature of things. Higher education may be provided for the third category of student.

Moral Education—The most important element in social culture, according to idealistic educational theory, is moral character; this means the practice of duty, virtue and conscience. The pupil should get accustomed to the idea of duty, although it may have agreeable or disagreeable results. Moral education falls into two classes:

Individual Responsibilities

(i) Physical and related to cleanliness, neatness, moderation and temperance in all physical satisfaction of desires, self-control, self-sacrifice, punctuality, regularity and avoidance of obscenity, profanity and immoral language.

(ii) *Self-culture*—The pupil is to learn polite behaviour, good manners, and have self-control. He should learn to be able to relate to his fellow-beings and to people in the community.

(iii) *Industriousness*—The school should aim at inculcating in the pupil a desire to work hard and to avoid idleness, by assigning definite tasks to each one of the students—the talks being suited to individual capacity, each pupil being made responsible for the performance and completion of the task assigned to him. Reliability, sincerity and perseverance are inculcated in him.

Community's Responsibilities

Aristotle and other philosophers after him, mention among the aims of education, the virtues of modesty, respect for the opinions of others, cooperativeness, liberality and generosity, which should be inculcated in the young.

Religious Education—Many of the idealistic philosophers give place to religious education as one of the educational aims. Since religion is based on the revelation of God to man, the student will find it helpful to discover reality for himself through religion. Religion will appeal through its forms of worship and ceremonies, to the imagination of the child.

Role of the Teacher

Education according to the idealist pattern is ideal-centred, not wholly child-centred, or subject-centred. Hence the teacher assumes a very important role in the education process. He becomes the key to educative process more than any other element comprising it. He is in the unique position of deciding what the students' opportunities for learning and growing shall be. He sets, to a large extent, the atmosphere of the learning environment. His personality is single most important influence in the pupil's learning experience. He is largely the mouthpiece through which the subject-matter is presented to the learner.

Teacher's Duties

(i) The teacher personifies reality for the pupil. The pupil understands and learns about the Universe through his teacher. The teacher is the GURU.

(ii) The teacher has to be a specialist in the knowledge of each one of his pupils. Just as one cannot teach a subject without a knowledge of it, similarly it is not possible to impart knowledge to a pupil without knowing him.

(iii) The teacher must have a great deal of knowledge and be widely read and thoroughly acquainted with all the techniques of teaching, to be able to teach effectively.

(iv) A good teacher commands the respect of the pupils by virtue of his own high standards of behaviour and conduct. He should lose himself in his selfless devotion and efforts to teach and guide his pupils.

(v) The teacher should be a personal friend of the individual pupil and should awaken and inspire in the pupil a desire to learn. His method of presentation of subject matter should attract the student. He is there to strive to bring about the intellectual, spiritual and moral progress of his pupils.

(vi) The role of imitation—Not only does a teacher initiate the pupil into the life of the intellect, but he provides standards of imitation. The social atmosphere of the school, patterns of speech, conduct and appearance encouraged in the school provide attitudes for imitation by the students. According to idealistic philosophy, the common habits are learnt, because children naturally imitate their elders. Since imitation is a natural tendency in the young, the school can utilize it for much-desired results.

Curriculum Development

Idealists approach the framing of the curriculum from the domain of ideas and ideals.

(i) The curriculum should represent the experience of the human race as a whole, relating to the physical and the social environment: the sciences and the humanities will thus be included.

(ii) Plato spoke of spiritual values which enable the pupil to pursue the good, the true and the beautiful. Thus intellectual, aesthetic and moral values will be inculcated through a study of language, literature, science, mathematics, art, music, poetry, religion, ethics, logic and metaphysics.

(iii) Physical education, which Plato called "Gymnastic" will be included in the curriculum. Athletics, gymnastics, health and hygiene will be taught along with intellectual, artistic and spiritual pursuits in the school.

Teaching Methods

What methods will the teacher use in idealism?

(1) Questioning and discussion are the techniques employed most often by a teacher in the classroom. Thought-provoking questions are asked, so that the content studied may have meaning and significance for the pupil. The teacher encourages the pupil to think for himself.

(2) The lecture method is of ten in evidence. Expository presentations are made by the teacher, in which accurate facts and objective information is supplied to the student.

(3) Single and group projects are undertaken by the class, for the performance of constructive tasks. These may be from the various subjects, and may involve excursions, creative writing, sketching, painting and science projects.

(4) Imitation is also used as a technique in teaching. The teacher sets before the students some models of distinct excellence, literary, artistic, musical, scientific or other, and direct them to observe and study these, and to

deliberately follow and reproduce their patterns. He does not encourage mere slavish imitation, but feels that the study of models might awaken the creative powers of the learner. However, the greatest use of imitation among the idealists, is in focussing the pupils' attention upon the life and work of great personalities. In Indian schools, emphasis has always been placed on the study of biographies, epics, and narratives, extolling the greatness, nobility, and sacrifices of heroes, martyrs and great scholars. Students are expected to emulate these examples and to imbibe some of the qualities of these great men.

Role of Discipline

Idealists believe that the pupil cannot realize his spiritual and moral possibilities without submitting to discipline and self-restraint. The teachers' guidance is necessary at every stage. The ideals of conduct presented before the pupil will guide all activities. According to Froebel, "Control over the child is to be exercised through a knowledge of his interests and expression of love and sympathy." Some idealists, on the other hand, recommend direct moral instruction as an agent of maintaining discipline. Honesty, humility, modesty and obedience to elders are virtues to be inculcated in the young.

Idealistic Power

(1) Idealism has attracted profound thinkers, and has been supported by many great philosophers. Idealistic philosophy has been written with great brilliance. Many educational schemes have had their beginnings in Idealism. For example, Plato's idealistic philosophy (as derived from the dialogues of Socrates), is written in the Phaedrus, Theatus, Phaedo, Timaeous and Philebus. This philosophy forms the basis of his great work The Republic which outlines a complete and remarkable plan of education, based on idealism.

(2) Education, until the advent of industrialism, was based largely on the principles of Klealism. Educators in India, China, Japan and many other countries in the east and the west, have formulated their plans of education on idealistic theory.

(3) The emphasis of idealists on personality has added an important dimension to education. The idealists' definition of personality proceeds logically from the assumption that human beings are not simply biological organisms, but are part of a spiritual universe. This logical implication, that human beings possess divine attributes, has brought greater respect and consideration for them from psychologists and educators. In recent years, this belief has permeated counselling theory, psychology and education. It has resulted into fresh look at human relationships in teaching.

(4) It is often felt that one of the important functions of a philosophy or a religion is to provide psychological comfort to its followers. This may very well be one of the strengths of idealism, for it provides such support in its belief that we are part of a spiritual universe. We are not part of a mechanical universe which is unconcerned about human welfare.

(5) Idealistic philosophy provides direct and clear guidelines for the aims in education, curricula, teachers' role and methods of teaching. There is no need of a search for the goals, meaning or methods, as there has to be in the newer philosophies. There are some schools (particularly those which are set up by religious organizations) throughout the world, whose functioning is the outcome of idealistic philosophy. Some of these schools have very high standards of scholarship, of intellectual and aesthetic pursuits, as well as an atmosphere of quiet order and peace within their precincts.

(6) In a world threatened by materialism, where technology has taken away much of man's individual freedom and dignity, idealistic philosophy restores man to his proper place in the universe. The school is not a place for learning the production of goods, but a place for thinking and creating beautiful ideas and things. The curriculum of studies is not utilitarian or materialistic, but dependent on the cultural heritage of man.

Negation of Idealism

(1) Idealism may be criticized as being out of tune with the prevailing scientific world-view and recent trends in education. Scientific research today, does not support the idealists view of a spiritual universe. The spiritualist theory of idealism with its subjective and mystical feelings, does not explain the objective world of biophysics, chemistry or space-science.

(2) Many of the terms and concepts used by idealists cannot be explained or described in simple terms, for example, the terms "spirit", "mind", "soul", "the cosmos", hence the danger that the teacher may be confused in the rendering of these concepts into objectives in classroom teaching. The teacher could contribute to the child's clear thinking and reasoning by a lesson in geometry or grammar, but how is he to go about giving instruction in the development of the child's soul? Should he give religious education for "the soul?" If so, which religion should be instruct in, since most religions make big claims?

QUESTIONS

1. The essentialists believe that there are some points of the educational compass which are more or less fixed. Discuss Idealism as a prop of educational essentialism.

2. Idealism is an advancement over realism by giving it a higher type of reality. Discuss the nature of reality in Idealism.

3. The underlying postulate of Idealism is that mind is the essential world-stuff. Discuss.

4. The idealistic philosophy of education considers human personality of supreme value. Discuss.

5. What are the essential features of Idealism? How do they help realise higher values of life?

6. Life is essentially spiritual. Discuss the fundamental principles of Idealism.

7. Spirituality is not a derivative of the physical. It is a product of man's creative activity. Discuss the nature of Idealism in the light of the above statement.

8. What are the educational aims of Idealism? Discuss.

9. For idealism learning is a process of unfolding. How would you construct a viable curriculum to achieve this end?

10. Freedom is the soul of discipline. Discuss the place of discipline in Idealism.

10

Values of Idealism

"Over against the philosophy of progressive education, with its main props in pragmatism, reconstructionism, and romantic naturalism, stands that of essentialism or traditionalism" (Brubacher). In the midst of the welter of change and diversity (as perceived by the pragmatists and naturalists), the essentialists believe that there are some points of the educational compass which are more or less fixed. Life is not all that fickle and fluid, it has substance and permanence which act as the needle of the compass and gives direction, stability and significance. "Essentialism has several philosophical props, one of the principal being Idealism." Accredited with high regard for individuality and freedom in education, its activity programmes are voluntaristic and developmental, and there is a measure of absolutism in the idealistic philosophy of education that brings it closer to the essentialists. Absolute is essential, remains constant in the midst of the welter of change, and should, therefore, be the object of pursuit of a meaningful educative process or activity. What is the nature and extent of the absolute may have to be understood and resolved in advance. According to Rusk, "Idealism contends that the material and physical universe known to science is an incomplete expression of Reality, that it exists but to subserve, and requires to compliment it a higher type of reality, a spiritual universe". In this manner, idealism is an advancement over realism by giving it a higher type of reality, over and above the plane of subservience and convenience: it is essential and is for its own sake.

The Concept

Born out of Plato's theory of ideas, wherein ideas are of ultimate cosmic significance, but they are not merely mental states as suggested by the term idea. In fact, they are the archytypes that give "form to the cosmos", and are the immaterial moulds "into which all matter is cast." In the matter-mind /content form controversy, idealism upholds the supermacy of ideas which act as ideals whereby acts of the senses, which concern matter, are judged. They are the standards: eternal and unchanging, which give form to the content presented by senses. Accepting the matter-content and mind-form equation, idealism gives credence to mind-form for its durability and universality. According to Ross, "idealistic philosophy takes many and varied forms, but the postulate underlying all is that mind or spirit is the essential world-stuff, that the true reality is of a mental character." If reality is mental, could man be far behind in the race for top honours because of his inherent intellectual endowments, sense of discrimination and facility of manipulation of situations, circumstances and environment thus giving him an edge over the physical, and a peep into the spiritual and sublime. According to Home, "educational philosophy of idealism is an account of man finding himself as an integral part of a universe of mind".

A long chain of great leaders of mind find its culmination in the wide delta of idealism where names such as Socrates, Plato, Descartes/Spinoza, Berkeley, Kant, Hegel, Richte, Schelling, Schopenhauer, Gentile and others amongst the westerners and a host of Indian thinkers finding inspiration from the Vedas and the Upanishads, shine like bright stars in a dark sky cutting across the barriers of space and time, region and religion, obsessed and possessed by a common bond of spiritualism.

The Definition: According to Brubacher "idealists point out that it is mind that is central to understanding the world [wherein]... nothing gives a greater sense of reality than the activity of mind engaged in trying to comprehend its world".

"Idealistic philosophy takes many and varied forms, but the postulate underlying all this is that mind or spirit is the essential world-stuff, that the true reality is of a mental character." (Ross) This is in direct contrast with the materialists who consider matter to be the stuff of which the external world is made.

Idealistic educational philosophy refers to a branch of thought which considers the ultimate reality as idealistic, hence mental and spiritual in character wherein the ultimate reality is not only monistic and absolute, unchanging and eternal, infinite and limitless, but also inherently essential and conscious. Hence, it is the essential and the absolute that should constitute education of a child. Idealism, therefore, considers the ultimate, fixed and eternal values and, enfoldment of a child in accordance therewith. As man is the embodiment of the Real, a lot of attention is focussed in idealism on the status of man as he could not be considered the "creature of his environment in the sense in which that term is applied to any other animal... man emerges in the course of evolution... he sets about to question, to inquire... and to strive after something better than the given". (Rusk) Idealistic philosophy of education, therefore, considers human personality of supreme value and constituting the "noblest work of God".

Basic Issues

1. Ideas are of ultimate cosmic significance.
2. Emancipation of spirit, as reality is spiritual and man is its manifestation.
3. Spirit and intellect take precedence over physical matter.

4. Realisation of higher values of life.

5. Ultimate aim is to achieve the three absolute values: Truth, Beauty and Goodness, which, in fact, are the consummation of the three domains of mind: cognitive, affective and, conative.

6. Higher rating to moral and cultural endowments.

7. As man is supreme, education should aim at study of mind.

8. Ideals do not happen, they exist, i.e., ideals are not the outcome of experience but are its very condition and man simply discovers them.

9. Ability of man to control and manipulate the physical environment through his spiritual, cultural and moral possessions.

10. Life is essentially spiritual.

Fundamental Principles: The following fundamental principles of idealism may be deduced from the above:-

Two Forms of Existence: Idealism believes in two forms of existence, spiritual and material. Nevertheless, it gives precedence to spiritual world which is real and ultimate and wherein the material world is transitory and finite. According to Home "idealism holds that the order of the world is due to the manifestation, in space and time, of an eternal and spiritual reality" and we would have never found it there if the nature of mind had not pre-imposed it in the very act of knowing it.

Ideas More Important: Ideas are ultimate whereas material objects are ephemeral. In fact, all objects of material world are embedded in ideas. "Ideas are of the ultimate cosmic significance... are rather the essence which gives form to cosmos... are eternal and unchanging" (Plato).

Man over Nature: Idealism considers man superior to nature as he has intellectual prowess to manipulate and control nature to his advantage. Man is not limited to experience alone but has ability to reorganise and recreate nature in order to create his own world of virtue and value. Spirituality is not a derivative of the physical, and Rusk rightly says that "the spiritual or cultural environment is an environment of man's own making: it is a product of man's creative activity."

Faith in Spiritual Values: Spirituality is an essence of divinity. Man, therefore, has a spark of divinity in him. Education should, therefore, help harness and realise the totality of mind on his way to self-realisation. "Goodness, truth and beauty are seen to be absolutes, each existing in its own right and entirely desirable in itself." (Ross) However, that beauty and truth could exist harmoniously without goodness is as debatable as existence of goodness without truth and beauty: the three are integrally related, so that "what is beautiful is inherently true and good, and vice versa. Idealism is marked by its faith in primordial values which are spiritual."

Importance of Personality Development: We had discussed somewhere that the aims and goals of education would differ with the meaning and significance one ascribes to self. Idealism considers man to be spiritual and as a manifestation of the divine. Man, therefore, should develop toward perfection of his true self which consists in approximation to the ultimate. Not only that, self-realisation is possible in a social context. As such, man should develop qualities of head and heart, such as love, sympathy, mutual well-being, cooperation and goodwill toward one and all. This emphasis on total development of man is characteristic of idealism. "The grandeur and worth of human at its best are emphasised by idealism. Human personality is of supreme value and constitutes the noblest work of God" (Home).

Unity in Diversity: Idealism reduces all diversities into divine consciousness which imparts spirituality to all natural entities, howsoever different they all may seem to be. The ultimate of this process is the fulfilment of man in universal consciousness, and is called self-realisation. All diversities of body-mind and matter-form get resolved in the Divinity of God.

Impact on System

Aims: "If the ideas conditioning the very pattern of the world in which the child lives are in fixed and final form, they must necessarily constitute the essentials of his education" (Brubacher). Hence, the aim of education should hover around total development of a child's spiritual nature which is universal, unchanging and eternal admitting, of course, the individual differences. As such, "the idea or ideal toward which his mind matures must potentially exist within the child before he starts to learn" (Brubacher). Education, therefore, should be unfolding of what is already in child, is bringing out and not pouring in, and should make "definite what formerly was incholate." As man is a spark of the divine, education should help him achieve that wherein its "objective is to strive to realize itself, to become what it was meant to be."

(a) Self-realisation, therefore, is the ultimate aim of idealistic education. According to Ross, "the aim of education specially associated with Idealism is the exhaltation of personality, or self-realization, making actual or real the highest potentialities of the self."

(b) *Spiritual Development:* Adam interpreted idealism in the form that universe is nothing more than a thought process: "it is rational, cosmos rather than chaos." As such, "attainment of rationality in universe should be the aim of education" and should enable "mankind through its culture to enter more and more fully into the spiritual realm, and also enlarge the boundaries of spiritual realm" (Rusk).

(c) *Health and Fitness:* The aspect of physical health and fitness of body receives due attention in idealistic education "for without such health and fitness the pursuit of spiritual values is seriously handicapped" (Ross).

(d) *Truth, Beauty, Goodness:* The educative process should be so designed that it helps one in realisation of the ultimate values of life by developing his moral and spiritual aspects.

(e) *Cultural Heritage:* Education performs a three-fold function in conserving, promoting and transmitting cultural heritage of a people. As such, education should acquaint children with cultural values and national heritage.

(f) *Sublimation of Innate Nature:* The emphasis on ideals should not be at the cost of man's innate nature which should be developed and sublimated into spiritual qualities and values. There should not be any repression and suppression in this regard.

(g) *Preparation for Holy Life:* Education should create conducive environment and situations in which one may be able to concentrate on spiritual development and self-realisation. "The object of education is the realization of a faithful, pure, inviolable and hence, holy life" (Froebel).

(h) *Develop Intelligence and Rationality:* There is purpose in the natural phenomena. Education should help one understand this purpose and help man mani-pulate and reorganise experience. A highly developed mind and intelligence can perceive and understand this all-pervading force. "In all things there reigns an eternal law... an eternal unity, God. Education should lead and guide man to face with nature and to unite with God" (Froebel).

(i) Character Building and Development of versatile interests (Herbart).

The Curriculum: Curriculum is the natural outflow of aims and ideals. Now, if the ideas "conditioning the very pattern of the world in which the child lives, are in fixed and final form, they must necessarily constitute the essentials of his education [and] there can be no avoiding them as the backbone of the curriculum." (Brubacher). They become a must for any worthwhile school programme in the idealistic context.

It, however, does not mean that education of the senses, and particularly physical and vocational education, is to be neglected. We have seen in the preceding section that physical health and fitness is as much essential for the well-being of an individual as "without such health and fitness the pursuit of spiritual values is seriously handicapped."

What it really means is that in any "hierarchy of education it will not be surprising if such fields of study occupy a lower status... as the formal intellectual studies and methods will rank highest." (Brubacher). Further, a child moves toward what must potentially exist within him before he starts to learn, making learning a process of unfolding. As such, curriculum should enable him to achieve the ultimate in this regard. "Now a man to be most truly and characteristically human must enter into his heritage, acquiring and recreating the common culture for himself and, if possible, adding something to the common stock" (Ross).

As idealism believes in acquainting the child with the created order of God, human history, cultural and spiritual heritage in and through experience, it recommends inclusion of sciences and humanities in his school programme. Culture, art, morality, history, philosophy and religion, poetry and music, as well as science and maths are necessary for a child to make him understand nature, and if need be, manipulate it, reorganise it. There may, however, be some difference in the weightage and priority.

The Procedure

Idealism did not cut much ice with methodology of teaching-learning. As such, it sticks to the old traditional and formal method of teaching which is generally verbose. Whereas idealism has fixed, specific and definite aims of education, as well as the corresponding curriculum, it does not have a definite method of teaching. Everything is fixed. It only has to be transmitted in a manner conceived best by respective thinkers except that an authoritative approach to teaching-learning is central as idealism considers classrooms as temples of learning wherein learning is intrinsic and not instrumental. Teaching-learning, therefore, is a formal, intellectual and autocratic pursuit wherein teacher and content take supremacy over the child. Teaching methods as advocated by some of the idealists are as under—

(a)	Socrates	Question-Answer
(b)	Plato	Discourse Method, Play
(c)	Aristotle	Inductive-Deductive Method
(d)	Hegel	Logical Measuring
(e)	Descartes	Simple to Complex
(f)	Pestalozzi	Training of physical organs; activity
(g)	Herbert	Instructional Method. Five formal steps
(h)	Froebel	Playway, Imitation

Besides, other idealists conceive of discussion, lecture, group-talk and a variety of other methods and techniques for teaching. The fact, however, remains that there is more stress on intellectual and formal mode of teaching wherein there is no fixed method of teaching in idealism. "Idealists consider themselves as creators and determiners of methods, not devotee of some single method"

(Butler). However, education advocates development of the whole child.

Controlling the Operation

Freedom is the soul of discipline wherein both should live in harmony. Education, therefore, should lead to freedom but this freedom should be curtailed and restrained: it should not be a licence, and should be an attitude of mind wherein a child is disciplined internally and not through extraneous means and consideration. Freedom, therefore, should guide and help in cultivating a disciplined mind engaged in the pursuit of the three highest values of life. Idealism believes in impressionistic discipline wherein teacher should be kind and sympathetic.

Teacher's Stature

A teacher should be a role model inspiring pupils to cultivate values in life. He should be morally high, intellectually developed, and culturally advanced, and be an impeccable and inexhaustible source of inspiration. According to Ross, "the educator constitutes the special environmental factor whose function is to lead the child nearer reality, and to guide him towards his utmost possible perfection".

According to Rusk, "it is to Greek thought that we turn when we wish to consider any of the problems of ethics, education or politics. Greek thought has in addition to its originality, a surprising universality." Plato was the foremost of the Greek philosophers and educationists, so much so, that even Rousseau said that, "if you wish to know what is meant by public education, read Plato's Republic." It is the finest treatise on education ever written. What a tribute!! Plato and Aristotle were the two most influential of all western philosophers, ancient, medieval, or modern; and of the two, "it was Plato who had the greater effect upon subsequent ages. I say it for two reasons; first, that Aristotle himself is an outcome of Plato; second that Christian theology and philosophy... was much more Platonic than Aristotelian" (Bertrand Russell). In Plato's Utopia, "the first thing to be considered is education... divided in two parts, each having a wider meaning than at present," and aiming at turning men into gentlemen as understood in high society today, all over the world.

Perception and Practice

Education is divided in two parts :

(a) Music, which means everything in the field of muses, fine arts, literature, general information about natural and social sciences, etc. culminating in culturising man.

(b) Gymnastics, means everything concerned with physical training and fitness, generally called athletic. So, Plato believed in a healthy mind in a healthy body and aimed at cultivating "gravity, decorum and courage" through his educative process, with strict control on the type of information/experience that the young may have access to in the early years.

Plato drew the line to only what was authorised. There was no poetry in his educational regimen hence no Homer and Hesiod for their poor portrayal of gods at times behaving in an unbecoming manner contrary to the general belief in their eternal goodness. God is the author of only good things and this position cannot be compromised under any amount of stress and emotion. Secondly, there should be no fear of death as sometimes suggested by Homer and Hesiod. Plato considered death as the reward of the brave. Thirdly, Plato lays stress on decorum and propriety. Any reference to or mention to the contrary is viewed as unbecoming of a gentleman. Fourthly, moderation in behaviour and conduct is the key to social grace, creating a desirable moral environment wherein lust, greed and cowardice have no place. The young one should see no ugliness or vice, but may be exposed to "enchantments", both in the "shape of terror that must not terrify and of bad pleasures that must not reduce the will." How tough and demanding rituals that one had to qualify before designated as gentlemen.

Thus, the two divisions of education in Plato produced men with clarity and depth of perception and thought and nerves of steel and courage.

Plato's philosophy rests on the "distinction between reality and appearance", with a religious overtone. He was an idealist giving his own theory of "ideas" which went for depth and gravity. According to him, "opinion is of the world presented to the senses, whereas knowledge is of a super-sensible eternal world," with fixed ideas and concepts. Idealism is a special gift of Plato to mankind.

Philosophy for Plato is a kind of vision, the "vision of truth." It is not purely intellectual and it is not mere wisdom: it is love of wisdom.

Plato distinguishes between the world of intellect and the world of senses, the world views which are qualitatively different. Intellect further is of two kinds, "reason" and "understanding". Of these, he considers reason as of a higher kind for its purity of ideas and dialectic methodology. Understanding is the kind of intellect which is applied, "it is inferior to reason in that it uses hypotheses, which it cannot test". Hence, not self-sufficient, whereas reason in all its purity and extent is based on the laws of self-sufficiency. Even Kant and Hegel rated it higher than senses and understanding which operate at the level of empirical reality and "creates objects out of Nature", or, in fact, creates Nature hence having limited use and import.

Curriculum Development

Music and Physical Training: During infancy or early years of childhood, Plato has suggested that music and physical training must be taught. He was of the view that education should begin with music and then should come the physical training. This will lead to harmonious development of the body as well as soul. He has himself said, "And, therefore, music training is a more potent instrument than any other, because rhythm and harmony find their way into the inward places of the soul, on which they mightly fasten imparting grace."

As regards the physical training, he remarked, "Now my belief is not that the good body by any bodily existence improves the soul, but on the contrary that the good soul by her own excellence improves the body as far as this may be possible."

Teaching of Mathematics and Geometry: Plato has also prescribed for the teaching of Mathematics and Geometry for early education. He believes that the teaching of these subjects leads to exactness in the children. He also suggested teaching of those subjects that lead to the formation of the background of philosophy. He had also suggested timely examinations in order to test the knowledge acquired by the children.

Curriculum for Higher Education: For the education of higher classes Plato has prescribed higher Mathematics, Geometry, Mathematical Music, Astronomy, Philosophy etc. Plato has praised Mathematics a lot. He has also showered a lot of praises on those who are good at Mathematics. After Philosophy, it is the Mathematics that he considers most important. He has himself said, "Have you further observed that those who have natural talent for calculation are generally quick at every other kind of knowledge and avoid delay if they have had Arithmetical training although they may derive no other advantage from it always become quicker than they would otherwise have been."

Similarly, he has praised Geometry when he says, "In all departments of knowledge, an experience proves, anyone who has studied Geometry is infinitely quicker of apprehension than one who has not." Plato has prescribed teaching of Astronomy for the farmers, sailors, and he has also suggested teaching of Mathematical music for them, perhaps, from the point of view of their utility in life.

Philosophy: Plato gave maximum importance to the study of philosophy for total comprehension of truth in all its forms. He was, as such, a rationalist. He, however, based study of philosophy on diathetic, and knowledge of other natural and physical sciences.

Method: Plato suggested only one method of teaching: Play, the most interesting manner of presentation of a subject-matter, in accordance with the natural faculties, interests and aptitudes of the children. His methodology, therefore, turns out to be child-centred.

Plato prescribes certain pre-requisites for initiation into the education activity. He is rather selective and for him, education is not for the masses. He restricts it to the class he calls as guardians, where it confines to men of "honour on the ground of a combination of intellectual and moral qualities" who must be just and gentle, fond of learning, with a good memory and a harmonious mind.

Plato rejects that perception is knowledge. He unlike Socrates says that we receive knowledge through sense organs rather than with them, and further, that some of our knowledge is not even connected with any sense organ, as mind "contemplates some things through its own instrumentality, other through its bodily faculties." We experience hard and soft through touch, but "it is the mind that judges that they exist and that they are contraries." Knowledge transcends perception, and consists in reflection. Here again he is emphasising the element of purity in knowledge to determine its origin, nature and extent, as later advocated by Kant when he spoke of empirical and pure knowledge, giving almost similar examples of number at both levels. Number is pure and a priori, but is known only through perception of things around, such as "ten fingers". Number, as such, are eternal, immutable, but at the same time are logical fictions, and can be known only through experience.

Various Theories

According to Plato "education consists of giving to the body and the soul all the perfection of which they are susceptible". Plato, therefore, is a perfectionist and views education to perform this function. It, therefore, has the following aims:

1. Inculcating the idea of good citizenship and virtues.
2. Development of body as well as soul: advocates the concept of healthy mind in a healthy body.
3. Provide vision of truth which is one of the absolutes the other two being beauty and 'goodness'. Plato, in this sense is an absolutist and an essentialist.
4. Inculcate feeling of appreciation for beauty, which is one of the eternal aims of life.
5. Self-realisation.

Plato's Teachings

1. Plato was one of the greatest philosophers of democracy and he has propounded democracy in its best form. He also believed that the government of the people, for the people, and by the people is the best government.

Teacher in the Emerging Indian Society 209 citizens are well equipped to live up the standard of democracy. They should be guided by reason and have a balanced personality. According to Plato, democracy should provide equal opportunities for all so that they may develop their faculties and abilities but he also believed that the government should be run by better people. He did not believe that four heads, even if they are dull, can surpass one head of a philosopher.

2. He believed in the balanced and proper development of the personality and has, therefore, prescribed for the education of the body as well as soul. In this regard, he

has given a psychological foundation to education which is considered important even today. He gave importance to the study of philosophy as well as Mathematics. He also prescribed for the teaching of moral values and religious concepts. He thought that these things would bring about the development of virtues in man. If men are virtuous they create a virtuous society free from evils. According to him preparation of ideal citizens is the real aim of education. That aim is still very valuable for all such countries that are wedded to democracy and democratic way of life. To create love for the absolute truth and democratic way of life. To create love for the absolute of truth beauty and goodness was also an aim of his education. He had this aim in view because he thought that this love can bring about the development of the social faculties of the child.

3. Plato was one of the greatest Greeks who really understood the requirements of human body and soul. He understood the importance of education as well as Philosophy and presented it before the world in a very skilful and nice manner. It was this exposition that forced Rousseau to remark. "If you wish to know what is meant by public education, read Plato's Republic... It is the finest treatise on education ever written."

The Analysis

The Demerits

1. It is an abstract and vague doctrine laying more emphasis on preparation for the next world rather than for the world here and now.

2. Avoids the realities, troubles and turmoils of the day to day living, whereas education should make one capable to solve problems and thereby live a happy and contended life.

3. More emphasis on intellectual development and strengths.

4. The concept of immortal values may be a dent into individual freedom and enterprise wherein one may evolve one's own sets of values depending on experience, needs and social interaction.

5. The focus of attention shifts to the teacher curriculum who becomes more central to the educative process, whereas child psychology stresses that the educative process should be child-centred keeping in conformity with his needs, interests and capabilities.

6. Formal and stereotyped methods of teaching laying more emphasis on rote and cramming.

7. Reduces science subjects to a secondary level in its curriculum.

Comments: The limitations mentioned above are not the demerits but reflect only the inadequacies of the doctrine which takes a side look at the educative process which points forward to the Absolute rather than the mundane, howsoever relevant and useful it might be.

The Merits

1. Idealism makes a salutary contribution toward the aims of education by giving an exhaustive account and description of what education should help a child achieve in the process of his overall development.

2. Pursuit of the ultimate, eternal and universal values of Truth, Beauty and Good will help one inculcate the best in him both morally and spiritually, in fact, the total development of all the domains of mind.

3. Aims at universal education in order to help self-realisation which is by one's own efforts and diligence.

4. Teacher acts as an inspiring role model by his kind, sympathetic and encouraging behaviour and leads and guides the child through the maze and intricacies of self-development. He is not a bye-stander but is fully involved with and seized of his responsibility toward his wards in the process of their overall growth and development.

5. By encouraging personality development of a child, idealism shows deference toward his individuality and stimulates his creativity and appreciation. Universality of educative process is subject to one's individual interest, ability, aptitude, needs and aspirations.

6. By encouraging impressionistic discipline, idealism makes a child realise the nature, need and meaning of self-discipline in the process of self-advancement wherein discipline is intrinsic and internal and very much integral to self-actualisation as virtues and values are perceived by a disciplined mind only. Discipline, therefore, is a means of self-control and self-development.

Comments: By emphasising the eternal and unchanging laws of nature, accepting a purpose behind all creation and by highlighting the innate and inborn capacities of man, idealism makes man the centre of existence wherein he moves toward self-actualisation and seeks his identity with the ultimate by sheer dint of his own initiative, effort and diligence at home, school and in society. It runs counter to blatant greed and material outlook and zeroes on the ideal and spiritual nature, needs and essence of man. Man is divine; man is power. These powers and their products are "peculiar to man, and differentiate him from other animals; they lie beyond the range of the positive sciences and raise problems which only philosophy can hope to solve, and make it the only satisfactory basis of education."

The Distinction

Idealism and naturalism have had a long-standing rivalry through the ages. While materialism, as we have seen earlier, characterizes naturalism, we may broadly say that the main feature of idealism is spiritualism. In the Western world, idealism began with Socrates and Plato, while in the East, idealistic philosophy characterizes the Upanishads. Plato indicates in his Dialogues the importance of mind and reason in the experience of man. He does not concentrate on the forces of nature as do the Greek physicists who went before him. One of Plato's central themes is the famous doctrine of ideas, which are at the basis of idealistic philosophy. These are ideas, according to Plato, which are so real and enduring that the material objects are fleeting and unreal as compared to them. In fact, according to Plato, physical objects are only imperfect representations of ideas. We come to recognize such absolute existences as true, through a process of recollection. That is, we remember the former knowledge of these absolutes that we had in our previous existence before we ourselves were embodied in human form. These universal ideas are not just convenient classes in Plato's thought, they are fundamental things, "ideas" or "forms" from which particular things are derived. Idealism may thus be termed Ideal-ism, because it points to ideas.

Evolution and Growth

Idealism as a school of philosophy is represented (besides Plato) by such thinkers as Berkely, Fichte, Hegel, Kant, Schelling, Gentile and many others. In India, idealism may be discovered in the works of Aurobindo Ghosh, Rabindranath Tagore and Mahatma Gandhi, in the modern era, while the Upanishads and the Bhagwad Gita, as well as the message of the Buddha display idealism in their philosophical approaches.

Main Principles underlying Idealism

(1) The mental or spiritual is higher than the material, the physical world is of less importance than the world of the mind, ideas and experiences. Reality exists in the mind of man, and not in the physical world. Idealism shifts the emphasis from the natural and physical facts of life to the spiritual side of human experiences. The material and physical world is not a complete expression of reality. It is subordinate to a higher type of reality, a spiritual universe, a universe of ideas and essences or archetypes, which give form to the universe. They are the ideals or standards by which material things may be judged. These ideas are eternal and unchanging.

(2) Beyond the physical and material world, there is a spiritual universe in which dwells the Universal Mind. The human mind is only a part of the Universal Mind and obtains its values and goals in life from the Universal Mind. Some speak of the Universal Mind as God or the Creator.

(3) Since the world of experience is more important than the material universe, idealists attach great signifi-cance to the study of man and his mind. They assert that man's nature is distinctive, and its distinctiveness places him on a different level from animals. It is spirituality, rather than animality which characterizes him and distinguishes him from the lower creatures. But man's spiritual nature is not something that has been superimposed on him, it is the very essence of his being. The biological explanation of man as the highest of the animals is inadequate and untrue. Man is a spiritual being, unlike animals. He can express himself in language and communicate through various forms of an and culture, which animals are incapable of. Man expresses his spiritual aspirations through morality and religion. These capacities exist in man alone, and cannot be explained by the physical and biological sciences.

(4) Idealists maintain that the distinctiveness and superiority of man's nature is apparent not only from his spiritual capacities denied to animals, but is also seen in his power and control over the environment. Animals have to survive or submit to their physical environment. They cannot alter it, but man can change and manipulate it, shaping is according to his needs. Apart from the physical and material environment which man can alter, he has also the power of controlling the spiritual and cultural environment and values. Not only do men inherit and common culture of mankind, they can also add something to it.

In conclusion, we may say that according to the idealistic philosophy, reality is spiritual; it exists in ideas, purposes, intangible values and internal truths. Thus, there is a measure of absolutism in a philosophy. Man possesses a distinctive nature, which creates the spiritual and cultural environment, and values represented by communication through art and culture, knowledge, morality and religion. The material of the physical universe described by the sciences is an incomplete explanation of reality.

11

Values of Humanity

Life with 'values' is all meaningful. Whereas life in the absence of 'values' is of no use and is not good at all. A person who gives importance to values is good, is considered good by others and is also held in high esteem in the social group he belongs to.

Every good person values time. Such a person is very mindful of time. He/she gives importance to it by giving the significance to every moment-minute or second. He/she is always keen to make the most of his/her time. Thus, whatever has its importance and worth may be called value. Truth, Honesty, Beauty, Goodness etc. are values, whereas a lie, dishonesty, badness, ugliness are disvalues. "The choice before present humanity is either total annihilation or coexistence through ethical and spiritual values"-Bertrand Russel.

According to N.T. Ram, "A value is what is desired or what is sought. Values may be operationally conceived as those guiding principles of life which are conducive to one's physical and mental health as well as to social welfare and adjustment and which are in tune with one's culture."

Manual work is important for every human being. In Indian culture, there is due emphasis on this value. Guru Nanak Dev advocated the value of 'Kirat Karna'. In this regard, Mahatma Gandhi said, "Those who do not work with hands soon lose the music of their life." In our system of education the dignity of labour is held in high esteem. Education Commission (1964-66) recommended work experience for the youth for the inculcation of dignity of labour.

Various Theories

(a) According to Clyde Kluckhohn, "Value is a conception, explicit or implicit, distinctive of an individual or characteristic of group, of the desirable which influences the selection from available-means and ends of action."

(b) R.K. Mukherjee says, "Values are socially approved drives and goals that are internalised through the process of conditioning, learning or socialization and that becomes subjective preferences, standards and aspirations."

(c) Allport observes, "The term value means the relative prominence of the subject's interest or the dominant interest in personality."

(d) D.H. Parker puts forth the views:" Values belong wholly to the inner world of mind. The satisfaction of desire is the real value, the thing that serves is only an instrument. A value is always an experience, never a thing or an object."

(e) R.B. Perry says in his general theory of values, "Any objective whatever it be, acquires values when any interest, whatever it be, is taken in it, just as anything what so ever becomes a target when any one who so ever aims at it."

(f) In this regard Edgar Brightman remarks, "In the most elementary sense, value means whatever is actually liked, prized, esteemed, desired, approved or enjoyed at any tune. It is the actual experience of enjoying a desired object, or activity."

(g) According to John Dewey, "The term Value' has two quite different meanings. On the one hand, it denotes the attitude of prizing a thing, finding it worthwhile, for its own sake or intrinsically. So value in this sense is to appreciate, but to value also means a distinctly intellectual act, an operation of comparing and judging to evaluate."

(h) Dr. Prem Kripal says, "Values may be defined as :

(i) what we believe (professed values);

(ii) what we practise (operational values); and

(iii) what we learn from experience in order to adopt and renew traditions received from the past (traditional values)". He further remarks, "Values should be operational and also relevant and dynamic. Values should not be crystalized and frozen to the point of rigidity, stopping further growth and renewal."

Different Categories

Before we classify values into certain categories or groups, let us try to enlist them. A few values are: truth, beauty, goodness, sincerity, obedience, respect, honesty, worship, devotion, service, satyam, shivam, sundram, purity, simplicity, acceptance of one's fault or mistake, universal love, brotherhood, broadmindedness, service to others and secularism. There can endless number of values if we consider it from various angles. It is rather difficult to put them in specific classifications. Surely many type of classifications will be required for presenting all of them.

Walter's Classification: Walter G. Everett in his book 'Moral Values' classifies human values in the following eight groups:

Economic Values. These are indicated by market price and they include all purchasable things. Economic values are instrumental in the sense that they are used as means to obtain other values. Some writers do not believe that these are values in the strict sense but only in a secondary or derivative sense.

Bodily Values. These values relate to the health efficiency and beauty of the physical life.

Recreation Values. These refer to the values of play and leisure enriching the life.

Values of Association. These may be called the social values as they include numerous forms of human association-from friendship and family life to world-wide relationships.

Character Values. Here we may include the whole range of desirable, personal and social virtues including justice, benevolence, self-control and truthfulness.

Aesthetic Values. Beauty of nature and works of art are the aesthetic values.

Intellectual Values. Values concerning knowledge and quest for an attainment of truth can be included in this group.

Religious Values. Religious values include worship, devotion etc.

Parker's Classification According to Interest: Parker has given another classification of values according to interest. The different groups suggested by him are as under:

(i) Biological values

(ii) Economic values

(iii) Affecting values

(iv) Social values

(v) Intellectual values

(vi) Aesthetic values

(vii) Moral values

(viii) Religious values

Classification in Terms of Ultimate Realities: Plato advocated another classification in terms of ultimate realities. These are:

(i) Goodness

(ii) Beauty

(iii) Truth

These values of life have been enunciated by Indian thinkers as Satyam, Shivam and Sundaram.

Origin and Development

Values are there within the individuals and they develop in them as are the situations all around and the circumstances they are placed in. A good person in the teeth of bad environment may become outlawed and shun his goodness, truth, honesty and sincerity.

Various sources of values are:

Religion. Different religions propagate different values. Analysed and properly understood, almost all religions lay emphasis on the same values.

Hindu religion advocates self-realization or MOKSHA. Everyone ultimately tries to merge his ownself with universal God.

Christianity, Islam, Sikhism emphasis a particular way of life based on the doctrines and principles of respective religions.

In the recent past, the new discipline 'Study of Comparative Religions' has come up in different centres of higher learning. In Punjabi University, Patiala, the Department of Comparative religions is housed in Guru Gobind Singh Bhawan. The very structure of the building shows different religions in human society and ultimately all merging into one. The basic philosophy behind all religions is that God is one and the same whatever may be His garb in different religions. Young scholars from India are seen going to foreign countries specially U.S.A. for their doctoral work in this new discipline. Surely this discipline will affect considerably in propagating right values among the youth.

All the religions of the world recommend the following common values of life:

(i) Simplicity

(ii) Pursuit of truth

(iii) Dignity of labour

(iv) Tolerance

(v) Broad Mindedness

(vi) Welfare of mankind

(vii) Attainment of bliss-Moksha

(viii) Holy life

(ix) Purity and simple living

Philosophy. Philosophy of life is another important source of values. Philosophy involves deep and critical thinking and thus it is able to have its own list of different values. Values of life change with the change of time and change of philosophy. For example idealism is in favour of values of life, such as truth, goodness, and beauty.

Literature. Literature is also an important source of values. Literature and social life are closely interlinked. Values of social life are reflected in different forms of literature, such as essays, stories, poems, prose writings etc. The study of literature affects the mind of the learner. The study of good literature has far reaching effects on the youth.

Social Customs. Social customs, social functions, cultural heritage, social beliefs, social practices advocate different types of values. Since the society goes on changing with the passage of time, the same way the values also go on changing.

Science. Apparently science seems to be against religious beliefs and thus there seems to be end of all good values. Actually it is not so. Science is rather an important social institution and is source of values. Through science, we are able to develop knowledge through observation, experimentation and rational thinking. Science provides us with a new set of values which have their own utility and usefulness.

According to Barber, the values more favourable for science are the following:

(a) Rationality.

(b) Utilitarianism.

(c) Universalism.

(d) Individualism.

It is true that science helps us to think scientifically and act rationally.

According to Russell, "The effects of science are various and of very different kinds. There are direct intellectual effects, the dispelling of many traditional beliefs and the adoption of others."

Destruction of Values

Different types of values make the individual grow and develop rightly. The values are the assets of an individual. In the absence of moral, social, cultural, and economic values, man has no worth, and is considered insignificant. The society whose individuals have lost values may be called a poor and backward society. Indian society has been a very good example of high traditions and conventions replete with all type of values. If we compare the present situation with that of the past, it is all depressive, and sorrowful. Over the years, there have been all types of deterioration. Too much erosion of values is seen all around.

The erosion of values is everywhere and at all levels leading to the spread of greed, self-aggrandizement, gross-injustice, abuse of human rights, perversion of power, callousness, insensitivity, depravity of taste and behaviour, pettiness, waste and plunder and man's wallowing for the low and dark dimensions of his consciousness.

S.N. Ghosh says in his paper 'Key to Value Orientation', " The more we pursue this fragmented science in the name of development or removal of poverty, the more we would proceed towards mass impoverishment and elitist parasitism, when more and more people are thrown in the vortex and have to compete for survival, all values, piety, compassion, spirit of sacrifice, truthfulness, independence, courage, fellow feeling, love etc. come under a blight from which only the very exceptional persons can escape." Dr. T. Ramji observes, "Man is the monarch of the external world of emotions and passions to a large extent. There is a crisis of character in our age, owing to deterioration of values in social, economic, political and religious spheres of life." He further says, "In the midst of material prosperity, there is a sense of frustration and gloom. In the midst of abundance, we find poverty in a large section of society."

Dr. Sampuran Singh has analysed the present position of Indian society and the erosion of social values. In his book 'The Holistic Education' in the foreword of his book Vimla Thakur remarked, "Thoughts, ideologies, codes of conduct and sets of values, psychological pattern of behaviour have failed in transforming man. Man with the help of thought organization has created a marvellous scientific and technological world, but human being, as an individual is unhappy and frustrated, not at peace with himself, not at harmony with the different layers of his being."

Why there has been erosion of values in social groups is a question which needs contemplation, and pondering over by one and all. Surely those who are responsible for it should reconsider everything and review everything with the motive of setting everything right. The educationist should also exert and think of ways and means for improving the deteriorated social set up of life. The research workers should also work in this area of crisis and help in bringing about improvements.

Why Erosion of Values? The erosion of values has started from the top and it has gone down through different channels causing havoc all around. Perhaps the only possibility is that a revolutionary type of change would be able to set things right. Erosion of values is discernible in the following institutions in the country:

Political Institutions. The political groups of the country ruling or the sitting has set many worst examples by showing erosion of values before the public. All types of quarrels among the different political groups, first verbal and then of physical type, are being noticed by the public. With the advancement of Science and Technology, the use of T.V. has now revealed the workings going on in different meetings to one and all in the public. One important person of the Govt. abusing the other or throwing a chair upon public others or beating them is seen by within the country or abroad. Persons of higher or lower ranks, and especially the youth and the budding children are adversely affected by this type of activities. The political groups have thus led to the erosion of values among masses.

Erosion in political standards and values are of the following type:

(i) The political leaders exploit the masses to achieve their narrow and selfish ends.

(ii) The so-called political people lack code of conduct and they indulge more and more in political corruption.

(iii) In the light of constitutional provisions and guarantees given there in, far less is actually provided.

(iv) The leaders keep their vested interest in the fore front and national interests are ignored.

(v) There is lack of true leadership. Many high-ups in the political circles don't deserve the rank but they continue holding it shamelessly.

(vi) Police atrocities and brutalities are committed on the advice of politicians.

(vii) Scandals, militancy, lawlessness, indiscipline are on the increase in the society. Often politics is involved.

Educational Institutions. The educational scene in its true sense can be seen in the universities (so called centres of higher learning), the colleges and the schools. Politics one way or the other has entered in the sacred profession of teaching. Elections of teachers and students are held there for which all types of political pressures are used. Quarrels, physical fighting, disrespect to the chair and to the high-ups can be seen. Then teachers going on strike, the students going on strike and sometimes both teachers and students going on strike together-all this is deteriorating the social values day by day. The educational institutions are meant for betterment of the individual and the society but they are now helping in creating an unwanted type of social environment. Every now and then, the Heads of the institutions are seen quarreling with the staff or the students. Corruption on the part of the authorities is spreading and making the younger groups imitate it. Some examples are given below:

(i) Selfishness on the part of teaching and administrative community is seen.

(ii) Co-operation, fellow feelings, brotherhood, social service, etc. are disappearing in the institutions.

(iii) All types of corruption, malpractices from the top to bottom are on the increase.

(iv) Self-discipline, hard-working, honesty, sincerity are disappearing.

(v) Disobedience is spreading all around.

(vi) Everyone is becoming more and more materialistic and money minded-all at the cost of values.

Scene at Home. The scene at home has also become similar to the ones being seen in politics and centres of education. Quarrel between the parents, quarrel of youngers with the elders, quarrel between different members of the family and same age group are now multiplying. Almost every home stands disintegrated as far as love, affection and respect are concerned, which is similar and parallel to the sight in educational institutions and Parliament House of the country. The situation at home and in family is reflected as:

(i) Self-centredness and selfishness are spreading.

(ii) Respect for others, obedience to elders are fast decreasing.

Neighbourhood Sight. The streets joining different homes present their own added gloom and deterioration in this direction. There is jealousy and hatred of one with the other. Mutual give and take relationship, the we-feeling etc. are disappearing. Help from one neighbour to the next can hardly be seen in times of difficulty. Respect of elderly persons living in the neighbourhood is also fast disappearing. This is evident from the following:

(i) Spirit of co-operation, fellow feelings are vanishing.

(ii) Individualised style of living and self-centredness are increasing.

Sight at Informal Social Gatherings. There are informal types of social gatherings in the bazars, on the railway stations, in the trains, in the buses, etc. The elderly persons are seen standing whereas the youngsters continue sitting occupying seats in the moving bus or the train. Gone are the days when people out of respect offered the seat to the ladies and surely to the aged and elderly persons. Now even on making special request nobody vacates the seats for the ailing person even. Respect for others, sympathy, kindness, etc. are now fast disappearing. The present trend is:

(i) Social sensitiveness is disappearing from the minds of the people.

(ii) The feelings of oneness, common brotherhood are matters of the past. None seems to be caring for others.

(iii) Respect for others, sympathy and kindness for those in difficulty are missing.

Religious Institutions. Religious institutions have also gone down in moral standards to a great extent. Politics has entered into these organisations and there are sights showing erosion of values. Sympathy for a poor person is no longer the consideration there. Give and take relationship has become the basis in matters of service rendered by the religious organisations. The present situation might have been caused due to ill-will and unwanted type of behaviour shown by the public or the so-called devotees.

Correcting Measures

Erosion of values in the social circles need be checked vehemently by one and all concerned. It is the duty of one and all to shoulder their responsibility with full sincerity and help in setting things right. Before we think of ways and means to check, the further erosion of values let us think of the sources of values.

Required Education

The social environment all around is deteriorating day by day. There is erosion of social, economic, political and cultural values. No doubt, there has been great advancement in the field of Science and Technology, but it has changed the attitude of the people considerably. People now have more or less materialistic attitude. It has led to different types of conflicts, such as old beliefs and new beliefs, old values of life and new values of life. Now only value oriented education can deliver the goods rightly and help to change things for betterment.

Views related to Value Oriented Education

Indian Education Commission. In this context, Indian Education Commission (1964-66) puts forth the views: "The weakening of social and moral values in the younger generation is creating many serious social and ethical conflicts in western societies and there is already a desire among some great western thinkers to balance the knowledge and skills which science and technology bring with the values and insights associated with ethics and religion at its best. In the situation that is developing, it is equally important for us to give a proper value orientation.

About value oriented education, Challenge of Education: a Policy Perspective mentions, "One of the major crises facing education in India is that of value orientation. It has been usually argued that the main focus during the last three decades has been on quantitative expansion and consequently adequate attention could not be paid to maintaining standards and quality of education. The output of the educational system is not only of poor quality but degradation of the moral values has also been noticed."

National Policy on Education (1986). Following points are mentioned in the National Policy of Education-1986:

"The growing concern over the erosion of essential values and an increasing cynicism in society has brought to focus the need for readjustments in the curriculum for the cultivation of social and moral values.

In our culturally plural society, education should foster universal and eternal values, oriented towards the unity and integration of our people. Such value education should help eliminate obscurantism, religious fanaticism, violence, superstition and fatalism.

Apart from this combative role, value education as a profound positive content is based on our heritage, national goals, universal perceptions. It should lay primary emphasis on this aspect.

Views of Educationists and Thinkers. Regarding value oriented education, different educationists and thinkers of India have put forth their-views as under:

Mahatma Gandhi wanted education should be for the hand, head and heart. Education for the heart was the spiritual training for him. According to him, the aim of education is self-realisation-the summum bonum of life and education.

Rabindranath Tagore said, "The greatest use of education is not merely to collect facts, but to know man and to make oneself known to man."

Aurobindo gave a higher and clearer dimension to education of values. He recognised the dormant spirituality in every individual. His scheme of education for spiritual values was two-faced. He believed that our education should provide the opportunity for teaching of higher values. At the lower level all should be educated in higher values. In the second phase only those who can pursue the spiritual values should be given spiritual education at higher levels.

Swami Dayanand laid emphasis on the role and responsibility of parents in the scheme of value education. According to him it is the duty of parents to give instructions in value to their children which draws injunctions from the tradition of ancient Indian education.

Swami Vivekanand defines education as "Education is a manifestation of divine perfection already existing in man." He further says, "We want education by which character is formed, strength of mind is increased, the intellect expanded and by which one can stand on one's feet."

Dr. Radha Krishnan says, "Education is not limited to the imparting of information or training in skills. It has to give the educated a proper sense of values."

The Characteristics of Man: A few characteristics of a man with values are listed below:

(a) A man with values looks fine. All tend to appreciate him as well as his activity.

(b) 'A man of words' finds appreciation all around. Whatever one says, sticks to it firmly.

(c) Respects the elders—considers them to be his guide, depends upon them and remains a person of their faith and confidence.

(d) Tolerance and patience are fully with him. He tolerates others and does not lose patience for a while.

(e) A true national worker for the betterment of society, community and the nation.

(f) Ever ready to help others, considers the service of others as his prime duty.

(g) Sympathetic attitude—he never scoffs or laughs at others in times of difficulty, rather he shares the troubles with a sympathetic outlook.

(h) Works diligently, never shirks work.

Values of life are, therefore, ornaments which shine like stars in the personality of the individual who possesses those values. It is therefore, very important that values be inculcated.

Significance and Importance

Approaches: There are different approaches for inculcating values. They are briefly discussed here below:

Direct and Indirect Approach. Direct approach means teaching values directly to others. Here efforts are made cautiously to teach different values to others. The approach may work for sometime but many a time, it has its disadvantages. There may be reaction of the learners and sometimes they may give opposite opinions. That can prove rather more dangerous.

Indirect approach of teaching values is more convenient, effective and lasting. Here, teaching is done indirectly. The learner reads books and is able to catch up values of life here and there. In day to day life situations, he learns values incidently.

Formal and Informal Approach. When the learners are taught about difficult values by using formal ways, it may not leave much effect. Here, materials from books are taught with a motive of teaching certain values. Television is shown by using formal situations in order to inculcate different values. On the other hand, in informal approach the learner or the receiver of values is unaware of values. He reads some material from the books and is able to pick up values of life incidently. This type of learning is of greater value and lasts longer.

Curricular and co-curricular Approach. According to curricular approach, separate syllabus is framed which aims at teaching values to the learners. The syllabus is prescribed and teaching is done to finish this syllabus. In the text-books, the values maybe integrated in different chapters. Thus, the students have curricular programme which helps them to learn different values.

In co-curricular programme, different activities such as singing, poem recitation, drama, debate, declamation contest, essay writing competition, etc. are organised with a motive of inculcating different values of life in the students. There can be social service activities, physical exercises, games and sports. Different activities will help in the inculcation of variety of values in students.

Ways and Means for the Inculcation of Values in Schools: The school authorities can organise various activities and functions for the purpose of inculcation of values in the students. The head of the institution and the teaching staff can plan and organise a number of programmes for this purpose. A few such programmes are briefly explained here:

(a) The text books prescribed for the students should contain stories with certain moral lessons. Teachers interested in writing text books for the children can help in making the text-books of this type. Even supplementary readers or books for the children may be written by some teachers in collaboration with others and help in the achievement of this goal.

(b) Prizes may be given to the deserving students for showing honesty, bravery, gallantry, truth, etc. The award of prizes be given to the students in social gathering or functions.

(c) Declamation contest maybe organized in the institution on themes related to values of life. The contest may be intra-school and inter-school. Participation in the contest by way of speakers and also by way of audience will have a good deal of impact.

(d) National Service Scheme (N.S.S.) need to be popularised and its programme of activities be organised vigorously. The students interested in social service at the railway station, at the general bus stand, in the social festivals, in the hospitals, in the villages, in the slum areas be able to do a lot. In this way they will imbibe values of life permanently.

(e) A few projects for value education may be started in educational institutions under the guidance of some teachers. The students may start their own canteen on no-profit no-loss basis. Different groups may control it turn by turn and make its functioning successful. Some students may start a co-operative store where books and stationery on wholesale rate may be purchased and sold to all the students studying in that school. The basis of the co-operative store should be no-profit no-loss. It will make the students hardworker and they will also understand tips of business and the margin of profit-loss, etc.

In the same way, students' co-operative banks, students' co-operative post office, etc. may be set up in the institution under the guidance of some teachers. All these practices will inculcate good values of life among the students. These students will come out as successful and worthy social beings.

Educational Institutions should shoulder the responsibility and strive in every possible way for the inculcation of values in students. The beginning years in the school are more conducive for it. The teachers will be able to achieve the aims while devoting less tune and by paying far less attention as compared to the situation which would be otherwise.

(f) Extension lectures based on morality or value oriented education may be arranged in the institution. Eminent persons specialized in this field may be invited. Listening to the lectures, discussions, etc. will help the students to have clarification with regard to values.

(g) The head of the institution and the teaching personnel should be the living examples of values. The institution in itself should be made a centre for moral instructions. It should propagate higher values of life.

(h) Book exhibitions on literature related to values be organised in the institution by extendable invitations to noted publishers/book-sellers of this area of knowledge. The exhibitions should be thrown open to the students and the community. It will have its effects on one and all.

(i) Educational TV can work wonders in this field. Some good teachers can bring out materials related to values in the form of TV serials. Showing such films to the students and the community be made a regular feature of the school.

(j) Art and painting exhibitions on themes like moral, social, cultural values, etc. be organised in the institutions. Paintings of distinguished artists depicting values be displayed. Such exhibitions will have their effects on the growing personalities of children. Some children might develop then-interest in this area of knowledge. On the spot, Art and Painting competi-tions may be organised on themes related to different types of values. Students of different age groups may be invited from institutions of the region or the state as may be considered proper. Prizes may be given for excellent performances in different age groups. It will highlight the themes of values among the children and through them to the families and the community.

(k) Some journal on the theme of values in life may be brought out by an institution. It can be done by some voluntary organisation also. Suitable articles can be invited for publication. The journal may be monthly or quarterly as is possible and its circulation should be popularised. It should be suitably priced so that it is within the reach of majority.

(l) Skit, drama, competition, etc. may be organised in the institution. Assistance may be sought from the District Public Relations Officers. The themes should have values in life-social, moral, cultural, political, educational, etc. The different institutions should be encouraged to participate in the competition enthusiastically.

(m) Value oriented education should be made compulsory in all the schools. One teacher may be entrusted with the duty of assessing the whole with teaching of the school in terms of value education. Strenuous efforts should be made to achieve the desired aims with the co-operation of the staff and students.

(n) Morning assembly should be made compulsory in all the educational institutions. It can be of half an hour duration. Apart from morning prayer, good thoughts may be read out by some students and staff members. Religious and national songs may be sung and poems may be recited.

(o) House examinations may be arranged in Value Education. All students may be asked to qualify it at junior levels say in standard V, standard VIII and also at standard XII. It should also be at degree level which may be organised by the university or by the college itself. No student should be considered to have passed the examination without having passed in Value Education or Moral Education or the so called Religious Education.

Views of Different Commissions on Education for Values: The importance of Value Education has been recognised by different Education Commissions and Committees appointed by the Government. Their views are as under:

(a) The Hartong Committee (1929) felt that religious instructions can be given in common schools outside the school hours.

(b) The Central Advisory Board of Education felt in 1946 that religious and moral instruction was important and that it should be left to community to which the pupils belong.

(c) The Secondary Education Commission Report in 1953 favoured that religious and moral instruction should be given in school, and outside school hours on voluntary basis.

(d) The Sriparkasha Committee on Religious and Moral Instruction had recommended that Religious and Moral Education should be imparted in all educa-tional institutions.

(e) The Education Commission of 1964-66 has also strongly recommended for the direct and indirect teaching of social, moral and spiritual values to our children. The Commission has recommended that the, University Department of Comparative Religion should produce suitable literature for teaching of universal social, moral, religious and spiritual values.

Value-crisis in India has to be checked by one and all concerned with it directly or indirectly. Then and then only we can hope to see the bright future of the countrymen and see India as prosperous nation. There is need of re-consideration, re-planning, restructuring and re-execution of educational programmes. Let us also follow the views expressed by different Commissions on education for the development of values and act wisely and rightly.

QUESTIONS

1. What do you mean by value? Explain moral, social and cultural values by giving suitable examples.

2. What do you mean by value-crisis in India? Explain the situations on the basis of which you can say so. As a teacher, suggest remedies to overcome it.

3. "In a democratic set up, the importance of Religious and Moral Education cannot be minimized." Discuss.

4. How can a programme of Religious and Moral Instruction be introduced in the schools when there is value-crisis all around?

5. India has been following a policy of secularism. Against this background, discuss the role of Religious Education in Indian schools and colleges.

6. How will you plan educational programmes in your schools as a Head of the institution to develop secular, moral and social values in your students?

12

Values of Naturalism

Naturalistic Values

Tholes, who lived in Miletus in Asia Minor in 600 B.C., observing water to be such a large constituent of many material and living forms, decided upon water as the one single substance common to all things. Thales found his final substance within nature, making him one of the earliest naturalists. Apparently, he did not need to go beyond nature to search for reality. Leucippius and Democritus in 500 B.C. explained the world by reducing it to empty space and atoms. As early as 600 B.C., at the time of the Buddha if not earlier, the Universe was classified by elements of which all Indian schools of philosophy recognized four—earth, air, fire, water. To these, orthodox Hindu schools and Jainism added a fifth, akasa, which is generally translated as ether. These five elements were thought of as the media of sense impressions: earth of smell, air of feeling, fire of vision, water of taste, and ether of sound. A single atom was believed to have no qualities but only potentialities.

Thomas Hobbes in the Seventeenth century, described nature as an aggregate of things moving from one place to another in that space which is beyond us. Space is defined by him as a kind of beyondness, which is quite different from the mental processes of the observer. Jean Jacques Rousseau (1712-1778) in his Emile describes the education of a child close to nature. He believed in the goodness of individual man. Nature yields all kinds of good things, but the society of man grasps them and perverts them to evil ends. Rousseau glorified nature, not as eternal and indestructible order of atoms moving in space, as did the ancients. Instead he exalted nature, considering it dependable and benevolent. Herbert Spencer, in the early nineteenth century, used the word "force" to describe reality. According to him, we came to be what we are now, by a process of growth and development. A single cell took in unrelated materials from the physical world, and organized them into our bodies. Spencer was not a materialist, as the ancient naturalists were, he was an energist identifying reality as force or energy. Rabindranath Tagore describes the child's active subconscious mind which gathers its food from the surrounding atmosphere like a tree. Natural surroundings and freedom were important factors in the development of the child.

Education and Naturalism

Rousseau gave us what may be called Romantic Naturalism in his programme of education for Emile. His was a cry of revolt against the corruption of human society. He glorified Nature, not as the ancients did. He exalted Nature, considering it dependable as contrasted with a society which is fickle. Nature is not evil and crafty as society is. Nature provides us freedom whereas there is only tyranny and authority in society. The romantic naturalist has a profound reverence for nature, and Rousseau believes that child nature is good rather than evil, as his contemporaries generally believed. The implication here is that human nature develops according to laws just as the laws obeyed by heavenly bodies as they move in their orbits. The duty of educators is to learn what these laws are. It is their further duty, once they know the laws, to make use of them, rather than interfering with their operation. For Rousseau, education does not mean merely imparting or storing knowledge from outside. It is development of the child's natural powers and abilities from within Rousseau made this point clear by saying that there are three sources of education, namely, nature, men and things. The education from nature consists in the spontaneous development of our organs and faculties. It implies the working of natural tendencies and interests. It means the expansion of the child's natural powers, besides, it connotes a love of nature itself and demands that educational materials should be the facts and phenomena of nature. Education from nature does not mean one of social life and institutions. It is to prepare a natural man. "The natural man is not the savage man, but man governed and directed by the laws of his own nature rather than those of social institutions", is what we read in Emile. Rousseau advocated that education from man and things must be subordinated to that obtained from nature. He preferred the latter because he believed that the natural powers, emotions and reactions are "more trustworthy as a basis for action than reflection or experience that comes from association with society". Herbert Spencer laid down five educational objectives in his famous essay "What Knowledge is of most worth?"

Self-preservation—In order to live completely, man has to continue his own existence, and education helps to acquaint the learner with the laws of health and enables him to earn a living.

Securing the Necessities of Life—It is in developing economic efficiency that education helps in preserving life. Education should train man to preserve and maintain his life.

Raising Children—Life must continue into the future in new generations. Spencer held that the most important function to be performed, is that of being parents. The case of children should be a subject of study in the curriculum: every one should study child education.

Citizenship—Effective social and political action should be taught in order to make good citizens.

Education for Leisure—Life is not merely a struggle. Complete living means that one should be able to enjoy one's leisure. Knowledge of the various sciences and arts and activities of mankind should enable us to choose from enjoyable leisure occupations.

Maria Montessori, in her approach to childhood, bases her method of education on naturalism. According to the principles of the Montessori method, we have:

Education as Development—She believes that the child is a body which grows and a soul which develops. We must not mar or stifle the mysterious which lies within these two forms of growth. She believes that in the child's nature, at birth there is already contained all that the child is to become, and the teacher should care for the child in a manner so that the natural growth is guided in the process of unfolding itself.

The Idea of Liberty and Freedom—Montessori's idea of freedom arises from her concept of development. Since the child's whole future development is already contained in his nature at birth, that nature must be allowed freedom to unfold itself freely. Her idea of freedom is a democratic one. She holds that freedom is the right of every child and every human being, and advocated the spontaneous development of the child through complete liberty.

The Principle of Individuality—The child's individuality must not be crushed through collective handling or conformity to rules. The teacher must know each child individually; physical records of his development must be kept. Not only mental development, but the child's physical development as well, should be the concern of the teacher.

Self-education—The teacher should not interfere with or force the child to learn in a particular way or at a certain rate. Each child should progress at his own rate and gain self-education through the apparatus provided for the individual child.

Training of the Senses—Sense training prepares the child directly for intellectual learning. The senses of touch, hearing, taste and smell are developed through the apparatus provided for the individual child.

Rabindranath Tagore's school in Shantiniketan upholds in many respects the chief principles of Naturalism. The features which characterize his philosophy are:

Freedom for the Child—According to Tagore, children should be brought up in an atmosphere of freedom. Too many restrictions should not be imposed on them "lest they have to sit like dead specimens of some museum whilst lessons are pelted at them from on high like hail stones on flowers". Without freedom, schools become, "education factories, lifeless, colourless, dissociated from the context of the universe, within the bare white walls staring like eyeballs of the dead". Freedom means the liberation of all aspects and powers of the child's personality, namely, the senses, the vital energies, the various mental capacities: imagination, intelligence and also the emotions of the heart, sympathy and love. According to Tagore, freedom also implies free, untrammelled interaction by means of the energies and powers thus released, with the perennial realities of the universe—Nature, Man and the Universal man who contains within himself and transcendes both Nature and man.

Active Communion with Nature and Man—Tagore believes that education should not take us away from our natural surroundings, nor should it divorce us from the stream of life.

Children should be brought into direct contact with nature. The child's mind is always on the alert, restless and eager to receive first-hand knowledge from mother nature. He wants the children to be struck by chance surprises from nature—"the coming of dawn, heralded by the music of birds and flowers, and a sight of the beautiful sunset leaving deep impressions of the children's minds". Tagore's school, Shantiniketan, the abode of peace is situated in idyllic surroundings, woods, grassy slopes and palm trees, amidst fragrant flowering bushes and trees.

A.S. Neills's school at Summerhill, illustrates the naturalistic philosophy. It is based on the principle that children grow naturally in an atmosphere of freedom. There are no fixed time-tables, classrooms, textbooks or curricula. The pupils and teachers mix freely, ask questions of one another and arrive at answers through discussion and common exploration, on various themes. The pupils are looked upon as potentially good and not evil. No adult standards are imposed upon them. The only discipline is self-discipline, which is achieved by the students through freedom and a sense of responsibility. Neill gives a new meaning to the words love, approval and freedom. He shows great respect for a life of freedom, and a negation of the use of force, in the education of the child. He points out that well-established systems of education with all their complexities and accessories are formal, rigid and artificial, and hinder the child's natural development. Hence, at Summerhill, he provides an education which is independent of text books and formal schooling.

Status of Child

Naturalists stress the importance of child-study. Pestalozzi, Froebel, Stanley Hall, Montessori, Tagore, Piaget and others, have emphasised the child's dynamic nature which grows and develops in distinct stages, each stage having its own characteristic: infancy, childhood, adolescence and maturity. Naturalism ushered in the psychological movement, and forms the basis for child-centred education stressing freedom, initiative, spontaneity and self-expression in learning. Direction is provided by the child's own level of development, and by the maturation process. The teacher or parent is like a gardener, whose task is to cultivate the environment and to destroy the weeds, so that the plant can unfold, according to its own inner developmental plan. The school must attend to the child, it must revolve around the child's needs and potentialities rather than around the subject-matter of instruction.

Stanley Hall the foremost American pioneer in genetic psychology (human development) emphasizes natural development in children, according to the recapitulation theory of human growth. Stanley Hall was influenced by Charles Darwin's theory of evolution and he applied this theory to psychology, in his beliefs about recapitulation. Stanley Hall, a great educator as well, believes that the object of the teacher should be to get the child in a condition of responsive sensitiveness to every aspect of nature. This contact with nature makes life larger and fuller. All education should be directed to the unfolding of the senses, so that the child can get as many sensations as possible, and thereby the widest development of the mind. Children will be selfish before adolescence, let them be selfish for a while. Do not impose upon them any artificial conformity to your standards. A little child is a bundle of sentiments: therefore appeal to the heart, which is the strength and source of life, in giving him education. The child repeats the race, he develops physically and mentally just as the human race developed in the early stages. Childhood embodies at different stages, the successive changes of the race.

Arnold Gessell is the most recent, noted authority on child development, in the tradition of naturalism. The child must do his own growing up, he says. For this reason, we should create the most favourable conditions for self-regulation and self-adjustment. He is a living, growing organism, an individual in his own right, to whom the culture must attune itself, if his potentialities are to be realized. Gessell emphasizes the concept of maturation. All development in the child occurs in definite, patterned and internally controlled sequences. These sequences apply not only to the growth of tissues and organs, but also to functions and behaviour. Forcing or limiting the child will only create negativism and a lack of productivity. Each child's individuality should be recognized, keeping in mind that certain types of behaviour will occur regardless of intervention.

Stature of Teacher

The teacher has a peculiar place and duty to perform in an educational system based on the philosophy of naturalism. He cannot interfere with the activities of children, nor can he impose his own ideas upon them. Their education is based on the free development of their own motives and interests. He has to provide opportunities for their growth and development in an atmosphere of non-intervention, and freedom. He does not expect deference or undue respect or submission from his pupils, nor does he pose as superior. He tries to understand the pupils and approves of their behaviours. He is on the side of the child. Rousseau and Fichte are in favour of such non-intervention, because they believe that the child's nature is essentially good.

Montessori considers the teacher's interference harmful, since the specially designed environment, through the use of the didactic apparatus, can evoke the right type of response from the children, and they can also correct their own errors. In A.S. Neill's school, Summerhill, a teacher does not use force against a child, nor has a child the right to use force against a teacher. A child may not intrude upon an adult just because he is a child, nor may a child use pressure in the many ways in which a child can. Closely related to this principle, is the need for true sincerity, on the part of the teacher. A.S. Neill says that during the five decades or so of his work in Summerhill, he has never lied to a child.

Role in Education

One might easily think that in the naturalistic philosophy, it is desirable for education to follow the order of Nature: parents and teachers should simply leave the children to Nature. Nevertheless, naturalism does not make such a proposal. The chief justification which Spencer offers for education as a deliberate and planned programme, is to point out man's long infancy and childhood, which need not only education, but a natural functioning. The distinctive characteristics of the educative process, as conceived by Spencer, have an inclusive significance, and have been adapted and followed by many educators after him.

(1) Education must conform to the natures, processes of growth and mental development—This root principle, already discussed earlier, comes from a desire to understand the nature of the child and is based on the naturalistic view of the pupil. It is the make-up of the pupil that determines the form of the learning process, and not the methods designed by teachers or society. The process of learning must match the experience of the learner, or, there will be no learning. In order to get into an understanding of the process of learning itself, we need to ask, "How?" How can education possibly follow the natural order? The following two principles answer these questions to some extent.

(2) Education should be a pleasurable activity for children—Children enjoy doing things which the present state of development of their body and mind makes them, ready to do. Their readiness to perform or undertake certain kinds of activities is shown by their interests and responses. Hence, interest in the subject and interest in ways of doing things should guide teachers and parents with regard to the topics of study and their methods of presentation to the child. The

child's interest in and readiness to learn a topic is therefore of prime importance.

(3) Education should engage the spontaneous self-activity of the child—The child educates himself in a great measure; most of his knowledge is based on what he discovers through his own relations with people and things. Tell the learner as little as possible, let him discover as much as-possible through his own perception and effort.

(4) Acquisition of knowledge as an important part of education—During the period of adolescence, Rousseau and Spencer both advocate a study of several subjects. Spencer advocates a study of the sciences, particularly of physiology, since this knowledge is helpful in the preservation of life. Knowledge of physics, chemistry, mathematics and biology will help the pupil to earn his living through an occupation, when he grows up. Psychology and sociology should also be learnt. For his enjoyment, he should learn sculpture, music, painting, drama and poetry.

(5) Education for the body as well an the mind—This should not be forgotten, there is no use gaining knowledge intellectually and neglecting physical fitness. Mind and body should be cared for and developed side by side; there should be a healthy balance of mental and physical activities.

(6) Methods of instruction should be inductive—This follows from the principle that teaching should make fullest use of the self activity of the pupil, telling him as little as possible and encouraging him to discover as much as possible. Children should master the art of independent observation and direct acquaintance with facts, in order to learn effectively.

(7) Punishment should be based on the consequences of wrong deeds, but should be tempered with sympathy— As we should teach with the rhythms of nature, so we should also punish as nature punishes. Anger must be avoided in punishment every time a child touches fire, he gets a burn. Nature quickly teaches a normal child the dangers of fire and this exemplifies for parent and teachers, what is desirable in corrective relations with children. Of course, in dangerous circumstances, the child has to be warned of the punishment from natural consequences. There are stages of development in wise discipline.

Naturalistic Hardness

(1) As a protest against the rigidity and formality of school instruction, naturalistic forms of education present a refreshing humanistic attitude towards learning and methods of instruction. Wordsworth wrote his famous "Immortality Ode" as a plea for the recognition of the beauty of childhood and as a protest against the adult standards imposed upon children:

"Trailing clouds of glory do we come.....

Heaven lies about us in our infancy.....

Shades of the prison-house begin to close

Upon the growing boy".

The inhumanity to children in schools, during that period is also portrayed in "Oliver Twist" and 'Tom Brown's School Days".

(2) The naturalistic movement in education brought to the forefront the importance of the recognition of the child, in the process of education, Rousseau, Spencer, Pestalozzi, Froebel, and Montessori, followed by the

psychologists Stanley Hall, Gessell and others, changed the environment of early childhood and elementary education in a dramatic manner. Child-centred education became an important feature of educational programmes in many countries of the world. Naturalism in education showed that the child was not "a little adult" but a being in his own right, with desires, needs, hopes and developing abilities.

(3) New schools gradually come into being as a result of child study—Froebel's Kindergarten, the Montessori Method and schools. Tagore's Shantiniketan, A.S. Neill's Summerhill, are representative of the very many new schools for children which were developed and established not only by private agencies but by educational authorities all over the world.

(4) In the simplicity of naturalistic educational practices, there lies a beauty. Many of the schools are located in rural areas and in natural surroundings, where first hand contact with natural phenomena is possible. Today, when, ecological problems and pollution are causing so much concern, schools located where children are away from these agencies are a distinct advantage.

(5) The concept of discipline, under naturalistic education, is one which is very desirable. Children are treated as equals by adults, and their personality and individuality are respected. They are not made to feel inferior by harsh attitudes and constant correction or reprimand. Children share freedom as well as responsibility with adults. They bear the logical consequences of their actions and learn much quicker than through lectures and advice from their elders. Self-imposed discipline becomes an accomplished fact, in a school where students are trusted and treated with dignity, and in an atmosphere of approval.

Naturalistic Softness

(1) The simplicity of naturalistic educational practices may not be possible in urban areas, where schools exist in crowded, noisy and dense population localities. The beauty of natural surroundings is denied to schools located in large cities, some of which are in high rise buildings. It is difficult to harmonize the concept of a school in idyllic surroundings influenced by nature, in the crowded city surrounded by the evidences of technology on every side.

(2) The leisurely pace of learning through experience, unaided by many books and other instructional formats, may not, in most instances be possible in present-day society where a fast pace, mobility and immediate reaction to every day life situations are required. The information overload today is so great that vast quantities of learning are needed in a short amount of time, if one wishes to keep pace with events in the world today. Whether we like it or not, modern media and technology, besides vast quantities of printed materials must enter into the educational process. Education under naturalism, would disregard these means to speeded-up learning.

(3) Naturalism in education has no explanation for a higher order, God, or something outside ourselves as something towards which man can strive. The physical world around, and the biological urges within, are all that naturalism is interested in. Only the epistemological question is answered to some extent. "How do we gain knowledge?" The metaphysics of naturalism, "What is reality?" and the axiology of aesthetic, religious and moral values are completely left out, the questions are not raised. Hence as a philosophy, naturalism seems, somehow, incomplete.

(4) Nature is not all rhythm and harmony, in relation to which one can find peace and beauty. Nature responds to effort and toil, the soil produces crops, water-systems provide irrigation from rivers, man now orbits the earth in a space lab, all is possible, because we have learnt to match our technology to the laws of the functioning of nature. Man has harnessed the forces of nature for his use, but there are times when the energies of nature become unfriendly; the tiny atom makes us fear unknown disaster. Industry and technology have results which can overpower this planet and make survival perilous for man. Thus, physical nature alone is not the power which can be used to control and direct education or any other human endeavour, there is something higher which can direct man's purposes and strivings, towards positive ends. Naturalism is not enough.

(5) While naturalism has been a great force of revolt and has focussed on the limitations of formal education in the past, bringing about many innovative practices in education, it has no constructive suggestions to offer regarding a goal for educative effort. Naturalism does not point to a higher end in view, in the educational process.

According to naturalism, nature is the ultimate reality. Nature alone contains the normal and the final answer to all philosophical problems. Nature is a self-sufficient entity having its natural matter, natural forces and natural laws. There is nothing beyond nature, behind nature and other than nature. Human existence should be in accordance with natural laws. Natural world is the real world.

Concept and Perceptions

James Ward: "Naturalism is the doctrine which separates nature from God, subordinates spirit to matter and sets up unchangeable laws as supreme".

Rusk: "Naturalism is a philosophical position adopted by those who approach philosophy from purely scientific point of view."

Perry: "Naturalism is not science but an assertion about science. More specially, it is the assertion that scientific knowledge is final leaving no room for extra-scientific or philosophical knowledge."

Adams: "Naturalism is a term loosely applied in educational theory to systems of training that are not dependent on school and books but on the manipulation of the actual life of the educand."

Hocking: "Naturalism is metaphysics which considers nature as the whole of reality." It exiles what is supernatural or other world.

Significant Features

Belief in Nature. It means belief in nature and return to nature. Ultimate reality is in matter and not in spirit. Life is another form of matter and is ultimately reduced to matter.

Belief in Science. Science is the source of all knowledge. Only that knowledge is true that is derived from science through scientific methods. Naturalism is simply philosophical generalisation of Science.

Laws of Nature. Laws of nature are unchangeable and entire universe is governed by them.

No faith in Soul. They do not believe in soul. Human life is to be interpreted in terms of matter.

Importance of Senses. Senses are gateways of knowledge. The final truth can be known through senses alone.

Material world. It is the real world.

Importance of Brain. Mind is the result of brain functioning. Brain is matter.

Mental Activity. Emergence, imagination, thinking, reading, etc. are all processes of mental activity, which are the functions of the brain.

Child is Born Good. Rousseau believes that child is born good. It is the society that makes him bad. Therefore, no established laws and values may be accepted by the child as those values may have an evil influence on him.

Supernaturalism. Naturalism emphatically reject supernaturalism. There is no such thing as transcendental self. No faith in God or religion. Divine inspiration, strength of prayer, and other world are all illusions and mislead human mind.

Heredity and Environment. Heredity and environment both influence the personality of a man.

Various Kinds

Physical Naturalism. It interprets the man and the universe in terms of physical science. It relegates man to the background and has little to contribute to education. All that it has done is to place knowledge of science above every kind of knowledge.

Mechanical Naturalism. It is also known as mechanistic naturalism. It believes that the entire universe is a machine made of matter and is possessed of a self driving energy. It is nothing but materialism which shows that anything which exists is a form of matter. Living beings are also small machines, complexes of atoms and molecules. Man is also a mechanical creature. He has no creative force, no purpose and no direction. The aim of education is to make him a good machine and to give him sufficient energy or stimulus for the purpose.

Biological Naturalism. It is also known as evolutionary naturalism. In the process of evolution, which starts with a single living cell, man has achieved the highest form of life. All living beings have an urge to live and for this reason life evolves from lower forms to higher and more complex ones. This process of evolution is continuous. Human nature is primarily animal. At the animal level, the process of evolution stops at the material or physical level, but in the case of human beings it is also manifested is the mental and Psychic levels as well.

It is this biological naturalism which has made the greatest impact upon education.

Naturalism in Education. Naturalism has come on the scene as a reaction against oppressive weight of tradition, stern discipline, formalism, rules of the school, dry curriculum, artificial behaviour of the teacher etc. Naturalism is a world applied to those principles of training which do not depend upon schools and books but upon the Laws of natural life of the child. The child and his nature occupy the central position. Back to nature and 'according to nature' are the slogans. Child is born innocent, simple and pure. Education should find its purpose, its process and its means wholly within the life and experience of the child and stresses the value of dynamic method. All artificial and of the child. It seeks to base education on the nature and psychology and unnatural classroom methods, the rigidity of time table and old ideas of discipline have no value in this system of education.

The following points emphasise the relation between naturalism and education:

Nature is the Base. This is the essence of naturalistic philosophy in education. Natural development of the child takes place in the natural environment. The word nature stands for two things—physical nature and nature of the child.

The child's nature is not static, but it grows and develops. The educator should mould his teaching according to the changes in the nature of the child. Rousseau has said "All things are good as they come from the hands of the author of nature, everywhere they degenerate in the hands of man."

Child Centred Education. The child occupies the central and pivotal place. He is in the forefront. The child is invested with all goodness, all that is necessary to protect him from a detective environment. The educator should pay full attention to the study of child psychology and then guide and teach him according to his needs and aptitudes. The child should be treated as a child and not as a man.

Freedom of the Child. It is through freedom that the child can grow in its natural way. Child should be left free in order to gather experiences and to understand his own mistakes and shortcomings. There should be an atmosphere of complete freedom for the growth and development of the child. He should have a free choice of activities.

Child's Happiness and Mood. Happiness is one of the chief requirements of the child. Education should generate happiness and good mood for him.

Instincts as Basis. The instincts of the child should constitute the basis of all education. They should be exploited fully to modify his behaviour. It is through education that child's animal behaviour should be transformed into human behaviour.

Role of Sense. Senses are the gateways of knowledge. For effective learning, sensory experiences should be provided.

Objectives and Goals

Fullest Development. It is the chief aim of education according to naturalism. The individual should become perfect after development because he is the highest creature in the world.

Self-expression. Education should develop self-expression in the individual.

Survival of the Individual. Naturalism believes in the struggle for existence and survival.

Sublimation of Instincts. Education should aim at the redirection and sublimation of instincts for socially desirable ends.

Adjustment. Education should enable an individual to live in harmony with his surroundings by teaching him the art of adjustment and thus ensure his health and happiness.

Social Progress. Education should accelerate the pace of evolution and thus achieve social progress much earlier than otherwise.

To Develop Individuality. The individual should be made capable of developing his own individuality according to his natural ability.

Future Happiness. Education should be a preparation for complete life and aim at achieving the present and future life.

Curriculum Development

Before we understand the implications of naturalism in curriculum, it is essential to grasp the concept of negative education given by Rousseau. No formal education is to be given to a child upto the age of twelve years. This is what is meant by negative education. Just do not tell the child to speak the truth but rather create situations where there is no possibility of telling a lie. There should be no classroom teaching. Let the child roam about freely. It is called learning by wandering. Let him learn from the members of his family. Formal education deprives him of his freedom.

To Plan the curriculum, Rousseau divided the development stage as under

I. 1-12 years Negative education-Training of senses

II. 12-15 years Training of intellect

III. 15-20 years Teaching of history

IV. 20-25 years Preparing him to be a father.

Subjects and activities will be like this :

Sciences. The Sciences which deal with nature to get top priority.

History and Social Studies. Naturalists lay emphasis on the past experiences of the race and suggest the teaching of history and social studies.

Mathematics and Language. Mathematics and languages are important because they are tools for understanding the sciences.

Physical Education. Rousseau speaks of many health rules. The child must be allowed utmost freedom of movement. For making him healthy he must be exposed to cold, heat and risks as far as feasible. Running, jumping, climbing and swimming should be encouraged as his natural physical activities.

Religious Education. No place for religious education. No mention of God which cannot be explained through scientific knowledge. Religion is to be felt and not be reasoned about. Therefore every child should be left free to develop his own concept of religion.

Moral Education. Moral education is a matter of experience rather than of instruction. Rousseau favoured moral training through the theory of natural experience.

Liberal Education. Naturalism does not believe in specialized education. It stands for liberal education i.e. free cultivation of all human capacities in the interest of perfect individual development. All men are equal and their common vocation is manhood.

Self-preservation. Self-preservation is the first law of life. Naturalists advocate the inclusion of those subjects which would submerge self-preservation. High place to sciences and no place to cultural subjects.

Traditional Subjects. Traditional subjects, conventional habits, knowledge and information built by the sophisticated society should not be given any place.

Broad Based. Naturalists emphasize harmonious development of the child, therefore curriculum should be board-based.

Activities and Skills. Naturalists lay emphasis on various activities and skills relating to self-preservation, rearing and discipline of children, social and political relations, glorification of tastes and feelings, etc.

Correlation with Life. To ensure his survival, the child must develop adaptability to his surroundings. Correlation of the curriculum with life around will be necessary to achieve this goal.

Emphasis on Present. Present is more important than the past and the future. Still the naturalists have not committed the mistake of neglecting the past and the future. Historical study is undertaken to enable the new generation to construct a new social order and thus plan for the future.

Teaching Methods

Naturalism has changed our entire thinking regarding methods of teaching. It emphasizes more dynamic and progressive methods in place of traditional ones.

Direct Experiences. Direct experiences with nature, things and men is the keynote of instruction.

Learning by Doing. Rousseau says, "Give your scholar no verbal lessons, he should be taught by experience alone. Teach by doing whatever you can, and only fall back on words when doing is out of question." Experience and activity are the fundamental bases of education under naturalism.

Use of Senses. We should have maximum use of senses through direct experience.

Observation and Experimentation. One of the important methods of imparting scientific knowledge is through observation and experimentation.

Direct Method. In the teaching of languages naturalists advocate direct method to improve the student's vocabulary.

Direct Study of Nature. In the teaching of science they advocate direct study of natural phenomena outside the school or in the laboratory.

Excursions. Geography should be taught through excursions and trips rather than from books and maps.

Heuristic Method. For science and mathematics, naturalists emphasize heuristic method also.

Practical Exercises. Geometry should be started not with arguments and problems of the text book but with practical excursion of menstruation.

Self-government. Subject like civics should not be taught through books but through the actual practice of self-government in schools.

Playway. It is play which help the child to express himself fully, to be creative and to acquire confidence for learning skills. Playway is regarded as the natural and outstanding method of creative education. It creates the spirit of joyful, spontaneous and creative activity. In Montessori schools, in boy scout movement, in school journeys and in other activities, playway method is strikingly in evidence.

Freedom. The child should not be kept under control. There should be an ideal environment of freedom for his development. Naturalists disfavour classroom methods and rigid time table.

Nature of the Child. Education should be planned according to the nature of the child i.e., according to his abilities, interests, aptitudes and needs. Thus individualization in education is another watchword of naturalism.

Co-education. Naturalists believe that it is unnatural to separate sexes. Segregation of sexes develops unnatural attitudes among boys and girls. Co-education will develop right type of sex relationship, family life and community living.

Residential Schools. Naturalists favour residential schools because here the teachers can easily provide a suitable environment and can put a check on undesirable external influences.

Maxims. Naturalism has provided a number of maxims for education. Some of them are simple to complex, definite to indefinite, direct to indirect, empirical to rational. These maxims have given new trends to our methods of teaching.

Role of Discipline

Individual is to be given unrestricted freedom. The checks on the child are also to be natural. Naturalism opposed the method of physical punishment because it gives rise to undesirable conflict in the child. Rousseau says, "Children should never receive punishment. Freedom and not power in the greatest good." The naturalists advocate discipline by natural consequences. In the child does something, the nature itself will reward him. Thus he will learn to distinguish between the right and the wrong through the consequences of his own actions.

Freedom is to be given in social context and not to an extent which results in disintegration of the society. The child is to be given liberty but not enough liberty to interfere with the liberty or activities of others.

Emphasizing discipline through natural consequences. Spencer writes, "When a child falls, or runs its head against the table, it suffers pain, the remembrance of which tends to make it more careful." In the same breath Spencer warns that this principle should not be applied during infancy. He says, "A three-year old child playing with an open razor cannot be allowed to learn, by this discipline for the consequences may be too serious."

The child should not be unnecessarily and unduly repressed. We should respect him and his personality.

John Stuart Mill does not agree with Spencer and says that child should be warned when necessary. We know that nature is blind. It does not distribute her penalties in a fair and just manner. It would be a sin to leave moral education upon nature. By committing a little mistake one may loose his life as a natural punishment. It is better to prohibit a child standing on the bank of a river. If he drowns by his own mistake, it would be only the parents who would get a lesson, and not the child.

Teacher's Role

Teacher does not occupy a high and respected position in naturalism. The naturalists think that teacher will interfere with the development of the child. The original glory of the child fades when a teacher interferes. However, certain less important roles are given to the teacher.

Teacher as Observer. Teacher's place is behind the scene. He is an observer of child's development rather than a giver of information, ideas etc. Naturalists consider that the child's nature is essentially good, and any intervention is therefore harmful. But the teacher must see that education of the child takes place in the form of free development of his interests and motives. The teacher must study the child's psychology and interfere in his activity only when some obstacles bars his progress.

Teacher as Protector. The aim of education is to provide the child with opportunities for complete understanding and self-expression. The table of the educator, therefore, is only to protect the child from representations and mental disorders of all kinds.

Teacher as Stage-setter. The teacher has simply to provide the stage for the child's acting, to create an ideal environment and to provide the child an opportunity to do as he likes. The teacher sets the stage, supplies materials and opportunities and creates conditions conducive to natural development of pupils.

Conditional Acceptance of the Teacher. Teacher is acceptable only on conditions or on terms. He will design situations which help in inculcation of right type of habits in the children. In playing his role is only as a director, the teacher should not over do or over-act his role.

The Analysis

Lack of Ideals. Naturalism is without any lofty aims of education. It regards human being only as an animal. It may produce a material man, but it cannot produce a full man, because his spiritual and moral aspects remain neglected.

Too Much Stress on the Present. It lays too much stress on the present and ignores the future.

Ignores Books. It asserts that education should be based on the activities and life experiences of the child. But we cannot afford to ignore books which are the medium of education.

No Vision of Goal. Naturalism does not provide any clear vision of the goal and proposes no destiny.

Stress on Heredity. It lays too much stress on heredity.

Confusion about Nature. The concept of nature differs from one naturalists to another. Some stress physical nature and others interpret it as human nature. There is often disagreement about what constitutes normality and abnormality in human nature.

Lack of Emphasis on Physical Education. Naturalism places little emphasis on physical education and ignore the importance of social education. Specialized development of one side of human nature is false and unnatural.

Over-emphasis on Sciences. Sciences get priority position in curriculum and subjects like art and literature find little emphasis.

Over-emphasis on Behaviour. Too much importance to behaviourism is bad. Naturalism explains man's behaviour as animal behaviour.

No Moral Law. It recognises no moral law, no sense of duty. Self-satisfaction is the greatest achievement. It is pure hedonism.

Unrestricted Freedom. It gives unrestricted freedom to the child. It is not practicable to give meaningful instruction without imposing some obligations.

Discipline by Natural Consequences. Every violation of natural law will bring pain to the child and thus compel him to change his pattern of behaviour. This is a very risky and dangerous position.

Conclusion: Naturalism, although an imperfect philosophy, has exercised a great influence on modern system of education. It has emphasized child-centred education, freedom for the child, and broad-based curriculum. It has given us a number of modern methods of teaching like project method, heuristic method, play-way method, Dalton plan etc. It also stressed the use of audiovisual aids to make education a matter of direct experience. The child and his natural development have become pivotal considerations in education.

13

Values of Pragmatism

The Perception

Pragmatism has emerged as a twentieth century revolution against nineteenth century dogmatism, rationalism, monism, etc. Vast industrial expansion, economic prosperity, social-protests and needed reforms have resulted into its formation. Charles Pierce was the first thinker to introduce the concept of pragmatism in his philosophy. Later John Dewey, William James and Schiler developed and popularized it in the field of education.

Different Views

Derivative Meaning. Pragmatism is derived from the Greek word 'Pragma' meaning action. It also means work done. Unlike idealists, pragmatists live in the world of facts and not of the world in ideas.

Reid. He says that the central theme of pragmatism is activity, engagement, commitment and encounter.

Titus. Pragmatism places greater emphasis on method and attitude rather than on systematic philosophic doctrine. It is a matter of attitude and method of scientific enquiry.

William James. Pragmatism is a temper of mind, an attitude, it is also a theory of the nature of ideas and truth; and finally it is a theory about reality.

Rusk. Pragmatism is nearly a stage in the development of a new idealism an idealism that will do full justice to reality, reconcile the practical and spiritual values and result as a culture which is the flower of efficiency and not the negation of it.

James Prett. Pragmatism offers us a theory of meaning, a theory of truth, a theory of knowledge and a theory of reality.

Pragmatism is an attitude, a method and a philosophy that uses the practical consequences of ideas and beliefs as a standard for determining their value and truth. It is based on the philosophy of change and experimentation.

Various Kinds

Humanistic Pragmatism. It means that every act should be for the benefit of man. Whatever fulfils man's purpose, satisfies his desire and develops his life, is true.

Experimental Pragmatism. It regards that as true which can be experimentally verified. Whatever works is true.

Biological Pragmatism. It has great faith in man's capacity for changing his own destiny in the environment. Man is strong enough to make a better environment for himself.

Basic Principles

Changing Nature of Values. The pragmatists say that philosophy in the past has made the mistake of looking for ultimates, absolutes, eternal values and fixed principles. Pragmatist does not believe in any set values of life. In the words of John Dewey, "Truth is made, just as health, wealth and strength are made in the course of experience."

In this ever-changing world nothing is true or good for ever. The old order changeth yielding place to new. The truth of an idea is not a stagnant property inherent in it. It is relative to time, place and situation. Workability, satisfaction, consequences and results are the key words in the pragmatic conception of truth.

Reality Still in the Making. Reality is not readymade, it is still in the making. The world or the universe is always in a state of change and flux. Individual is ever concerned with making it better and better still.

Importance of Experience. Human experience is the centre of reality. It is the human experience which is the determiner of values in life. Only human experience is reliable, which is intensely practical and active.

Faith in Experimentation. William James insists upon the truth's cash value in experimental terms. Only that thing is good and beautiful which emerges out useful after experimentation.

Pragmatism is Action. It emphasizes action rather than thought. Between theory and practice, pragmatism states that practice comes first and theory afterwards. So learning by doing or learning by activity is the watchword of pragmatism.

Development of Personality. Pragmatists believe that development of personality is possible only because of interaction with environment.

Faith in Flexibility. Pragmatists believe that nothing is fixed and final in the world. Life is ever-changing and self-renewing process. Change is the law of nature. Values also change with time and space.

Faith in Social and Democratic Values. Pragmatists are essentially democratic because democratic society is the best means of achieving humanitarian ideals.

Faith in Present and Immediate Future. Pragmatists do not believe in the past. They remain confined to the immediate problems and look forward to the immediate future. They believe that tomorrow is another day with its own problems and requiring some new methods of solution. They live from moment to moment and do not plan for life.

Faith in Humanism. Pragmatists are humanists. They believe that science should be utilised for social welfare and solution of human problems.

Moliorism. There is moliorism in pragmatism. James supported this doctrine which holds that the world is not completely evil nor completely good but is capable of being improved.

Role in Education

For Pragmatism, education is a laboratory in which philosopher's dictums becomes concrete and are tested. In the words of John Dewey "Philosophy is the theory of education in its most general phase". Pragmatism stands for progressive trends in education. It emphasises freedom to the individual child, his interests and social interests.

Significant Features

Education as Life. Education is life itself and not merely a preparation for life. Life is a by-product of activities and education is born out of these activities. Education should give an opportunity to the child to face problems of actual life.

Education as Growth. Growth is the real function of education. It should enable the individual to grow to his maximum. The teacher has to facilitate the process of growth.

Educator as Social Efficiency. Education is a socializing agent. It is the social continuity of life. Through it the man develops social relations and becomes specially efficient.

Education as Continuous Reconstruction of Experiences. Education is by experience, for experience and of experience. Experience is the only source of true knowledge. One experience leads to further experiences. The experience is revised, re-organised and reconstructed. This revising of experience is education.

Objectives and Aims

Pragmatists are opposed to any kind of fixed and static aims of education. According to John Dewey, educational aims must possess the following three elements:

(i) Aims are based on the educand's actions and needs.

(ii) They elicit the educand's cooperation.

(iii) They are specific and temporary, not permanent and general. Thus, in pragmatism we can arrive at the following aims:

Creation of Values. Pragmatism does not believe in preconceived values. Education should develop an active, dynamic adaptable and enterprising mind which may be resourceful enough in creating values.

Maximum Growth. Education is to provide conditions for continuous and maximum growth. All growth should be conducive to the welfare of the individual and society.

Harmonious Development. Education should ensure harmonious developments of the man-physical, intellectual, aesthetic, social, moral and religious.

Satisfaction of Needs. The child should be enabled to satisfy his need in his environment.

Social Efficiency. Education should cultivate the power to join freely in shared or common activities. It should impart traning for complete living in the social world of today. Social efficiency includes economic and cultural efficiency, as well.

Proper Adjustment. Education should enable the human being to be fairly adjusted in his existing environment.

Rich Life. To sum up the aims of education we can say that the chief aim of education is to make the present life of the child rich and abundant for a successful creation of values and continuous progress.

Educational Rules

The following also emerge as the educational principles of pragmatism from the above discussion.

1. Education should be child-centred.
2. Education should be both for the betterment of the child as well as the society.
3. There should be full respect for child's freedom.
4. Education should be based on child psychology.

Pragmatism and Curriculum: The curriculum should provide the educand to develop all his qualities and obtain all knowledge which may help him in the creation of values, gaining social efficiency, development of harmonious personality, making proper adjustment and solving the problems of life.

Knowledge is not for the sake of knowledge alone. It must meet the needs of the day. The following principles can be enlisted for pragmatic curriculum.

Principle of Utility. Those subjects should be stressed in the curriculum which are useful in solving human problems and meeting life situation. Technical and scientific education forms an important part. Home science for girls and Agriculture for boys.

Principle of Child's Interests. Curriculum should be governed by the child's interests, aptitudes and tastes at the successive stages of development.

Principle of Child's Experience. Pragmatic concept of curriculum is dynamic. Curriculum should provide to the child actual experience rather than rote learning.

Principle of Integration. Pragmatists believe in the unity of knowledge and skill. Subjects should not be segregated from each other. They should be integrated into a single unit.

Pragmatic curriculum would include apart from practical and scientific subjects, the subjects like mathematics, language, hygiene, geography and history. The elementary stage curriculum would involve reading, writing, counting, nature study, handicraft, drawing and painting.

Teaching Methods

Pragmatists reject all the traditional methods of teaching. Child is the centre of educational system. Therefore, the whole emphasis of pragmatism in methods of teaching is on the child. The method of teaching should be based on the following principles:

Principle of Action or Learning by Doing. The pragmatists believe that the child learns best only through his activities. Child is spontaneously active and therefore activities that are purposeful, efficient and orderly should be preferred in his case. Experiment is the first and the best method.

Principle of Establishing Relation with the Life of the Child. The method of teaching should be forged afresh in the light of real life situations. They should help establish a relation with the life of the child his desires, interests, needs and activities.

Principle of Integration. They advocate the methods which promote integration and correlation of knowledge.

In the light of these principles, the pragmatists have suggested project method and experimental method as the two methods:

Project Method. It is not possible to discuss this method in detail here. We give below only its brief description:

Meaning of Project Method. According to Kilpatrik, project is a unit of whole-hearted purposeful activity, carried on preferably, in its natural setting.

In this method, the activity is chosen from the real life of the children. In this method, he would really do and learn. He will be active both physically and mentally. He will be provided opportunities of work and play. A project is a problematic act and not merely an ordinary activity. The problem requires reasoning, imagining, evaluating, calculating and judging. It is not a mechanical activity, it is a meaningful act. The project is carried out in social environment. It inculcates in the student cooperation, mutual help and sympathy. Thus the learners become socially efficient citizens.

Kinds of Projects. Projects are generally of four types, i.e., producer's type, consumer's type, problem type and specific learning projects. We are primarily concerned with the specific learning projects.

Principle underlying the Project Method

The Principle of Purpose. The protect must be a purposeful activity. Aimless activities cannot be treated as projects.

The Principle of Activity. It must suit the active nature of the child.

The Principle of Freedom. The desire for activity should be from within the child's mind. It should be spontaneous and not forced. There should be no imposition by the teacher.

The Principle of Experience. The project is carried out as a experience for the learner.

Principle of Reality. The project should create a real life situation for the learner.

Principle of Utility. The project should be useful in every way. The knowledge gained from it must be such which can be of use in later life.

Stages of the Project Method

Providing a Situation. The teacher has to provide a suitable and interesting situation preferably a social one.

Choosing a Project. Out of this situation, emerges a project. Only that project should be chosen which satisfies some real need of the students.

Planning. The project is planned after a good deal of discussion, suggestions and counter-suggestions and modifications. The teacher guides them in proper planning.

Executing. It is the putting of plan into action or practice. The teacher should ask the pupils to assign duties and distribute work amongst themselves. The duty allotment should be according to interests.

Evaluating. The project is judged, evaluated and reviewed. The students examine it critically. The mistakes are noted. The students have to see whether they have worked according to the plan.

Recording. Record of all the activities is maintained by the pupils in the project book. Important points are noted down for future reference.

Merits of the Project Method

Based on Laws of Learning. The method is based on psychological laws. In the project books important points are noted down for future reference.

Learning by Doing. The method is based on learning by doing.

Training for Democratic Way of Life. All children work together each making his contribution for the success of the project chosen by the group. They work for the common purpose, learning thereby responsibility, cooperation and tolerance.

Education Related to Life. Knowledge is related to life. Therefore knowledge gained through project method is practical and useful.

Encourages Correlations. It removes the water-tight compartmentalization of subjects. Unity of knowledge is achieved in a project.

Cramming Discouraged. It encourages reasoning and discourages cramming.

Dignity of Labour. The students learn to work by their own hands for execution of a project.

Demerits of the Project Method

Taxes the Teacher. The teacher remains under great stress. Much is expected of him as the planner of the project.

Costly. Lot of material and equipment may be required for carrying out projects.

Unsystematic. It may plunge the school routine into a chaos. It disorganises school work and class-work.

Unsuitable in Large Classes. In large classes it will not be very useful as most of the students will not get any share in its activities.

Inadequate Progress. The method may not show regular and adequate progress in learning

Haphazard Learning. It involves incidental learning which may not provide compact body of knowledge.

Conclusion. The project method possesses many merits. It can be ideal method if it is protected from its drawbacks.

Pragmatism helps us more in the methods than in the aims of education. In this method, knowledge is acquired after experimentation. It wants us to be experimental in our learning. Pragmatists want the pupils to think and act for themselves, to do than to know, to originate rather than to repeat. This method will demand practical work in the laboratory or in the field to try out better methods of solving the problems confronting them.

Pragmatism and Discipline. Discipline is primarily social and it emerges through happy, free, purposive and cooperative activities of the school. According to Dewey, 'Discipline is a mental attitude and in order to maintain this attitude, socialized activities are essential. Social projects will lead to moral training or character training. These activities will result in permanent attitudes of cooperation, sympathy, self-reliance, independence and initiative.

Freedom is an important element of this discipline. Education is to generate democratic qualities in the individual. There is innate relationships between freedom and discipline. Social consciousness is created which prevents the child from indulging in anti-social activity. This discipline is not the outcome of external forces. It is backed by social consciousness, freedom and joy.

Pragmatism and Teacher. The teacher is neither superfluous nor the supreme authority. He is a friend, guide and counsellor of the child. He educates the child in self-discipline and active participation. He has to be active, alert and arrange situations so that children also remain active. He wants his pupils to think and act for themselves to do rather than to know, to originate rather than to repeat.

A teacher has to be embodiment of knowledge. He should be intelligent, efficient and practical. He should have the knowledge of the child's interests and changing needs of the society.

The teacher should have sympathetic and personal relations with the child. There is no spoon-feeding. He should create a problem solving attitude in his pupils.

Criticism: Every philosophy has its negative points. Pragmatism is also not free from defects.

Negation of Values. Pragmatists do not believe in eternal values. It may be true, but still there is something which is constant otherwise there will be no concept like common good or common bad. Idealists strongly oppose this concept of pragmatism because they believe that truth is eternal and we cannot allow it to become relative and subjective.

Negation of Pre-determined Ideals. Pragmatism emphasises that ideals and values are man-made and changeable. The reality is that values like truth, goodness and beauty are good for ever and do not change.

Negation is Spiritual Values. Pragmatists neglect spiritual values. Without spiritual values, we cannot gain happiness, contentment, and peace of mind.

Negation of Fixed Aims of Education. Pragmatism gives no fixed ideal to education. Such an education is bound to be aimless. Some predetermined aims and ideals of education are necessary.

Absence of Food for Soul. Humanities do not find a place in pragmatism scheme of education. Their absence is sure to lead to the starvation of the soul.

Utilitarianism. There are many cultural pursuits which have to be pursued for their own sake. There is a joy in losing itself in vast realms of knowledge but pragmatists do not believe in it.

Interests Change. Interests of a child are the greatest basis in pragmatism. But interests do not remain constant and change from time to time.

Difficulty in Curriculum Construction. Pragmatism advocates that knowledge should be acquired through experiences. It is very difficult to construct curriculum and make projects on the basis of life experiences.

Non-practicability of Project Methods. As already discussed, project method suffers from many drawbacks.

Conclusion: Rusk says "If culture is to be saved, it must be by developing in pupils a love of knowledge for its own sake." But it must be accepted that pragmatism stands for progressive trend in education. Pragmatic education is neither teacher-centred, nor curriculum-centred but it is pupil-centred. Aims of education have to be flexible and adaptable. It stands for experimental method of teaching. It has ensured the place of democracy in education. Correlation and integration of subjects gets a prominent place. It lays stress in dynamism and flexibility.

14

Religious Values

The *Concise Oxford Dictionary* defines religion as a "particular $ystem of faith and worship—human recognition of superhuman controlling power and especially of a personal God or Gods entitled to obedience and worship". The main components of any religion are theology, rituals and code of conduct.

It is believed that in India, the conception of Supreme Being, the first cause of the universe i.e., the Brahma, had a great impact on the moral code of the Aryans. Starting from the worship of various elements of nature such as the sky, the earth and various forces of nature, there was a trend towards finding unity in them. Polytheism was correlated to monotheism just as forces of nature namely, heat, light, electricity to one single thing 'energy'. This Single Cause of the universe, was impersonal, absolute, passionless and beyond consciousness, just like energy in this material world, is the primal cause of the universe. This chain of thought led our ancestors to one of the greatest philosophical conceptions—that the whole world was one.

The concept of religion is bound to vary from person to person and from society to society. For example, in Hinduism, the equivalent of religion is 'dharma', which is far more a comprehensive word than the word religion. The word 'dharma' is from the root 'dhra', which means something which holds the society and this universe together. As such, 'dhama' lays greater stress on one's goals, functions, obligations and duties. It is, difficult to say which conception of religion (which) the respondents had in mind when reacting to the following statement:

It would be appropriate to impart moral education,

(a) Without reference to religious teachings;

or

(b) With reference to teachings in various religions.(G-2)

Positive Role of Religion: Thus more than 50 per cent of the respondents favoured moral education with reference to religious teachings. There could be several reasons for it, some of which may be as follows:

(i) Religion plays a positive role in the moral uplift of man. It may, at times, be the fear of gods which may be the motive factor for individual's right conduct. William Newton Clarke considered the role of religion in imparting moral education as that of a school master. He wrote in his book *The Christian Doctrine of God*.

" Doubtless the ethical life of the world has suffered much from religion, but it owes to religion immeasurably more than it has suffered from it. Faulty enough indeed the influence has been, but the ethical life of the world has on the whole been greatly reinforced and purified by its religions."

(ii) All religions are creations of superb minds. Religious writings are replete with episodes which have great moral lessons far man. It would be lack of wisdom on the part of man not to benefit from the wealth of experience stored in the religious books.

(iii) We, in India, are not trying to create an irreligious society. What we have accepted is a variously religious society, and not a society which has nothing to do with religion. Therefore, religion cannot be rejected merely on the ground that we are a secular state.

The Perception

Those who are opposed to assigning any role to religion in the sphere of moral education may have some of the following arguments in mind.

(i) According to Article 28 (1) of the Constitution of India,

"No religious instruction shall be provided in any educational institution wholly maintained out of State Fund."

This, of course, does not apply to the educational institutions run by private trusts. In regard to such institutions, Article 28(3) of the Constitution lays down the following policy.

"No person attending any educational institution recognised by the State or receiving aid out of State funds shall be required to take part in any religious instruction that maybe imparted in such institutions or to attend any religious worship that may be conducted in such institutions or in any premises attached thereto unless such person or, if such a person is a minor, his guardian has given his consent thereto."

(ii) Religion is identified by some people more as theology, a set of rituals, fear of God and greed for heaven rather than a code of, conduct evolved over a period of years. Such people see no link between religion and morality. In his work 'Christianity and Hinduism', Bishop Caldwell writes:

"We meet with a moral Hindu who has broken altogether away from religion and, what is still more common, still more extraordinary, we meet with a devout Hindu who lives a flagrantly immoral life. In the latter case no person sees any inconsistency between immorality and devoutnes."

'The Karma Theory' which is one of the fundamental principles of Hinduism proclaims the importance of virtuous acts. The following legend in a Hindu sacred-book brings out very aptly the higher place of a kind act than the performance of rituals. A rich man, once, performed the ritual of offering 1000 mangoes to the sacred Ganges. One of these mangoes was picked up by a poor beggar to satisfy his hunger. The same night, the rich man, in his dream saw the goddess Ganges who told him that she had accepted the offering of the mango only! The 'devout Hindus' of Caldwell experience are therefore, not truly religious.

(iii) People project their moral conceptions in the shape of gods; but once created these divinities react on the conscience of their creators. Examples are not wanting where divinities created by the priest class and other powerful sections in the society have had an adverse influence on the morals of the society. It is in the name of some divinities that injustices are perpetrated on the weaker sections of the society.

(iv) To many people, religion has meant forcible proselytisation at the point of bayonet or economic and social exploitation of others. Religions have led to feuds among the co-religionists as well as between people of different faiths.

(v) Communists as well as many other people have no faith in any religion. Religions like Buddhism make no reference to God. If moral teachings are to be based on religion, it would amount to imparting no moral education to persons who do not believe in religion.

(vi) Some of these people hold that moral education should be based on rational thinking only. In ancient Greece, where there was no priestly class, the country had no theocratic morality. Aristotle discussed only scientific foundations of morality. In ancient Rome, morality was based on patriotism and not religion.

(vii) The great Hindu codifier of values, Manu, makes no reference to rituals and supernatural things in his definition of dharma.

Those who hold that moral education should be imparted independent of religion argue that if some day a person rejects his religion (and this can happen with the growth of materialistic values), he would reject morality also. It would, in a way, amount to throwing the baby along with the bath tub.

(viii) Today, many societies are pluralistic and have a markedly different value-system arising from their respective religions. Therefore, there is an inherent difficulty in linking morality with religion.

Critics and scholars have also pointed towards several disintegrating factors in various religions. For example, Judaism, Christianity and Islam, which have a common catchment area, believe in an exclusive God. Their God brooks no rival, whereas according to Hinduism, all Gods are manifestation of the same Brahma; only the sages have described Him differently. The Judaic God commands his worshippers that when they enter the land of their enemies, they will "destroy their altars, and break their images, and cut down their groves, and burn their graven images with fire". (Bible, Deut 7.5). Iconoclasm, temple razing has been preached and practised by Islam to a similar degree. It is told that Walid was sent by the prophet to destroy the idol of al-Uzza at Nakhle worshipped by the tribal people there. Wherever the followers of Christianity went, they destroyed gods and religious places of the 'nonbelievers'. When America was discovered, the

Benedictine monks who came in the train of Columbus boasted of having destroyed single-handed 170,000 images in Haiti alone. Juan de Zummarage, the first Bishop of Mexico, writing as early as 1531 claimed that he destroyed 500 temples and 20,000 idols of the heathens. In our own country, in Goa, Jesuit fathers destroyed many Hindu temples. The Hindus, at one time, had to pay 'Jazia, only because they were Hindus and not Muslims. A law laid down that infidels could not build their temples. The Laxmi Narain Temple in New Delhi is reported to have come up in the country after a lapse of about 700 years. Various religions, thus, appear to have been reduced to mere denominations only.

Conveying Vehicles

In case educational institutions adopt an attitude of indifference to religion, it would mean leaving the interpretation of religion to the reactionaries and half-educated people only and jeopardising the process of social evolution.

The works of the religiously inclined saints and sufi poets and philosophers like Namdev, Tukaram, Kabir, Kurral, Jaisi, S. Radhakrishnan and others in different languages express moral truths in epigramatic phrases. All such works have had a great moralising influence on the society and it would be a mistake not to make use of them for their literary and moral value.

Every religion lays down some code of conduct for its followers and contains in its books numerous legends to inspire its faithfuls to observe certain norms of behaviour. It would be useful to make use of this heritage, for imparting ethical education to students.

Each religion preaches spiritual fulfilment, withdrawing from the lower pulls to higher recesses of mind, prayer, meditation, inculcation of virtues like compassion, contentment, good actions, self-surrender, service of mankind and all that can elevate man and the society.

Elements of Faith

To the statement that—"Students should be given an intelligent understanding of the codes of conduct of various religions", (G-9), the respondents reacted as follows:

S. No.	*Category of Respondents*	*Number Agreeing*	*Number Undecided*	*Number Disagreed*	*Number of persons who expressed no opinion*
1.	Total population	798	39	44	—
	(881)	(90.6)	(4.4)	(5)	
2.	Age-Group 18-25 years	43	4	5	—
	(52)	(82.7)	(7.7)	(9.6)	
3.	Above 40 years	532	20	22	—
	(574)	(92.7)	(3.5)	(3.8)	
4.	High School	115	1	7	—
	(123)	(3.5)	(0.8)	(5.7)	
5.	MA or above	414	27	23	—
	(464)	(89.2)	(5.8)	(5)	
6.	With income from Rs. 1000-1999 p.m.	88	6	4	—
	(98)	(89.8)	(6.1)	(4.1)	
7.	With income of Rs. 4000 p.m.	369	16	22	—
	(407)	(90.7)	(3.9)	(5.4)	

All the categories of respondents listed above lent a high degree of support to the statement.

Whatever be the source of the material employed for moral education, all discussions on the value-system should be on rational basis only and not wrapped in meaningless myths and superstitions. For example, it would be an incorrect approach to say, 'Respect women because it is written in *Manusmriti.*

yatra nariastu poojante, ramante tatra devata,

yatraiatastu na poojante, sarvaatatraphala kriya.

'Homes where women are worshipped become the abode of gods but where women are not given respect, all the actions of the people there end up in failure'.

Instead, students should be told with examples that whenever and wherever women have been given an opportunity in education, services or other spheres,, their contribution has been no less than that of men. On this account as well as on account of the sacrifice which women make as mothers, they are worthy of great respect.

It would be wrong to attribute some of the existing social ills solely to religion. Foreign aggressions, alien rule, present day consumerism and absence of developmental work over long periods are vital factors responsible for moral decay of the society.

Religion has played a central role and is still playing an important role in the life of the Indian people. All our works of ancient art, literature, dance, music, etc., are intimately interwoven with religious myths and thought. Sciences such as astronomy and geometry, etc., were cultivated in India initially for religious purposes only. Therefore, it may not be possible to eliminate religion from our lives without the grave risk of cutting ourselves from our roots. According to a news-report, a record number of 19.92 lakh pilgrims visited the holy shrine of Vaishno Devi during 1988, exceeding-the previous year's mark, by 1.35 lakhs. These pilgrims came from all over India. Even a number of politicians who swear by secularism visit the holy shrines located all over India. The visit by these leaders may be politically motivated, but they indicate the 'direction of the wind' in our country. Due to great appeal which religion has for the Indian masses, religion was used as an effective weapon during the freedom struggle of the country. V. Subramaniam writes :

"Annie Besant's use of the *Bhagvadgita* and theosophy appealed to the urban high-caste Hindu—while Tilak widened the base of appeal through using the Ganesh Puja as an instrument of politico-cultural revivalism quite apart from his Karmayogic (activist) reinterpretation of the Bhagvadgita. Bengali radicalism drew inspiration from the Mother Goddess right from its early days—and Gandhiji's efforts to appeal to the widest public included the slogan of Ram Rajya and the singing of Ram Dhun. In short, the nationalist movement though never exclusively Hindu nor theocratic, nevertheless used Hindu religion cultural symbols and slogans as the most practical instruments of mobilisation of the Indians-in spite of strong criticism both from the Right and Left, from Liberals such as Sapru or Kunzru and Leftists such as Jawahar Lal Nehru, the from Socialists and the Communists."

The motif 'Yoga is efficiency in action' '(Yoga Karmasu Kaushlam) adopted by the National Academy of Administration and the National Productivity Council is from the holy Bhagvad-gita. Of course, the choice of the motif would have been on account of its appropriateness and eloquence and not religious considerations but this is all the more reason that the students should be given an intelligent understanding of various religions and the useful messages contained in the religious text.

"The Indians," remarks Sir Harcourt Butler, "are as essentially religious as the Europeans are essentially secular. Religion is still the beginning and the end, the alpha and omega of Indian Life". This belief finds expression in a bitter satire of the Urdu poet Akbar, of which the gist is " The East is spiritual, the West is material. Mansur (the Sufi Pantheist who was executed in Baghdad in A.D. 922 for blasphemy) declared, 'I am God.' Darwin announced " I am the son of an ape".

Religious Strength

As regards the role of the religious institutions, the questionnaire for the students carried the following statement :

"Religious institutions such as temples, mosques, churches should play greater role in propagating moral values in the society". (S-11)

Agencies in Operation

(a) College students agree with the statement to a greater degree than do the school students.

(b) Male students are more in favour of the idea that the religious institutions should play a greater role in propagating moral values than the female students.

(c) In each case the degree of agreement with the statement is less than 75 per cent.

More than 25 per cent of the respondents were undecided on this issue or were opposed to the idea of religious institutions taking up the work of the propagation of moral values, possibly due to the fact that the respondents were skeptical about the ability of the religious institutions to achieve results. Some of the following steps could be considered for equipping the religious institutions for working effectively in the sphere of value-education.

(i) It should be ensured that the temple-priests or other similar personnel involved in the work take a progressive and not an obscurantist's view of religion. For this purpose, a system would have to be evolved on a national basis for entry to priesthood. Individuals wishing to become priests should go through an adequate course of training and education. In the USSR, prior to glasnost and perestroika, notwithstanding that communism is antagonistic to religion, the priests; before they could take up priest-hood, have had to go through a course of adequate training and education in religious and other allied texts. If government can successfully intervene with the administration of the Vaishno Devi temple in J and K State, there is no reason why a similar system cannot be introduced or at least experimented in India.

(ii) The education programme of the priests must drill the trainees in the concept of oneness of the Supreme Being and certain degree of the comparative study of various religions. *Ahura Mazda* in Zoroastrianism, Allah in Islam, Heavenly Father in Christianity, Iswara in Hinduism, and Sunyata in Buddhism are only different names given by different people in different geographical and linguistic regions for the same cosmic, creative, infinite and eternal energy. The leaders of religious institutions should be trained to remain free from bigotry.

(iii) The people in religious institutions, like all other people, should bear in mind that as a society evolves intellectually, spiritually and socially, its value-system undergoes a metamorphosis. In case religious institutions refuse to accept this logic, they would lose their credibility. A couple of examples of a progressive and a rational approach in this regard are given here.

Example-I : Among the Muslims it was held for a long time that the *Zakat* or the *Wakf*, i.e., the money collected for charity purposes, is to be spent, among other things, for religious education only as distinct from secular education. In recent years, rational Muslims have justified the utilisation of Zakat for secular education. According to these progressive thinkers, the Holy Prophet Mohammad had sent a number of people to India and China to receive education. Evidently these people had not gone to these countries to receive Quranic education. Therefore, it is perfectly in accordance with the Islamic thought to utilise Wakf for imparting secular education.

Example-II: Islamic tenets, on theocratic basis, divide the world into two sections-Dar-al-Islam and Dar-al-Harb' It was said that no taxes be levied by Muslim countries for imports from the former category of countries whereas taxes maybe levied in the case of the second category. The rationalist Muslims have, in recent years, changed this view in this manner. They say that Islam upholds the essentiality of survival. As money is necessary for survival, therefore taxes maybe levied in the case of all categories including the first category.

Example-III: According to Islam, Muslims are not allowed to charge interest from anyone, even from banks. The modern thinking among some Muslims is that banks invest money-deposits of the individuals in various projects and business deals and earn profits. As sharing of profits is not specifically banned by Islam, the depositors can accept these profits. The issue is still a debatable one as Muslims of the conventional types view that trade has an element of profit and loss and risk. As bank deposits do not have this element, bank interest cannot be equated to trade profits. They argue that this is a circuitous way of accepting the bank-interest by changing its nomenclature; but then if religious leaders refuse to accept these changes, the changing society would just ignore them and their sermons as well.

Forwarding the Message

There was the following statement in the questionnaire relating to mass-media.

"Indu and Joginder Singh were discussing radio and T.V. coverage of such programmes which are religious in character. Indu justified such coverage whereas Joginder Singh felt that such coverage violated the principle of secularism. Who, in your opinion, was correct?

(a) Preventing the mass-media from doing such a coverage would, to some extent, mean working for a closed society. The endeavour, on the contrary, should be to depict all religions, cultures as well as sub-cultures rather than drawing a curtain on them. India's mission to evolve a society with composite culture and not one which is indifferent to all cultures.

(b) Any belief or custom which becomes a part of the mainstream of life no longer remains exclusively religious. It becomes a part of the social life of the community and deserves to be depicted by the mass-media. The immense popularity of the *Ramayana* and the *Mahabharata* T.V. serials from the Doordarshan network amply establishes the justification of projecting such programmes through the mass-media.

(c) Secularism has two forms. There is the 'absolute secularism' which is practised in the communist world where religion has no place in the planned affairs of the country. There the religion is a totally private affair.

The Indian view of secularism is, however, different. In India, all religions can flourish. The government does not give preferential treatment to any particular religion. Therefore, if a balanced coverage of important programmes of all religions is undertaken by mass-media, it would lead to better understanding of all cultures by different communities inhabiting the country.

Those opposed to the use of mass-media for religious programmes primarily may be of the opinion that the Preamble of the Indian Constitution declares India a secular state, therefore the government should not dabble with religion. They may be interpreting secularism as communist societies do this. Some persons in this category also have a feeling that the government massmedia occasionally, give a preferential treatment to the programmes of one religion vis-a-vis programmes of other religions. Difficult as it may be to totally ward off such an imbalance or an error of judgement in the selection of programmes for the mass-media, its incidence can be reduced by drawing up a clear and a well-thought out policy. The question is—which is more hazardous in a multi-cultural society—to deprive the people of the chance of having an intelligent understanding of the cultures and religions of other communities and interaction with them, or taking a calculated risk of the consequences which would flow if there is some error in the choice of programmes for dissemination through massmedia. Perhaps, the latter course may be a better choice.

It may be argued that human-kind had started observing some kind of moral code earlier than it evolved any kind of religion. Merial Downey and Av Kelley held that:

"..... morality has to be seen independent of religion. If there is a connection it is not that morality is dependent on religious beliefs, it is much more likely that man's religious beliefs are a result of his moral awareness". As Kant said, "Belief in God is grounded in moral consciousness rather than moral law on belief in God."

The question, however, is not if the moral code preceded the evolution of religion or it was viceversa; but whether in the present context moral education should be undertaken with or without reference to religion. In this context two things are to be kept in view:

(a) Have we evolved adequate secular literature for imparting moral education?

(b) If religion is divorced from theology and belief in supernaturalism, is there any harm if its moral code, and fables, stories and other relevant material are used for imparting moral education?

In this connection one cannot overlook that only 532 per cent of the respondents supported the application of religion for moral education, whereas 43.3 per cent supported that moral education should be imparted without reference to religious teachings. However, it is not known what was the picture of religion that the respondents had in mind while reacting to this statement. If the picture of religion before them was that of bigoted priests, performance of unmeaningful rituals, sermonising doctrines, one would agree that religious teachings should be kept aloof from moral education; but if religion means harmony of the individual with all forms of life and matter in the cosmos, religion provides a sound basis for moral education.

In view of the above, it would be desirable, as corroborated by about 90 per cent of each category of respondents (in G-9) to give students an intelligent and a rational understanding of the code of conduct of various religions, so that students are not deprived of the wealth of experience stored in these books.

If our dilapidated value-system is to be restructured and saved from decaying further, it is essential that religious establishments should also play their full role in this regard. For this purpose, it would be necessary to have an educated priesthood which has a comprehensive view of various religions and can see the elements of unity behind all religions. The mass-media should also take a balanced and a rational view while projecting customs, traditions and programmes, etc., connected with various religions and intended to impart information to the viewers on different aspects of the national and cultural life and for inculcation of moral values among them.

15

Values of Buddhism

Buddhism is the philosophy based on what Buddha said in his lectures to the people of this world. Buddha was born in 562 B.C. at Kapil Vastu one hundred miles in the north of Kashi on Nepal border. He was the son of Raja Shuddodhan of Shakya dynasty. His original name was Siddhartha and Gautam was the name of his family line. His mother died seven days after his birth and he was, then, brought up by his step mother Maha Prajavati. He was married to Yashodhara and had a son Rahul born of them. Right from the beginning of his life he was highly religious-minded not, at all, attracted by worldly pleasures. His father made herculian efforts to turn his mind away from Vairagya. But, he did not succeed and Buddha left home for forest life at the age of twenty nine. He came to be the disciple of two Sanyasis, Aalar Kalam and Ram Putt. He could not be satisfied with their teachings and went with five of his disciples to Urubella for rigorous penance to achieve realization. There Buddha immersed himself into deep meditation and harsh penance. He crossed the four stages of meditation and finally at the peak of it achieved self-control and stability. He realised that the whole of the universe was a well-regulated system of beings and saw higher and lower beings experiencing worldly pleasures and miseries leaving one form and taking another form. In the last hours of the night his ignorance vanished and true knowledge emerged. He became Buddha. He decided, instead of becoming indifferent (Virakta) to life, to give that knowledge to the people who had a desire to get freedom from miseries of the world and were eager to know what the reality was. He delivered his first lecture at Mrigdav of Samath. He had then, gradually, a large number of his disciples who went out to spread his message in all corners of this and other countries.

Buddhist Philosophy

Buddhism is more a philosophy of practical life rather than a philosophy of ideas and ideals. Buddha was a Karamyogi and he actually carried the teachings of Karam-yoga into practice, into perfect practice. Unlike many prophets of the world who held that they were either incarnations of God on this earth or were messengers of God and who drew their impetus for work from outside, who expected reward from outside, Buddha was the only prophet who said "I do not care to know your various view and theories about god; what is the use discussing all the subtle doctrines about the soul; do good and be good. And this will take you to freedom, to whatever truth there is." He was absolutely without personal motive in his life, the great philosopher preaching the highest philosophy of life. Yet, Buddha had the deepest sympathy for the lowest animal and never put forth any claim for himself. He was an ideal Karam-Yogi acting entirely without motive.

Buddha is the name of the infinite knowledge. Buddha did not want to go to heaven, did not want money: he gave up his throne and everything else and went about begging his bread through the streets of India preaching for the good of men.

Ultimate Truth

Buddhistic philosophy is revealed in the *Tri-pitakas*, the compilation of Buddhas teachings, ideas and ideals made by his followers after hundred years of his death. Buddha himself did not write any book. It was his disciples who passed on his teachings from one generation to another till they were finally put in the book form. The *Tri-Pitakaas* (three books or boxes) are: (i) Vinay Pitaka, (ii) Sukta Pitaka, and (iii) Abhidhamma Pitaka. The Vinay Pitaka is the code of conduct for the monks of both the sexes. The Sukta Pitaka is the store-house of religious rules and their illustrations. The Abhidhamma Pitaka contains Buddhas teachings and his philosophical ideas. It is these Pitakas which constitute the source of Buddhistie philosophy. Each Pitaka contains several parts.

Four Great Truths: Buddha's teachings and ideals had their origin in the attainment of *Buddhatwa* i.e. wisdom or infinite knowledge enlightenment which was possible for him through his deep and continuous meditation resulting into his inner experience. The world outside was real and objective for him. This reality appeared to him as:

(1) Full of miseries.

(2) All world miseries having a cause

(3) All miseries being possible to be eliminated

(4) Consisting of certain ways and methods through which these miseries could be eliminated.

Buddha said birth leads to pain, old age means pain; disease means pain; death means pain; attachment to the undesirables is painful and parting with the loved ones, too, is painful; failing to achieve the desired is painful; love and hate are universal truths. They disintegrate the life and create imbalances. Man's struggle to live is the cause of this misery. Freedom from this misery is possible; men must make efforts.

Buddha said that everything has a cause and also an effect. The phenomenon of cause-effect is found operating everywhere in the universe. It applies equally in case of human life and its history, human actions and events of human life. If we know the cause of human misery and make effort to free ourselves from that cause, we will not suffer any more. The cause of human misery is desire, desire to live. Desire and ignorance are two sides of the same coin. Ignorance leads to extreme individualism, selfishness and revolt against universal good. This results into desire and greed, which prick into the soul and make it difficult to get rid of the misery. Buddha said that ignorance is destroyed by knowledge and wisdom; desire and greed are destroyed by moral consciousness.

Another aspect of reality as described by Budhists is the principle of *Pratityasamuttapannvad* (die cue), the cycle of life and death. This is also a cause of human misery. The man dies and is born again. This cycle of dying and taking birth again goes on forever continuously. All our lives past and present and fixture form an infinite chain without beginning and without end, each link of which is one life with two ends, birth and death. According to Buddhism the cause of this birth-death cycle is man's own desire, the man himself. Buddha told that man himself is the master of his fate, fortune maker, God and protector. He had strong faith in rebirth phenomenon.

Buddhism denies that there is something behind both body and mind which is an unchangeable and immovable substance and emphasizes that there is no such thing as immovability and unchangeability in the universe; it is all change, nothing but change. The Buddhists advocate this as the principle of Kshanikvad or Anityavad i.e. momentariness, meaning thereby that all things that are caused exist for some time and, then, vanish. Nothing exists permanently. Everything is perishable and, hence, momentary. Nothing is eternal. It is an illusion that things appear to us as permanent. Change is the hard reality of human life and of this universe. The outside world is an objective reality to Buddhists. Universality of things is denied by them.

Buddhism believes in the theory of karma. It says every individual comes in this world with all the past on him; the infinite past ushers the present and the way in which we use the present is going to make the future. Thus, everyone born in this world has a bent, a direction towards which he must go, through which he must live. There can not be a cause without an effect. The present must have had its cause in the past and will have its effect in the future. The body has to remain under the power of past karmas.

Basic Principles

Buddhism advocates a principle of Artha-Kriya-Karitwa which means existence is purposive. Everything exists for some purpose and is transitary and changeable. The seed exists to germinate and having done that it gets destroyed. Buddhism is Anatmavadi philosophy as claimed by many writers. They say that the soul has no place in Buddhism. Essence of Buddhism is according to Dr. Radhakrishnan (p. 56) (i) Swarga (heaven) devoid of God, (ii) immortality without soul and purity without worship and prayers. But several other writers hold that "Buddhism can not be considered anatmavadi" (Devendra Muni Shastri, p. 99). Even Dr. S. Radhakrishnan said when Buddha called the soul as "Aatmadip", "Aattadip", "Aatmasharan", "Aattasharan", he was pointing out to the eternal soul, Universal soul within us (p. 64). In general the concept of soul in Buddhism is that "it is neither a unity of elements, nor different from elements, nor it is a synthesis of mind and body; nor it is a wholly unperishable substances; what it is can not be described. Yet, there are five material elements which are said to make the soul. These are:

(1) Form (Roop) including earth, sky, air, fire, water.

(2) Pain (Vedna) which means experience of pain (Vedna Skandha)

(3) Name (Sangya Skandh) which enables a person to recognise a thing

(4) Impression (Sanskar Skandh) which means impre-ssions of things, events, etc. Left on the person after experience. They are of three kinds: action, speech and image.

(5) Vigyan (Vigyan Skandh) which means knowledge of external objects through 'self, through form, taste, touch, smell, etc., in other words all sensory and perceptual knowledge:

All of these are inter-related and constitute components of the soul.

Significant Elements

Thus, the Reality (or Truth) as implied in Buddhism has following characteristics:

(1) The world outside is objective and real. The real is what the individual experiences. But, it is not desirable to be attached to it.

(2) There is no eternal or universal principle underlying this objective world, no God, no Brahaman or any ultimate principle.

(3) Life is full of miseries; and the cause of all miseries is ignorance.

(4) There is no such entity as the soul.

(5) Cause-effect principle is controlling and regulating all that happens in the universe and in the life of the human being.

(6) Birth-death-rebirth cycle is incessantly going on. But, there is no external cause of this, such as God or Brahman.

(7) Change is the law of nature. This is a reality. Everything on this earth is changing every moment. Nothing is unchangeable or immovable. The reality is dynamic. It appears to be immovable due to ignorance.

(8) Man himself, the suffering man is the reality. His own desires, greeds, and worldly attachments are the cause of his miseries; and this reality alone has to be faced with true knowledge so that ignorance is destroyed and man attains salvation and is freed from these miseries. Man, according to Buddhism, is neither a purely physical being nor he is a being with a permanent soul within him. He is rather a combination of the physical and mental forces, a *sanghata* (aggregate) of five *skandhas* (elements) such as *Rupa* (matter) *Vedna* (sensation or feeling), *Samjna* (perception), *Sanskara* (dispositions) and *Vignana* (consciousness).

(9) None can help man in this struggle for liberation. He alone can help himself. He has to work out his own salvation. Perfection comes through the disinterested performance of action.

(10) The only dependable truth in this world is Dharama Religious insight (Budhwatva). Attainment of this insight is the highest level of spiritual development and is the ultimate aim of humanity. Buddha suggested eight-step practical method for achieving this excellence, the salvation.

Buddha suggested following steps for achieving enlightenment:

(1) *The Right Insight (Samyak Drishti):* To keep in mind that life is full of misery which has a cause, which can be eliminated and that there are definite ways to achieve this. These are four truths which one has to keep in mind.

(2) *The Right Will Power (Samyak Sankalp):* For observing the four truths.

(3) *The Right Speech (Samyak Vak):* To be faithful to one's words.

(4) *The Right Deeds (Samyak Karmas):* This includes foresaking of violence and stealing, observing celibacy and detachment from worldly pleasures.

(5) *The Right Vocations (Samyak Aajivika):* It means earning one's living by right conduct.

(6) *The Right Exercise (Samyak Vyayam):* Adopting good ways and to give up bad ideas.

(7) *The Right Memory (Samyak Smriti):* To remember things correctly.

(8) *The Right Meditation (Samyak Samadhi):* This is essential for attainment of salvation.

Following above principles one can get freedom from worldly miseries. These principles are, generally, classified under three heads: (a) morality, (b) meditation, and (c) wisdom or intelligence.

The concept of salvation as implied in Buddhism is different from that ordinary one which is based on the concept of sin of ethic of intention. Buddhism advocated that sin is not the final power inimical to salvation; not "evil" but ephemeral life is the obstacle to salvation; salvation is sought from the simply senseless unrest of all structures of existence in general. Passion of any kind, Passion for God, even in the form of the loftiest enthusiasm is absolutely inimical to salvation because all desires mean attachment to life.

Buddhism is a salvation religion, an ethical movement without a deity and without a cult, an ethic with absolute indifference to the question of whether there are "gods" and how they exist. In terms of the "how" and "from what" to "what end" of salvation Buddhism represents the most radical form of salvation. It is solely personal act of the single individual. There is no recourse to a deity or savior, no prayer or religious grace, no destination of any kind. According to karma doctrine of the universal causation man's ultimate fate depends entirely on his free behaviour. It says that it is senseless to be attached to all or any inclinations, hopes and wishes connected with belief in this-worldly or other-worldly life.

Perception of Awareness

In Buddhism 'knowledge' is considered a means of attaining salvation. But, this is not 'in the sense of broad knowledge of earthly or heavenly things. Early Buddhism put restrictions on the quest for knowledge, the knowledge which concerned the search for what would occur after the death of the individual. It said that a concern for knowledge was also a "desire", "thirst" and did not benefit the holiness of the soul. Inquiry into the nature of *nirvana* was regarded by early Buddhism a heresy (Weber, p. 209). Buddhism also rejected speculation because it would imply an attachment to mundane intellectual knowledge which is of no use for future perfection. "The salutary" knowledge is exclusively the practical illumination by the four great truths of the nature, origin, condition and means of destroying suffering" (Weber, p. 209).

Buddha never wrote any commentary. He never claimed that he descended on the earth with some universal knowledge. Whatever he said was the result of his accumulated experiences of life. He never presented before his disciples any theory or "ism" or any sectarian belief. He presented only a way, a plan for the spiritual and moral development of man. The teachings of Buddha are connected with his attainment of Buddhatwa which is such a spiritual experience which can not be described in words. The whole of knowledge that was implied in Buddha's teachings is related to these experiences only. The aim of his teachings was only to suggest a new novel way of living.

According to Buddhism true knowledge is that which destroys ignorance which is the cause of all human miseries, pain and grief. Nothing happens without a cause and so miseries of life also have a cause and that they can be eliminated by following a particular way of living. Man can attain freedom from life's miseries by not only knowing, For that experience and practice are needed. Apart from this any other knowledge is useless. "The true holy seeker is not attached even to the desire of knowledge", said Weber (p. 206).

The kind of knowledge which is emphasized by Buddhists is the knowledge about the ways of attaining salvation, freedom from birth-death cycle and, thus, suffering miseries endlessly. Buddha said "when ignorance and desire are ended, then purity and inner awakening take place". That is the state of the soul when it is in complete peace and joy. How to achieve that requires full knowledge of self-control and practice of meditation.

For achieving self-control and spiritual development Buddha described the eight-step method. Full knowledge of these along with practice is what is most essential.

Besides this, Buddhism throws light on what is man, what is this universe, what is spiritual development, what is self, what is soul. These have already been discussed. The eight step method of practising penance has also been discussed. The only way of acquiring knowledge as emphasized by Buddha is experience gained through meditation, which leads to Bodhisatwa

Value Perception

What are the values which can be derived and lived from Buddhism is a natural question. The question may be put in a slightly different way as "what are the things that are prized most by Buddhism?" It seems following values may be inferred from Buddha's teachings and literature on Buddhism.

Spiritual Development: Buddhism stresses the fact that human detachment from worldly pleasures and attractions is necessary for getting freed from the tensions, unhappiness and miseries of the world. As human life on this earth is full of pain and grief of various kinds, the individual must find a way out. And the way suggested is spiritual development through self-control and right conduct. Buddha advocated attainment of divinity in the present life only. His Ashtang-Bidh method describes the procedure of step-by-step attainment and purity of heart and perfection leading ultimately to a stage where salvation awaits the man.

Means, not the Ends are Important: Generally, in the march to human development, it is the goals, aims or objectives which are focused above all. In case of Buddha's teachings more valuable are the means than the ends. He emphasized on living a life of purity' which is based on non-violence, sacrifice, unselfishness, desirelessness, doing always good to others without caring where they will lead to. Ultimately, you will be bound to reach the stage of perfection. Thus, practice of "good" is a value rather than the "good" itself.

Non-attached Actions: According to Buddhism non-attached actions (*nishkama karma*) is a great value of life. Buddhism does not teach inaction. This is true that Buddhism strongly held a belief that actions (karmas) bind and are the root cause of suffering. But, this was said about the attached actions, not about non-attached actions which do not bind.

Attainment of Nirvana: This is the final destiny of man according to Buddhism. This is a state of spiritual freedom and life also. if one is able to detach himself from all sorts of worldly passions completely by the observances of the eightfold path of discipline and self-control.

Buddhism: Like existentialism, teaches self-help and self-reliance as the most effective means of attaining perfection. At the same time, unlike existentialism, it also believes in the humanistic virtues of interdependence, mutual help, universal service and brotherhood.

Universal Salvation: Buddhism stresses universal salvation also. It teaches that it is not sufficient for anyone to attain his own salvation. After achieving his own *Nirvana* one must work for the Nirvana of others. This is the ideal of Bodhisattva in Buddhism.

Some of the Ethical Values: Buddhism repeatedly emphasize are those of non-violence (Ahimsa), truth (satya), kindness to all beings, self-restraint, nobleness, charity, etc. Out of these Ahimsa is most emphasized.

Discipline: The discipline that leads to the complete cessation of suffering and attainment of *Nirvana* is contained in the fourth noble truth of Buddha's famous eightfold path, the middle path as it is, generally, called. Buddha declared that those who wished to attain the ideal of life should avoid the two extremes of self-indulgence and self-torture because, as he said, "self-indulgence is low, vulgar, ignoble, harmful, and self mortification is painful, ignoble and harmful. Both are profitless." The former retards one's spiritual progress and the latter weakens one's intellect.

The eightfold discipline is very much emphasized in this context.

The Eightfold Path: All the elements of this eightfold path are values as advocated by Buddhists. These include (i) Right view or right understanding, (2) Right thought, (3) Right speech, (4) Right action, (5) Right livelihood, (6) Right effort, (7) Right mindfulness (having a constant vigil over the body, the feelings, the mind, and concentration. Of these, first two constitute what is called *Prajna,* the next three constitute what is called *Shila,* and the last three are called *Samadhi.*

There are two branches of Buddhism-Hinayan and Mahayana, "Yan" means vehicle. So Hinayan means small carrier, while Mahayana means the great carrier. Mahayana brought many changes in original Buddhism to accommodate many things which could appeal and attract ordinary religious people. The Hinyanas remained strictly loyal to the original principles of Lord Buddha. Consequently they remained small in number.

QUESTIONS

1. What are four great truths ?
2. What are the principles of Buddhism ?
3. What is eightfold path ?

16

Values of Jainism

As a reaction to Vedic Ritualism are two forces, Buddhism and Jainism. Although like Buddhism, Jainism could not free itself from the essentials of Hinduism. The founder of Jainism is Lord Mahavira whose childhood name was Vardhman. There had been 23 religious teachers prior to Mahavira Swami who was the twenty fourth one. The religious teachers of Jainism are known as Tirthankaras (perfect soul) or Jin, i.e., the one who has conquered passion. The first Tirthankara was Rishabhdeoji; and the 23rd one was Parsuadeo. But, Swami Mahavir is regarded the propounder of the essential principles of Jaina philosophy. Mahavira was a Kshatriya by birth and was an elder contemporary of Buddha. After 14 years of ascetic life he felt that he had gained enlightenment. After that he devoted his life to preaching his messages to people. He preached a non-theistic religion of moral purity and excellence.

Hinduism, Buddhism and Jainism all aimed at liberating man out of the degradation and suffering in which he is fallen. But, they differed in their approaches to enlightenment and solution. Buddhism and Jainism, however, both emphasized that their objective could not be achieved by worshiping gods and goddesses, nor by performing various rituals. They advocated that liberation from suffering and attainment of enlightenment could be possible simply by following the path of pure ethical conduct. Jainism rejected Vedantic and Samkhaya philosophies, though it was closer to samkhya doctrine in some of its metaphysical presuppositions, particularly in its view of the soul.

Ultimate Truth

According to Jainism the world in which the man finds himself is perfectly real. It is a function of six eternally-existing substances, five material and one spiritual. The five substances are: motion Principle of rest space time, matter. The sixth substance was, then, added to explain conscious beings which was named as Jiva.

The matter is said to be composed of atoms which form the basis of all material objects. These possess the qualities of touch, taste, smell and colour. It is believed that space is infinite and gives room for the *Pudgalas.* Time effects change. Dharma and Adharma are the principles of motion and rest, respectively. The Jainism holds that the world is not created by God or any supreme eternal Being from without. It exists by itself and is infinite, eternal and real, structured and functioning solely on the basis of ever moving and changing atoms of Pudgalas. In its essence every substance remains the same but in terms of its modes it changes. Every substance has two qualities essential and modes. This ascribes two qualities to this world also, both permanent and changing. In its essential aspect it is permanent, eternal and in its modes it is changing. The world is real, but not a place for enjoyment; it is a place for moral living.

Jainism denies any Reality beyond this objective world. It does, not believe in God or Brahaman as the creator of this world. It says that the physical world is governed by the Law of Karma. No God is required to govern the physical or the moral world. Thus, Jainism is a theistic religion, denying the universal eternal principle or God being behind this world. It, however, says that the man himself can attain Godhood by following the path of moral and spiritual discipline.

Man is another true Reality for Jainism. In Jainism man is himself given the status of God because, potentially, he is perfect, though he can not create the world. He is all perfect capable of attaining infinite power, infinite knowledge, infinite faith and infinite bliss. Thus, man is given the highest status in Jainism. He has a soul within him which is imbued with infinite potentialities. Though every *Jiva* has a soul, it is in the most manifest form in man. Soul is the eternal conscious substance in man which puts him highest among all the Jivas, the living beings. The present state of man is the state of bondage which is due to his own past karmas, actions with passions. Man has an immortal soul within him which does not die with physical death.

Another Reality, according to Jainism is the existence of soul in all living beings who make this world. It is this conscious principle in man which makes him suffer or helps him rise high on way to liberation. It is this conscious substance (Jiva) which underlies the phenomenon of rebirth or its transmigration from the old body to a new one, or *moksha,* the ultimate liberation from the chain of birth-rebirth cycle. Jainism is realistic and pluralistic. It believes in the reality of the world with all the plural objects in it. About man it says that his present state is not his real or natural state as his soul being associated with physical body (pudgala) has lost its original character. The real cause of man's imperfection is this soul's association with the body, causing its bondage. The cause of this association or soul's bondage is undoubtedly the ignorance (*agyana*). It is influenced by the passions of man due to ignorance. Good and bad actions of man leave an impression upon his soul which go on accumulating and constitute what in Jainism is called karman body which remains attached to the soul. After death it goes alongwith the soul. Godhood or man's godliness is the most developed state of the soul, a stage where a person's actions done with passion and past karma's influences are totally exhausted.

Law of Karma is a Reality in Jainism. Like Buddhism and Vedanta, Jainism believes that man is a product of his own past Karmas. At the same time it says that karma-bondage can be destroyed or its influence can be minimized and man can improve his lot by his sincere efforts in the present life. By purifying the soul through annihilation of the matter accumulated with the soul (*nirjara*) and preventing further influx of matter from without (*samvara*) man can get rid of the constant chain of birth and rebirth. For this Jainism has recommended specific methods and ways and means. Immediately after death of the physical body the soul transmigrates to a new body; The kind of a body and all conditions of new life are determined by the karmas of previous life. Life after birth is unavoidable unless *Moksha* (complete cessation of birth and rebirth) is attained.

Perception of Awareness

"For the Jains, too, knowledge is the supreme, in fact magical means of salvation" said Weber (p. 195). The Jainism has described two levels of knowledge-(i) relative knowledge (sapeksha Jnana) and (ii) absolute knowledge (nirapeksha Jnana). Man, while he is in bondage, is capable of attaining only relative knowledge. But a liberated (Kevali) attains absolute knowledge, "Whoever in life has attained the proper intuitive knowledge sins no more" (Weber, p. 195). According to Kalpa Sutra knowledge is classified into seven levels or statuses or stages. These are: supernatural knowledge (first stage), then ability to have vision, possession of magical powers and the ability of self-transformation, knowledge of thoughts of all living beings (the second stage of supernatural wisdom), freedom from all suffering (6th step), and finally (7th step) enlightenment stage. Thus, knowledge is graded and related to levels of spiritual development and progress. Attainment of proper intuitive knowledge leads a person to the realization that he is all-knowing and that he has all duties at his feet. Path to supreme knowledge in addition to study and meditation is asceticism of a high degree.

Knowledge, according to Jainism does not mean mere intellectual or scriptural knowledge. Knowledge to Jainas means inner realization, i.e., experiencing and seeing things for himself so that he is not attached to passions.

Right knowledge is the knowledge of nature of things, objects, events and happenings in the real perspective. It is understanding what exactly is nature of living and non-living beings, in other words of the objective material and non-material world. Jainism has described five non-living substances and one living substance, the soul. Knowledge about the true nature of these is considered very important in Jainism. Understanding of the difference between the living and non-living is emphasized.

Right knowledge of the nature of man, the soul. the karma doctrine, life after death, ultimate destiny, man's suffering and its cause, etc is essential for attaining *moksha* as is emphasized in Jainism. It is essential because the root cause of man's suffering and bondage is ignorance. Knowledge destroys ignorance. Knowledge is said to be, according to Jainism, the real *tapas* (penance), because it burns the karmas to ashes.

Real knowledge, as implied in Jainism, is that which helps in controlling the mind and purifying the self. For that knowledge acquired from scriptures only is not useful; only knowledge realized, experienced, felt within self is needed. Only self-realized knowledge is virtue, true and meaningful. So, it has stages and grows along with the stages of self enlightenment.

Value Perception

Values of Jainism are reflected in the threefold discipline taught by the Jaina Tirthankars, particularly Swami Mahavira. They called it a discipline of three jewels. To live life according to these three jewels was considered essential as following these one could get rid of ignorance and bondage and could attain liberation. These three jewels are; (i) Right faith, (ii) Right knowledge and (iii) Right conduct. All these three observed and followed jointly and in coordination was necessary for attaining *moksha*. They are inescapable as none is possible without the other.

Right Faith is defined in different ways. But, more rationalistic is the belief that it is faith in the Dharma including Ahimsa Dharma is the way of life as prescribed by Jaina Tirthankars or Jainism. It assumes importance as a value if respect and regard for Jaina principles are considered its essential characteristics. Jain Philosophy emphasized that faith in the spiritual principles taught by the Jains and other siddhas was the first requisite in the march towards Moksha. Without faith in the principles of Jainism even right knowledge and right conduct will not be possible. Faith in spiritual truth as advocated by the Jaina Tirthankars and their scriptures is considered, therefore, the most important value. But, certainly by faith Jainism does not mean blind faith. It must be based on one's own realisation, thinking and experience. Eight qualifying characteristics of faith are given by Jainism as follows: They call it Samyagdarshan the Right faith. It consists of— (i) *Nissankila* absence of doubt about scriptures, (ii) *Nihkankshita* absence of desire for the worldly pleasure, (iii) *Nirvichikitsa* absence of doubt about the attainment of spiritual path, (iv) *Amudhadristi* a clear vision of the ideal, (v) *Upabrhana, i.e.,* augmentation of spiritual qualities, (vi) *Sthirikaran* re-establishing deviation from truth, (vii) *Vatsalya* affection for true followers, (viii) *Prabhavna* preaching the importance of truth.

Right Knowledge has already been discussed. It is an important value because in the absence of right knowledge freedom from ignorance is not possible and the path to *moksha,* the highest spiritual aim of life is blocked and no progress on way to enlightenment is possible.

Right Conduct is the third jewel, i.e., third essential value of Jainism most needed for liberation. It is living a detached life. It consists of five vows known as Panchmahavratas These five are: (i) Non-Violence, (ii) Satya, (iii) Asteya, (iv) Brahamcharya and (v) Aparigraha (non-possession or non-attachment).

Ahimsa (non-violence) is a general principle and an important value according to Jainism. It is a great moral virtue. In its extreme form even not cooking and eating food after sun-set because of the fear of killing worms unknowingly and keeping the mouth covered are practised. Ahimsa has a very wide connotation in Jainism. Even talking against a person, forcing him to do something, self-praise, depriving someone of his freedom are considered acts of violence in Jainism. Similarly, negligence attachment, aversion and any action caused by them is violence.

Satya or truthfulness is another virtue considered very important by Jainism. It means falsehood should be avoided and truth must be spoken with good intention. It should not be harmful to others. Criticising others, to look down upon others, rebuking and abusing others, teasing others, etc, all are examples of untruth.

Asteya (non-stealing) means keeping away from all sorts of dishonesty and conceit, Stealing is considered in Jainism a kind of violence as it deprives others of their belongings. Even purchasing of stolen things amounts to stealing.

Brahamcharya (celibacy) means keeping away from illegal relationships with women other than one's wife. In its extreme form it also means abstinence from excessive desire for any sort of sense-enjoyment or indulgence.

Aparigraha means non-attachment to material possessions. Excessive desire for money, things of comfort, clothes, food and other avoidable things is considered undesirable. It requires that attraction for worldly pleasure and possessions should be avoided.

Besides these there are a number of practices that are recommended to be followed by the householders as well as for the monks such as:

(1) Digvrata restricting movement of the householders to specific directions.

(2) Desavakasikavrata indicating area or territory of movement of the householders and monks.

(3) Anarthadandavrat abstaining from harmful activities such as evil thinking, evil doing, giving weapons for violence, involving oneself in non-vigilant activities; etc.

(4) Samayika Vrata practising peace, inner-centeredness of the soul twice or thrice a day and imbibing the spirit of a monk.

(5) Prasadopvasa Vrata fasting including abstinence from bath, perfumes, physical adornment, sex, etc.

(6) Bhogopbhoga Vrata minimizing attachment to worldly objects, needing and using only things which are very necessary and unavoidable.

(7) Atithisamvibhaga Vrata prescribes qualities of givers and the recipients of alms as well as the process through which it is to be given.

These were considered most cherished values to be followed by the Jaina householders and the monks.

QUESTIONS

1. Explain the Jain concept of reality.
2. What is the concept of knowledge ?
3. What is concept of values ?

17

Values of Hinduism

There are six schools (Sad-Darshana—six in rights). These are: Nyaya, Vaisesika, Samkhya, Yoga, Mimansa and Vedanta. The real founders of these are not known. This is also controversial as to where and when they were reduced to writing. Together, they form a graduated interpretation of the Ultimate Reality. They all subscribed to the view that there is only One Ultimate Reality, though their interpretations of this reality does not remain exactly the same. But, in no way they are contradictory or antagonistic to one another for they all lead to the same practical end, knowledge of the absolute and liberation of the soul. They all grew out of the Upnishadas, the philosophical portions of the Veda. They are all written in the form of Sutras (aphorisms) which are extremely concise. They all accept the eternal cycle of Nature, which is without beginning and end and which consists of vast periods of creation, maintenance and dissolution. All of them accept the principle of regeneration of the soul that maintains that life and death are but two phases of a single cycle to which the soul is bound and to which it clings because of the ignorance of the true nature of things. All of them accept Dharma as the moral law of the Universe that accounts for these eternal cycles of Nature, as well as the destiny of the human soul. All of them agree that knowledge is the path to freedom and that the yoga is the method to attain final liberation.

Nyaya was founded by Gotama. It is concerned with the means of acquiring right knowledge which is classified under sixteen topics. It is purely a system of logic. Samkhya was founded by Kapila. This system comprehends the universe as a sum total of twenty five categories. It emphasized that all derived things in this world are produced from two realities, Spirit and Matter which are the ultimate Realities. It asserts that all things are evolved out of pre-existing material which is the static background of the universe and which simply unfolds itself as a rose unfolds from its seed. Yoga was founded by Patanjali. Here the concern is with the ways and means by which the individual can know Reality by direct experience. Mimansa was founded by Jaimini and was concerned mainly with the correct interpretation of vedic ritual and texts. Vedanta was founded by Badarayan and is an enquiry into the nature of the Ultimate principle of the Universe (Brahman).

Philosophy of Vedas

The word Vedanta literally means the end of the Vedas, the scriptures of the Hindus mainly divided into two portions—the Karma-Kanda and the Jnana-Kanda, the work-portions and the knowledge portion. To the Karma-Kanda belong the famous hymns and the rituals. Those books which treat spiritual matters apart from ceremonials are called upnishadas which belong to the Jnana-Kanda or knowledge portion. The term Shruti meaning that which is heard is chiefly applied to the Upnishadas said to be one hundred and eight in number. The Upnishadas are also called Forest Books or Aranyakas.

The Vedanta forms the basis of all systems of Indian philosophy, though they are named differently. From the interpretation of the opening sutra of Vedantasutra, the classic text of the Vedanta system written by Badaravan three schools developed, the Advaita (non-dualism). Vishishtadvaita (qualified non-dualism) and Dvaita (dualism) founded separately by Sankara (8th C.), Ramanuja (11th C.) and Modhava (12th C.).

The name of Samkara has become almost synonymous with Vedanta for his commentary on the Vedantasutra is the foundation for the largest and most popular religious sect of modern Hinduism called Vedanta. He was the greatest advocate of the teachings of the Upnishadas. Ramanuja stressed the theistic aspect of the Upnishadas while Samkara was strictly intellectual. Ramanuja was the great intuitionalist, surrendering to his feelings and setting forth his religious views, He admitted that the Ultimate Principle is real and exists, but said that the souls are also real, though their reality is dependent upon this Ultimate principle. He emphasized that the spiritual principle is the basis of the world and is not an illusion as held by Samkara. He insisted that. the existence of individual souls continues even after its release from worldly chains. He agreed that in the end there is nothing but the Ultimate Principle but emphasized that during the period of manifestation the world and the souls are separate in order to serve the Ultimate Principle. Madhava's system is known as dualism (Dvaita). He denies that the Ultimate Principle is the cause of the world and contends that the soul is a separate principle having an independent existence of its own: but it is associated with the Ultimate Principle

The Vedanta is technically called as Uttarmimansa, i.e., the last investigation, discussion, analysis or consideration of the Vedas, the end of the Vedas. The names *Brahamsutra* and *Brahamumimansa* are also used for the same as the central theme of the Vedas is the Universal spirit called *Bruhama* in sanskrit. Some scholars contend that Badarayan is an alias for Vyasa who is said to have originally arranged the Vedas, the *Mahabharata* the *Puranas* and Vedantasutras.

Ultimate Truth

According to Vedanta there is only one Ultimate Reality. This is accepted by all other schools of philosophy too, such as the Nyaya, Vaisesika. Samkhaya, Yoga, Mimansa. But their interpretations of Reality, though not contradictory, are different. Together they form a graduated interpretation of the ultimate Reality so interrelated that the hypothesis and method of each are dependent upon the other. In no way, they are contradictory or antagonistic to one another for they all lead to the same practical end, knowledge of the Absolute and liberation of the soul. They all grew, out of the upanishadas, the philosophical portion of the vedas. They all accept the eternal cycle of nature which is without beginning and end, and which consists of vast periods of creation, maintenance, and dissolution. They all accept the principle of regeneration of the soul that maintains that life and death are but two phases of a single cycle. All accept *Dharama* as the moral law of the universe. All agree that knowledge is the path to freedom and that yoga is the method to attain final liberation.

According to Vedanta there is only one Ultimate Reality (Brahaman) which makes its appearance to the sense as an illusion (maya). It shows how the world with its infinite variety is only an appearance and that all things are one and the same only appearing differently. The *Advaita* school of Vedanta contends that all phenomenal existence is an illusion called Maya, and that only the Ultimate Principle (Brahaman) is real. The *Pishistudvuitu* system maintains that there is only one Reality, but that in the objective world it manifests itself as a duality. The Dvaita school treats the evolutionary scheme in the same way as *Samkhya,* saying that the Ultimate Principle is not the cause of the world; soul is the separate principle having an independent existence of its own and is only associated with the Ultimate Principle.

The principal question raised by Vedantasutra is "what is the cause of the Primal Motion in Nature?" The Vedanta, however, advocated that there must be an intelligent agent behind this world which is so wonderfully designed and constructed. It is this agent which guides and directs the working of the subtle forces of the universe. This agent is called by the Vedanta as Brahaman, the Ultimate Principle which is beyond human intellect and reasoning. The inner matter becomes active only when there is the directive action of intelligence in it. To the Vedantists Brahaman causes the initial impulse in nature. He is the cause of the Prime Motion in Nature.

According to the Vedantists Brahaman is the Ultimate Reality, the Ultimate Principle which is defined in the sutras as "Man from whom proceeds the creation, preservation and reconstruction of the universe is Brahaman". It is considered by them the self-existent, the Absolute, the eternal, not only the object of worship but, rather, the object of meditation and knowledge.

The Vedanta also assumes that there is the "universal self or soul", sometimes called "Pannataman" (soul of the universe), the supreme spirit (the general vital principle). This serves as the efficient or instrumental cause of the manifest world. It brings about all the changes by its mere presence as the sun brings forth the spring flower. It is also known as Cit, universal consciousness, as contrasted with the "matter" called Acit (without consciousness). It is permeating all space and manifesting itself in all things. When a part of the soul enters the protoplasmic environment which it animates it is called Jiva, the life. Man is, therefore, only a spark of the infinite. This is the Reality as maintained by Vedanta.

The Vedantists also advocate that the Ultimate Reality is enveloped by delusion called maya. It has two functions, one to conceal reality and the other to project the unreal. It pervades the universe and is inferred only from its effect. It is identified with Prakriti, the universal matter and is said to be the material cause of the universe. This is the universal force operating in the mind of the individual and is, then, called ignorance (Avidya).

Thus, the reality, according to Vedantists is That knowing which we know everything in the universe. The idea of the Advaitists is to generalize the whole universe into one, that something which is really the whole of this universe. They claim that this whole universe is one, that it is. one Being manifesting itself in all these various forms. They admit that what the samkhya calls nature, exists, but say that nature is God. It is this Being, the Sat which has become converted into all this, the universe, the man, the soul and everything that exists. Mind and Mahat (Samkhya's concepts) are but the manifestations of that one Sat. The whole of this universe is the evolution of primal nature, God. God is the material cause of this universe. It is only name (Nam and Rupa) and for that one thing is differentiated from another. The Advaitists hold that in the lowest worm as well as in the highest human being the same divine nature is present. When a person has realized his own nature, the whole world has vanished for him.

All the Vedantists agree on three points. They believe in God, in the Vedas as revealed and in Cycles. The principle of cycle implies that all matter throughout the universe is the outcome of one primal matter called Akasha: and all force, whether gravitation, attraction or repulsion or life, is the outcome of one primal force called Prana. Prana acting on Akasha is creating or projecting the universe. Both the Akasha and Pran are resolved into a third thing called Mahat, the cosmic mind, which does not cause Akasha and Pran, but changes itself into them.

Significance of Awareness

Knowledge means knowing something or understanding something. To know means to understand what is what. This has been an innate desire of the human being, a metaphysical hunger to know and understand what lies beyond the mysterious and illusive veil of Nature. The beginning of India's historical past was marked by this vigorous quest for knowledge through which the great rishis (saints) tried to bridge the gap between the seen and the unknown. They also tried to explain the cause of inescapable experiences of sorrow and suffering that engulf mankind. What these great teachers of the ancient India experienced, speculated and said about various aspects of the existence of the universe and human life forms the content of ancient knowledge. It covers answers to such questions as: What is the nature of Reality? What is the nature of human experience? What is the cause of pleasure and pain? How can liberation be attained? These questions have been answered in different ways by different people and their views constitute their theories. In the. west man's perceptual knowledge forms the basis of their theorization. The West has, always believed that man can not know metaphysical truths by direct experience, while the orientalists hold that the world of mind and matter is but an appearance of a deeper Reality and that man can know metaphysical truths by direct experience. He need not depend upon speculation, inference or faith. Acquisition of knowledge is, to the ancient Indian sages, an unavoidable means, or method of getting rid of sorrow and sufferings. Knowledge helps man to be free from the bondage of ignorance which is the cause of all sufferings.

In Mundaka Upnishad it is proclaimed that there are two types of knowledge, one the supreme (Para) and the other the ordinary or relative (Apara). All the knowledge of the time, science, literature, and arts including the knowledge contained in the sacred Vedas was relegated by the Upnishada to the category of ordinary or 'Apara' knowledge. That alone is of Para" (supreme) knowledge which helps to destroy spiritual blindness and reveals the ever-present spiritual reality behind man and nature. Supreme knowledge is seeking the meaning behind all words, thoughts, all appearance. i.e., the supreme truth of Being. Supreme knowledge is the basis of all forms of knowledge, the knowledge of That by which all else is known and as such is synthetic and comprehensive. In other words, it is Wisdom that goes beyond knowledge and awareness, that by knowing which all else becomes known. It is obtained through the practice of self-control and self-transcendence (indriya-samyama and Yoga). It is anchored in the inner-self, the fountain of all strength, resource, and joy. This is the great idea that the Bhagavad Gita expounds with force and lucidity. This is the concept of knowledge which is advocated by Vedantists also. They also emphasize that spiritual awareness alone can transform all knowledge into Wisdom and into peace, happiness love and sacrifice.

According to Vedanta Philosophy supreme knowledge is beyond the perception of our sense; it is attainable only through direct experience. For that we need not depend upon speculation, inference or faith. Knowledge as advocated by Vedanta philosophy, means knowledge of the true nature of things. It is this knowledge which aims 'to free man from the bondage of ignorance which is the cause of human suffering. It is not discovery. It is understanding the Truth. Understanding involves process of analysis aimed at arriving at the rational and logical conviction and ultimately' realizing and becoming one with the Ultimate Reality" which is accomplished by practising Yoga. Knowledge to the Vedantists means knowledge of the Absolute and Liberation of the soul. Knowledge is path to freedom and yoga is the method to attain final liberation.

The theme of the Upanishadas is to find an "ultimate unity" of things. Knowledge is nothing but finding unity in the midst of diversity. The Upanishadas have this one theme before them. "What is that knowing which we know everything else?" All human knowledge, according to Vedanta philosophy, is based upon the finding of unity in the midst of diversity. Knowledge of the Supreme Ultimate brings enlightenment during this lifetime. The Vedanta endeavours to sum up all human knowledge presenting as Truth all that is universal and reconciling all that is different. Thus, the purpose of all knowing is to realise the Ultimate Principle (Brahaman).

The Vedanta emphasizes direct intuition or experience as the method of knowing or realising the Ultimate Principle. Badarayan maintained that the human intellect can never fathom the nature of the Ultimate Principle (Brahaman). Reasoning can be used only for secular matters, never for transcendental matter such as the existence of God, the existence of an afterlife, the nature of final emancipation, salvation or release. Here the human intellect is helpless. Such truths or realities can be accepted only on faith from those who have gained spiritual insight into the eternal scheme of things, and have recorded their experiences in the ancient body or literature called "Shruti" that is revealed. For that reason only the Vedanta contains Specific knowledge of the ultimate principle. Towards this ultimate goal one is required to pass through the four fold discipline which consists of (i) Viveka (ii) Vairagya, (iii) Satsampat (high-conduct including Sama. Dama, Uparati, Titiksha. Sraddha and Samdhana). Sama means tranquility or control of thought by withdrawing the mind from worldly affairs. Dama means self-restraint or control of conduct restraining the senses from external actions. Uparati means tolerance and renunciation of all sectarian religious observances and acquiring wisdom. Titiksha means endurance bearing heat and cold. Sraddha means faith. Samdhana means balanced mental-equipoise, freedom from much sleep, laziness and carelessness. (iv) The last step is Mumkshutva which means right desire consisting of earnestness to know the ultimate principle and thereby to attain liberation.

Significance of Morality

What the man should value in life is the question which can be answered by drawing inferences from what Vedanta stands for. The most fundamental teaching of Vedanta philosophy is that "man is to become divine by realising the divine": The essence of Vedanta philosophy, therefore, is centered in realisation. This is the most cherished value according to the Vedanta. The man must constantly make efforts on realising his divine nature, grasping and realising the infinite and rising higher and higher on spiritual plane. As said by Swami Vivekananda, "He must not stop anywhere. External worship, material worship is the lowest stage, struggling to rise high, mental prayer is the next stage, but the highest stage is when the Lord has been realized" (collected works, 1989, p. 12). A spiritual orientation of India's people is of supreme value. Practice of spiritualism, living spiritual life and striving for spiritual excellence are the values which Vedanta philosophy seems to emphasize.

Emphasis on spiritual values as its essential corollaries gives rise to the values of self-discipline and self-realization. The Vedanta considers all ethical and aesthetic values as by-products of man's spiritual growth (Swami Ranganathanada, 1986). Control of thought (Sama), self-restraint or control of conduct (Dama), tolerance and renunciation of all sectarian religious observances, endurance; faith and balanced mental equipoise all leading to right conduct are the eternal and universal values underlying all human endeavour according to the Vedanta. As conceived by Vivekananda these values alone can ensure stability and can supply the driving power for progress towards spirituality which is a dynamic force expressing itself as an unfailing basis of continuous advancement towards the only human goal, realization of God.

Attainment of human excellence which, consists in the manifestation of the Divine within man is the essential value of life to be lived by all men. Spirituality is the bedrock on which human excellence and ethical character can be raised. Religion is the discipline that makes it possible. Thus, religion (its study and practice) emerges to be a value from Vedantic philosophy.

Attainment of freedom, freedom from tensions, conflicts, bondage is another value which is considered important and is possible only through vedantic way of life. It can be attained only in the inner life, of man through utter purity of heart.

To conclude, spirituality is the goal of human life: and is also the eternal truth of vedantist philosophy.

QUESTIONS

1. How many schools are there ?
2. Who founded Nyaya ?
3. What is ultimate reality ?

18

Values of Islam

Islam had its origin in the teachings of prophet Mohammad (Pbuh) who was born in Arabia in 570 A.D. At that time polytheism was in vogue in Arabia and many kinds of rituals and idolatry were found to be in practice. As against this Mohammad preached a religion which was strictly monotheism. It was a religion which emphasized rigorous discipline devoid of any ritual or idolatry. Islam takes Mohammad as the messenger (Rasul) of God (Allah), though it does not discard other prophets such as Abraham, Moses and Jesus. But, of all these Mohammad is regarded to be the last and the most powerful. Teachings of Mohammad are regarded most trustworthy and are followed by all Muslims.

Mohammad had a divine nature from the beginning of his life. He was highly introvert and preferred solitude. Often he would retire to the forest caves for prayer and meditation. When he was forty he heard in his revelation a messenger of God, Gabriel telling him that he was the Apostle of God. Mohammad, then, began to propagate his message, But, in the beginning there were very few of his followers. The first person to believe in his teachings was his wife Khadijah herself. Afterwards as a result of political patronage and military conquests Mohammad's religion based on his teachings and called Islam spread very swiftly. Mohammad died in 632 A.D.

Islam is based on Quran which, it is said, contains God's message which came through revelations of Mohammad, Gabriel being the agent revealing to Mohammad. Quran means recite. Mohammad recited and the followers wrote it, Quran is regarded as eternal, uncreated and Allah's words. It is divided in 114 Chapters which are called Surahs. It contains all the basic teachings and principles of Islam in verses. It is supplemented by a less important text, the Hadith which is said to consist of the sayings (Ahadis) and practices (Sunnas) of prophet Mohammed and his companions.

Ultimate Truth

In Islam "Allah" (God) is the ultimate reality. The world around man is also Real, but it is the creation of God. All of the things around man are real; but all of them have been created by Allah. The Quran repeatedly reminds man that everything on this earth is the creation of God. There is nothing around man which is not created by God. Islam, however, is silent, on the point as to how this world has been created by God. It only says that Allah has created the heaven, the hell, the earth and all that is there on this earth; Allah is the lord of all of these sustaining and maintaining everything everywhere. Islam does not explain, as was done by samkhya, how this world was created. Yet, the world, according to Islam is real, not illusory. It can be destroyed by Allah any time when He wants. Everything on this earth has its life and continuity dependent on Allah's desire and sweet will. Allah is present everywhere and in everything.

God (Allah) is the ultimate reality on this earth according to Islam. Islam believes in only one God. He is supreme and the creator of everything on this earth including the man. In a number of Surahs one after the other in the Quran, it is repeated that there is no God except the one called 'Allah'. And this is what, every Muslim has to repeat before every prayer *"La Ilah a Ila' llahu Mohammad Rasulu'llah* (There is no god but Allah, and Mohammad is His Prophet). Also every morning and evening at the time of Namaz (Prayer) the Imam or the Mullah reminds every Muslim by speaking loudly *"Allahu Akbar, La Ilaha Ills.' llahu, Mohammad rasulu' llah* (God is great: there is no God but Allah, Mohammad is the prophet of God). Thus, Islam is a Faith that believes in God as One who is all powerful and the creater of every thing, He is divine and his Divine will is supreme, absolute and perfectly arbitrary. But, Allah is separated from his creations, maintaining a distance from man and everything else. God is described in Quran as All knowing, All-hearing. All-subtle, All-glorious, All-aware, All-powerful, Omnipresent and unique. He is also regarded as having such qualities as having will and power, but no form and shape, being compassionate, merciful, just and kind. He reveals himself, sometimes, to men through his messengers, speaks to them through his messiahs. God is also, according to Islam, the final judge of all the good and bad actions of human beings.

According to Islam, man is the real unit of existence. Though created by God, he is regarded to exist as a separate reality under the authority of the Almighty God. Islam as a word means "submission", hence the man in Islam has a duty to serve God in humble submission. He has no power, no right, no will of his own against God. Islamic prayers are said to be reverential only during which the man has not to ask for anything except God's grace and guidance. It seems there is nothing like human free will in Islam. This point is controversial, however.

The concept of Reality about life after death is quite unique in Islam. It is believed that after death the physical body of the man is consumed by the earth in the grave but the soul rests for a period of time in a place called Al-Berzahk till the day of judgement which is not known to anyone except God. On this Day of Judgement all the dead rise from the graves. Their souls reunite with their bodies and are brought before the Allah by his angels. Their deeds are, then, scrutinized. Those whose good deeds are more than evil deeds are rewarded by God by placing them in the heaven, while the others are sent to hell. Heaven is said to be a place where there are beautiful gardens, running waters, orchards with ripe fruits and green meadows, etc. Besides, there is said to be plenty of wine and beautiful girls. There are seven heavens described in the Koran representing seven stages of celestial bliss. Similarly, there are described seven hells also. These are places where scorching tires are burning everywhere; burning winds, thorns, smokes, scorpions everywhere. These are places of extreme torments.

The Reality pertaining to human destiny is related to the concept of life after death. It is said in Koran that the ultimate destiny of man lies in assuming the eternal membership either of heaven or of hell depending on his good or bad deeds. In the heaven the man lives in the company of God and his angels in eternal pleasure in pure spiritual form without any physical body. He is free from all bodily limitations, though not freed from his finiteness. But, he never is equal to God or attains a status equal to God. Islam, definitely, believes in a life after death comprising of the resurrection of the dead on the day of Judgement.

Perception of Awareness

What is knowledge & how knowledge is obtained ? What is true knowledge? etc, are nowhere expressly discussed in Islam. This may however, be inferred from the various aspects of Islam discussed in various texts.

The true knowledge, according to Islam is the knowledge about Allah, the creator of this world, knowledge about the man and his relation to God, knowledge about man's duties towards God, knowledge about man's destiny and life after death. All these aspects of knowledge have been discussed in the foregoing sections.

The source of this knowledge is just one book, the Quran which is said to be the word of God revealed to Mohammad through Gabriel, the angel. For this reason Islam is said to be the religion of the Book, Quran is said to be the eternal and uncreated eternal word of Allah. Islam is a legalistic religion laying down rules to be followed by those who have faith. It teaches people specific ways of sincere devotion and prayer to God, ways and importance of self-purification and liberality, religion and ethics etc. Knowledge of all these is considered important. This is what Islam means by true knowledge,' which is believed to be contained in the Quran.

Value Perception

Dr. Mohammad Iqbal as quoted by Saiyidain (1966, p. 65) once said that the teaching of the Quran which believes in the possibility of improvement in the behaviour of man and his control over natural forces is neither optimism nor pessimism. It is 'meliorism' which recognizes a growing universe and is animated by the hope of man's eventual victory over evil which is a value very much emphasized by Islam.

A distinctive feature of Islam is its great emphasis on rigorous discipline of daily life that it prescribes for its followers. Following these disciplinary rules strictly constitutes life's values for every Muslim. Islam is a legalistic religion in the sense that it prescribes rules of conduct for Muslims, almost for every sphere of life, And all these may be taken as values of life in Islam. Much of Islamic discipline consists of techniques related to sincere devotion and prayer to God. Self-purification and liberality are. therefore. considered the highest values of life. The following five values constitute "Five Pillars" of Islam:

Daily Prayer: Namaz is highly valued in Islam. It is emphasized that five times a day (at day break. at noon, at mid afternoon, at sunset and at early night) prayer should be observed by everyone having faith in Islam. And this observance has to follow "set procedure, for example. the face of the person praying should be towards Mecca, it should begin every time with the proclamation "Allahu Akbar" meaning thereby, that God is great, a set devotional posture has to be followed. The complete set of prayer consists of eight separate acts of devotion. Each Prayer is ended with the utterance of *La llaha ila' Ilahu, Mohammad Rasulullah*. It is considered more pious and important to pray in a mosque, though a Muslim is advised to do so wherever he happens to be at the time of Namaz. Daily prayers are considered of a great value as they are regarded as paths that lead to heaven.

Absolute Oneness: With Allah is the basic value of Islam. So before every prayer, the Muslim is bound to recite *"La Ilaha Ila' Ilahu, Mohammad Rasulullah"*, i.e., there is no god except Allah, and Mohammad is his prophet. It is emphasized that this should be recited with the wholehearted conviction that God is supreme, the creator of everything on this earth. Feeling within self oneness with Allah is more important than just reciting the words.

Alms-giving: It is another important value of Islam. All Muslims must give alms to the poor and the needy. It is considered a duty of all who have faith in Islam. And certain specific rules have been laid down in this regard. For example, sometimes one-tenth and sometime or e-twentieth of one's land income must be gifted as Zakat for supporting and helping the poor. Those who have a better financial status, are advised to give even more.

Fasting (Roza): It is another value which is much emphasized. During the month of Ramazan all Muslims are advised to observe fast. In the day they are not to eat or drink anything, It is only at night they eat. Besides, they have to observe a few more rules of conduct and avoid impurities during this whole month of Ramzan; for example, drinking wine, having sex, killing any human being, stealing, lying, etc. This value is so important that, as is believed, its observance can remit all kinds of sins committed by the person during that whole year.

Pilgrimage: Haji is an Islamic value which every Muslim considers as a religious duty to Undertake at least once in his life. It is a journey to Mecca taken during the sacred month of Dhul-Hijja. A large number of Muslims gather at Mecca coming from all parts of the world during this month. The congregation of Muslims has a great social value also. It caters to the unity of the Muslims of the world. Several kinds of rituals are performed by the pilgrims at Mecca. Dressing themselves in a prescribed manner they go seven times around the *Kabba,* kissing the black stone each time, casting stones at three pillars at Mina; they sacrifice a sheep, goat or camel, meat being given to the poor. They are there for ten days in their sacred robes (Ihram) which are put off only after ten days when they wear their normal dress. It is believed that pilgrimage to Mecca secures a place for them in the heaven.

Holy War (Jihad): It is also considered a value in Islam, though modern Islam does not seem to subscribe to this view. However, Quran says "Fight those who believe not in God, and who forbid not what god and his apostle have forbidden, and who do not practise the religion of truth." Quran also says that who die in this holy war are assigned places in the paradise.

Besides these major values, certain social and ethical values are also advocated by Islam. For example, hospitality, brotherhood of man and service to humanity, obedience to parents, avoidance of adultery, cheating and lying, avoiding stealing, murder, etc., are very much emphasized as values to be lived.

The virtues of renunciation and non-attachment to worldly objects are also recommended to be cultivated by all Muslims. There are rules prescribed by Islam to regulate marriage, divorce, dowry, inheritance, funeral ceremonies, etc. In fact, Islam is a legalistic religion and prescribes rules for almost all occasions.

QUESTIONS

1. What is reality, as per Islamic ideology ?

2. What is the concept of value ?

3. What is the concept of knowledge ?

19

Culture as Wealth

Culture is the level of sophistication achieved by a community in various fields of human activity, including politics, economics, religion, arts, sciences, lilterature, etc. There is a fine distinction between civilisation and culture. All that we possess in concrete shape is our civilisation but the abstract permeating the concrete is our culture. The houses that we have, the dress that we wear are parts of our civilisation; but the design and the abstract planning behind them signify our culture. Similarly, the values that we observe in our speech and conduct are the constituents of our culture. All our cultural-possession is either a result of our own efforts or it has been passed on to us by our ancestors. As culture is the sum total of the rich experience stretched over centuries of our human existence, there is no reason for us to remain indifferent to it. The Constitution of India, in Article 29 (1), gives every section of the citizens the light to conserve its own culture. Article 51 A assigns to every citizen, as one of the Fundamental Duties, 'to value and preserve the rich heritage of our composite culture'. The Union Ministry of Human Resource Development has a full-fledged department as well as a Cultural Heritage Division for the promotion of arts and culture.

S.No.	Category of Respondents	No. Agreeing	No. Undecided	No. Disagreeing
(1)	Total population (881)	833 (94.6)	24 (2.7)	24 (2.7)
(2)	Age-group 18-25 years (52)	49 (94.3)	1 (1.9)	2 (3.8)
(3)	Above 40 years (573)	54 (94.4)	17 (3)	15 (2.6)
(4)	High School & equivalent (123)	435 (96)	12 (1.6)	16 (2.4)
(5)	M.A or above & equivalent (463)	435 (94)	12 (2.6)	16 (3.4)
(6)	With income from Rs. 1000-1999 p.m. (98)	92 (93.9)	5 (5.0)	1 (1.0)
(7)	With income of Rs. 4000 p.m. and above (406)	380 (93.6)	14 (3.4)	12 (3)

S.No.	*Category of Respondents*	*No. Agreeing*	*No. Undecided*	*No. Disagreeing*
1.	Total population	256	6	5
	(267)	(96)	(2.2)	(1.8)
2.	School students (M)	64	3	3
	(70)	(91.4)	(4.3)	(4.3)
3.	School students (F)	84	0	2
	(86)	(97.7)	(0)	(2.3)
4.	College students (M)	33	1	0
5.	College students (F)	69	1	0
	(70)	(98.6)	(1.4)	(0)
6.	African students in Indian colleges (M)	6	1	0
	(7)	(85.7)	(14.3)	(0)

Significance of Culture

A statement was included in the questionnaire for the general category of respondents to know the public opinion in regard to one of the aspects of the Indian culture. The statement was as follows:

"Indians need to be made better aware of their cultural heritage." (G-6)

More than 90 per cent of respondents in each category have expressed agreement with the statement.

It would be interesting to also study the responses of the student-community giving identical statement which is reproduced below:

"Students should be made aware of Indian culture through history, literature and other books".

Importance of Books

The pattern of students' reaction to this statement is, more or less, similar to the one indicated by the general population to statement G6, which has been analysed earlier. There are, however, differences in the responses of school-students when compared to those of college-students. Fewer male school students agree with the statement.

The Education Commission (1964-66) had urged Indian Universities to ensure "that every student who passes out of an Indian university takes with him some understanding of India's cultural heritage, its past achievements and triumphs in the field of art, philosophy, science and so on. He should, in other words, know what he is heir to. This could perhaps, best be done at the first degree stage where such a study could form a part of a programme of liberal education. It is noteworthy, in this connection, that all university students in America have to take a course in Western civilisation".

The Programme of Action published by the Government of India for implementing the National Policy on Education 1986, elaborates this point at some length in the chapter on 'The Cultural Perspective'. It speaks of several strategies intended for creating better awareness among students of the country's cultural heritage. A few strategies are summed up below:

(a) A suitable hand book should be prepared for the guidance of teachers of each stage of education. Reorientation programmes should be organised for them and audio-visual and other material such as musical instruments, pictures, posters etc., should be prepared for students. A separate room in the school, could be earmarked for cultural exhibits, wherever it is possible;

(b) One teacher for culture should be provided in each institution.

(c) Distortions in curriculum, particularly in social studies and history should be corrected. Value-orientation should be given to lessons by drawing material from Indian heritage and great classics.

(d) Exhibitions of the work of local artists should be organised.

(e) Students should be encouraged to undertake the conservation of local historical monuments.

(f) Inter-school cultural meets should be arranged so as to bring out India's rich cultural diversity.

The programme of action makes the following suggestions in this regard for university stage:

(a) Broad-basing and diversifying cultural courses as of fine arts, music, dance, etc.

(b) correction of existing historical and cultural distortion in the courses of study such as of social sciences, humanities and languages etc. In this regard a *tour d' force* would have to be attempted but this is necessary in order to rectify the faulty perspectives;

(c) developing special courses in technical and professional institutions for conservation of monuments which are of immense importance as country's valuable ancient heritage;

(d) forming clubs and societies devoted to the promotion of various cultural aspects;

(e) earmarking incentives, fellowships, scholarships, etc., for creative work and research in the field of culture.

New Dimensions

The dissemination of India's cultural heritage should aim at acquainting students with:

(i) Customs, traditions and festivals, etc., of various ethnic, religious and linguistic groups inhabiting the country.

(ii) Works of ancient rishis, sufis, saints, insight into all-time epics, and other great classics.

(iii) Contributions of great men in various fields of the country's national life.

(iv) Cultural wealth contained in our works of religion.

(v) Intelligent interpretation of myths and poetic fantasies.

Religion is an important part of the cultural heritage, and more so in the case of India where fine and performing arts and literature have a strong spiritual/religious basis. However, while debating cultural themes related to religion, theocratic education should be excluded.

Myths form an important part of India's, or for that matter, any culture. Some of the writings described as myths have proved to be meaningful today, whereas others are meant to convey some message to mankind. Pushpak Viman was a myth a century ago; but today one can perceive it as it'might have been a reality' also. In the great work of the Sufi poet Malik Mohammed Jayasi, the heroine Padmavat is found talking to a parrot and the bird is talking to her. This might have been a total myth; but it points towards the level of sensitivity of the people towards birds in those times. In Kalidasa's famous work *Meghdoot*, the clouds are taking the message of a lover to his beloved. It is unbelievable and cannot be taken as truth; but it shows how a poet could conceive nature as part of man and man as part of nature.

The stories in the Puranas may have more or less as much element of imagination as of truth; but such writings have a great cultural significance.

They have been called by Socrates as noble lies and have their place in the cultural heritage of man and deserve attention by framers of the educational curricula.

In this context, we may keep in mind a couple of other things also in mind. Firstly, the study of Buddhism in India can be very must a part of the cultural heritage of India; but study of the Chinese or the Japanese version of Buddhism does not constitute a part and parcel of the Indian cultural heritage, though the merit of these studies otherwise cannot be denied. Secondly, there might be certain aspects of the cultural heritage which must have had their value and importance in the past, but stand invalidated today. For example, the practice of 'devadasis' in some Indian temples had the merit of promoting vestal virgins and dance as a part of worship; but it has degenerated and has become an anachronism today. Similarly, caste which was evolved as a measure to promote professional excellence stands condemned today on account of the infiltration of many evils into it. Any debate on cultural heritage must discuss all such issues objectively and rationally and ought not to unduly support degenerated practices.

The Heritage

One of the important functions of the Indian missions in other countries is to project India's image abroad. It is sad to note that our Embassies, High Commissions and Consulates are totally ill equipped for dissemination of India's rich cultural heritage in the countries to which they are accredited. These Missions neither have suitable personnel nor adequate material which could provide information on India's diverse and rich cultural heritage. India needs to follow the example of other countries in this respect and establish richly equipped and properly-functioning cultural centres in all foreign countries. In the present-day world rendered smaller by communication facilities, there is scope for greater interaction between peoples of the world. Widening of the scope of cultural interaction through our embassies is bound to enhance India's prestige.

The popularity and esteem of India's culture in other lands is likely to influence, to a certain degree, the attitude of her own people to their own cultural heritage. Thus the investment in projecting India's culture abroad would serve several purposes, some of which are—

(a) a boost in India's prestige, as her cultural achievements excel most, rather all countries of the world;

(b) infusion of a sense of self-esteem among the people of India and thus also lead to greater enthusiasm among the Indians for imbibing their own cultural values;

(c) dissemination of India's cultural message for the benefit of mankind as was done by her predecessors in South East Asia, China, Japan, Mexico and elsewhere.

Culture is the totalilty of thoughts, symbols, beliefs, sentiments, etc., which a group has developed and refined over a period of time and with which it has enriched its material life. Indian culture, broadly speaking, has material, spiritual and intellectual aspects. The historical remains and ancient writings testify to India's material progress since time immemorial. The Vedas, and the Upanishadas which are the oldest philosophical works in possessions of mankind today indicate the occupation of the Indian mind with the intellectual and spiritual aspects of culture. Hegal says, "A civilisation without a philosophy is like a temple without the holy of the holies". The speculative aspect of Indian culture first dived into the mystries of nature, as in the Vedas, and thereafter it tried to unravel the mystry of man, universe, matter and energy through the Vedanta. In this connection, Max Muller writes in his work Six Systems of Indian Philosophy (p.182):

"It is surely astounding that such a system as the Vendanta should have been slowly elaborated by the indefatigable and intrepid thinkers of India thousands of years ago, a system that even now makes us feel giddy, as in mounting the last steps of the swaying spire of an ancient Gothic Cathedral. None of our philosophers, not excepting Heraclitus, Plato, Kant, or Hegel has ventured to erect such a spire, never frightened by storms or lightnings. Stone follows on stone after regular succession after once the first step has been made, after once it has been clearly seen that in the beginning there can have been but one, as there will be but one in the end, whether we call it Atman or Brahman,"

On the glory of the Upanishadas, Schopenhauer says, "In the whole world, there is no study so beneficial and so elevating as that of the Upanishadas. They are destined sooner or later to become the faith of the people."

According to Deussen, "The Upanishadas formulate philosophical conceptions unequalled in India or perhaps anywhere else in the world."

Thus, the Indian culture is very rich. It is, therefore, surprising that Indians themselves should not be able to fully appreciate the worth of their own achievements. This can be, to an extent, attributed to centuries of foreign rule which tried to demolish the vestiges of India's culture. The absence of a culture base in education, which unfortunately continues even now, could be the other reason. Afterall, Macaulay, on whose Minute, the foundation of India's modern system of education was laid, believed that a few shelves of English literature were sufficient to contain the totality of India's literature. Whereas a section of the population under the influence of foreign education moved away from its rich cultural values, the village folks and the women, who were somehow left out from the western and other foreign influences, adhered to the old cultural values and preserved them. Unfortunately, these people having been relegated to a subservient position, were preoccupied with the struggle for existence and did not have much power to contribute to cultural regeneration of the country. Through folklore and religious practices, however, they contributed to the preservation of culture and the values which are so characterstic of the Indian psyche.

Today, India's cultural heritage is mostly treasured in our ancient books, subsequent commentaries of scholars on this literature and with the village and the women folk. The government, has, in recent times, initiated steps to preserve the contributions that were made in the past. These include preservation of monuments, support of performing and plastic arts etc. A number of organisations are also now engaged in the work of dissemination of India's past cultural heritage as well as of its present achievement. It is for the educational institutions to carry forward this work with speed and in a big way.

20

Evolution of Physical Power

As far as physical growth is concerned, it goes on from birth onwards in tissues, muscles, bones, height, weight, strength, sense organs, brain or inner organs and, in fact, in every physical aspect, function or formation. A child grows in every system of his body simultaneously, although this growth in every system cannot be described simultaneously.

The bones of the body grow in length, width and thickness as children mature. Long bones become, generally, longer in adolescence and there is final articulation of all the bones at their respective joints. Teeth grow and face changes; strength and agility increase. Each child's growth in weight, height and motor skills, as in other spheres, is unique with his own rate of growth and cannot be judged on standards based on group averages, although if a child does not increase his stature, his internal organs do not increase in size or his body is not enlarged with greater weight and height, there is something wrong with him and he will not be a fully grown individual in his own way to take his place in adult society.

Physical growth is affected by various factors such as inheritance lying in the genetic constitution, nutrition, living conditions and medical facilities and timely help. It is, for example, made out (Cole and Hall, 1970) that due to better food, better living conditions and better medical care, boys and girls are found to be taller, heavier and healthier than their counterparts during the last half century in the world as a whole. As described by Meredith (1949) man's height and weight are said to have increased from earlier decades to more recent years, as from 1927 to 1937 and 1947 mean weight varied from about 51 to 53 and 55 lbs in order and height increased from 47 inches to 48 and 49 inches in the case of 7 year olds. Gordon (1965) showed that any prolonged deprivation has its retarding effect on the rate of growth and on the development of personality traits. The retarded are noted to suffer from inferiority leading to over-compensatory behaviour and even rebellion or domineering way of dealing with others.

Basis of Geography

There is no doubt, that a person may be tall or short, thin or stout, healthy or unhealthy, handsome or ugly with respect to the quality of the genes. But physical development is affected by many environmental conditions such as supply of food, accident or disease. Even geographical conditions (as the type of environment) influence physical appearance and health. A man's skin becomes darker in strong sunlight of tropical countries. The somatic character of an individual is determined, to a certain extent, by the region in which he lives. Since the materials which his body uses are supplied from the soil where, if there is a deficiency or excess of any minerals or chemicals, important physical and physiological changes may result. The absence of calcium, for example (needed by bones and the blood), produces weak legs and rickets. The absence of iron and copper salts causes anaemia. The absence of iodine deteriorates the thyroid glands, leading to enlarged necks with goitre (McCollum, et.al., 1939).

Although natural and other differing environments produce differences in bodily and physical characteristics, the body of man is not like mere clay in the hands of surrounding conditions. The reasons for the limits to the modification of man's constitution lie in his congenital structure. "Long-headed and round-headed men and women live in the same location in Central Italy. Geographical influences do not make their head forms the same. The hereditary endowment on the physical and physiological side determines the body structure and the whole organic functioning. The nervous system and the organs and glands of internal secretion are the most important inherited mechanisms in the physiological make-up.

Basis of Biology

The nervous system is a mechanism capable of receiving and responding to stimuli, both from within and from without. The stimulations are transmitted by the nerves to centres in the spinal cord or the brain, where the impulses are transferred to nerves of control going to the muscles or glands. Thus, responses such as withdrawing the foot from the source of pain, the placing of food in the mouth or increasing the heart beat, are achieved. The glands of internal secretion called the endocrine glands pour their secretions (hormones) directly into the blood stream. These hormones go a long way in determining physical appearances, physiological conditions, temperament and mentality in general. Their hyper or hypo activities determined both by heredity and by environmental conditions, produce these differences. Thyroxin—the hormone from the thyroid gland located near the larynx, for example, helps in regulating oxygen consumption and hence in energy output. Persons suffering from hypothyroidism (thyroxin deficiency) show inertia, dullness and sluggishness, and in some extreme cases they become cretins—dwarfed in mental and physical growth. Hyperthyroidism (excess of thyroxin), on the other hand, leads to nervous tension, excitement and anxiety. Adrenalin, the hormone of the adrenals located near the kidneys releases the blood sugar from the liver and excessive adrenalin secretion leads to high blood pressure, perspiration and nausea accompanied by anxiety and nervousness. The pituitary gland located near the centre of the head at the base of the brain secretes growth-stimulating hormone which, if in excess, produces large limbs leading to gigantism. Pituitary giants are known to be absent-minded, unable to concentrate and very irritable. Stagner (1948) has shown that a deficiency of the pituitary hormone may check physical growth leading to dwarfism which is generally characterized by an excess of aggressiveness. The gonads secrete the important sex hormones. Biologically all human beings are bisexual, and some male hormones are produced by adult ovaries and some female hormones by adult testes. Some personality traits are related to the balance existing between these male and female hormones in the blood stream. Castration, as commonly observed in the case of animals, makes the male more docile, less aggressive with reduced emotional responsiveness. Hyperactivity of the male sex glands leads to an increase in sex drive with a more dominating attitude. The gonadal hormones affect immensely psychological characteristics and normal personality traits. The interests and attitudes of maturing boys, for example, are, to a certain extent, found to depend on the amount of sex hormones secreted by them, though many males with undeveloped testes develop mature interests and are brilliant in their fields.

There is no doubt that nervousness, irritability and over or under-activity may result from a variety of glandular states; and abnormal conditions of certain endocrine glands can produce distortions in personality. Some endocrinological disorders may lead to changes in general efficiency of bodily functions which in turn may give rise to feelings of insecurity or frustration as the internal balance is disturbed. But as held by Berman (1928) it would be an error to hold, as endocrine enthusiasts do, that the hormones determine the whole personality including one's opinions, habits and skills. It has still to be shown that the glands have anything to do with an individual's being altruistic or selfish, hospitable or niggardly, dutiful or treacherous. Only the future, if at all, could show that the glands are related to sympathy, suggestibility, memory and to other traits of personality. Freeman, studying the endocrine constitution of 1400 abnormal personalities of psychotics and epileptic cases, came to the conclusion that though many of the glands in these cases were abnormal, yet in no case could any consistent parallel between mental pattern and glandular make-up be established.

There is no doubt that hereditary endowment and physical environmental conditions influence the secretion of the endocrine glands. The effect of social environment and the psychological experiences of people may also be potent factors in the functioning of the endocrine glands. Conditions of town life, for example, are shown to produce excessive stimulation of the adrenals leading to increased strain and worry which are experimentally shown to decrease if the nerve connections to the adrenals are severed (Crile, 1934).

Some children are known to be nervous and irritable and others are quiet and calm. These temperamental differences cannot only be attributed to inheritance. The circumstances attending the experience of birth which may be easy or trying for the infant, some pre-natal conditions affecting the nervous system of the child and later other environmental factors in the family or other group relations may have been determining factors; and there is no assurance that the behaviour noted is not due to culture. But, in any case the temperamental differences are largely produced by changes in the functions of the ductless glands. If, for example one of the adrenals in a dog is removed, the reduced supply of adrenalin (the emergency hormone which prepares the animal to fight by releasing sugar from the liver) will make the dog docile and his fighting capacity would be reduced by one half. The removal of the gonads in a youth produces characteristics of a eunuch. If the parathyroid glands (attached to each thyroid), which regulate the consumption of calcium are defective, the individual becomes emotionally unstable and easily irritable.

From this discussion of the biological foundations determining the physical and temperamental qualities, attention for a moment may be concentrated on the process of physical development itself, as it appears in different individuals or groups of individuals. It has been a popular belief that growth in children as a group follows a set pattern from infancy to adolescence. The importance of the growth process has not been quite realised. At present scientific investigations have emphasized a wide range of variations at each age for each bodily dimensions such as height, weight, masculinity, etc., and each individual requires the personal history of several such measures for a full description of his bodily build.

Physical Alterations

There comes a period when physical growth is most rapid. In many physical dimensions this period coincides with the advent of the menarche in girls and of pubescence in boys (perhaps more due to endocrine secretions) when rate of growth is accelerated with the appearance of 'spurts' in the curves of growth.

During this period of pre-adolescence followed by puberty or adolescence quick and farreaching changes take place in the development of secondary sex characters in boys and girls. Hairs grow under arms and around the genitals. Boys grow beard and moustache and more hair on the body than girls. Second molars erupt in both, larynx grows more in boys and their voice becomes hoarse when the voice of girls is low. There is widening of shoulders in boys and hips in girls and their breasts develop quickly, though boys also have slight development on the chest round the nipples.

The sex organs in boys increase rapidly, they begin to have nocturnal emissions and girls begin menstruating. They both tickle: their genitals or masturbate, boys more actively and even may have ejection. This is a normal and passing phase and there is no physical damage done to the genitals. The only damage, if at all, is emotional, because masturbation being a selfish act, one may feel guilty or ashamed and some may have been frightened being insane or impotent when they grow-up.

Their attitudes towards each other and towards themselves change due to their bodily changes. The interests and behaviour of both boys and girls change after puberty and their adjustment is also influenced in school and society.

In the Harvard Growth Study (Dearborn and Rothney, 1941) it was found that the age at which maximum growth occurs on the average was 12.5 years in girls and 14.8 years in boys. But the early increase in physical growth of girls does not mean that all girls are taller and heavier than boys. Standard deviations of each sex show that the most advanced and the most retarded of each group differ much more than the averages in the two sexes. (Fleming, 1948).

Individual differences within each sex are greater than inter-sex differences for human behaviour. Whatever significant mean differences between male and female there are, these reside in the sex chromosomes. Sex differences in, for example, play, exploration, assertiveness, docility and intellectual performances, have generic basis on which human cultural practices are built.

Rough-and-tumble play is more observed in males and boys are typically rougher and more assertive than girls and this difference may be hormonal which in turn may be genetic. So also exploratory behaviour is more characteristics of the male. Boys in nursery schools are noted to be more exploring and playing about vigorously while girls better sit and play with toys requiring fine muscle coordination. Girls prefer sedentary activities than active play, and have more docile behaviour.

However, there are always individual exceptions. Repeated measures of a random sampling of some 50 girls in the Harvard Growth Study showed that though every girl made a more intense spurt than the averages within the period of a year or so, this period in individual cases ranged from 9 years to 15 years (Dearborn & Rothney, 1941). Apart from this variation in growth in different individuals, the analytical findings of this growth study cast a doubt on the conception of the 'constancy of physical size' and served as a corrective to such a statement as that of Hollingworth (1930) who said: "On the whole size at any age predicts size at all ages. The short remains short, and the tall remains tall throughout the whole course of growth and at maturity. The idea that there is likely to be some reversal of affairs at puberty whereby a tall child will 'fall off in growth and become short, while the short child is likely to 'spurt' at that time and grow tall, has been shown to be a superstition, founded on nothing more substantial than human longings. Such a reversal almost never happens".

In contrast with this, no two of the 266 cases studied regarding consistency in growth of stature, had identical standard scores at each age from 7 to 17. There were many cases that were parallel in development, but none was exactly the same throughout (Dearborn & Rothney). These 266 cases revealed that individual members particularly on the extremes tended to approach the mean. There appeared a levelling process at work. The taller tended to move down towards the average, and the shorter to move up towards the average, whereas those near the average tended to remain in their original position. (Dearborn & Rothney, 1941). An intensive study of individual cases revealed that no two individuals had the same developmental history as portrayed in their deviation in relation to the mean of the group. Moreover, the individual growth data were so varied over this period of growth that it did not offer much promise of reliable prediction in individual cases (Dearborn & Rothney, 1941). The growth curves in any dimension like height or weight give a generalised picture that tends to conceal differences among groups or individuals.

There was evidence of earlier and late maturing in certain cases. On the basis of variability of growth there was reason to believe that growth was quite frequently characterized by cycles, as it were, and that these cycles, though determined by biological mechanisms, seemed more to be caused by environmental factors (Courtis).

With regard to physical growth, it is out of the scope of this discussion to go into the details of all the changes in the bodies of boys or girls from childhood onward. What is important for this discussion is to recognize over-lapping in actual dimensions from one year to another, and wide differences in individuals at each age. This is probably the most important finding of the more recent years. (Fleming, 1948).

As every individual follows his own pattern of growth, there is the individual growth curve as an indicator of any unexpected change. Such an indication of variation in growth is important for educationists to note. If a pupil, for example, obtains quite a different measure at one time, it points to the desirability of a careful investigation into his physical health, his social environment, emotional upset or glandular changes. In the case of early maturing when children attain adult proportions more quickly, there is a longer period in which social adjustments are made. These children may pass through a period of considerable loneliness, until their contemporaries catch them up. Parents and teachers who can sometimes draw attention to this variability and who are themselves convinced of its unimportance for the future happiness of the children, can remove the apprehensions of the growing pupil who imagines himself to be so different and unattractive in comparison with his fellows. According to the old notions of regularity of growth based on averages obtained from measurements of large number of children at various ages, these variations in individual growth may be labelled as abnormal, but teachers are required to read these pronouncements of abnormality with great caution.

The deviants in growth process are troubled not so much by the disability or variation, as compared to the normal but more by their emotional reactions of resentment, fear or dependency. These variations should not be tormenting to the youngsters and the teacher should also keep an even and accepting emotional atmosphere in the classroom and should help them by even referring to better informed persons such as doctors, psychologists or social workers and should take these variations not abnormalities as such, but as facts of life. (Cruickshank, 1956).

Every individual pupil has a pattern of his growth which cannot be predicted either from the averages of the group or from his own record at one time. No one, however, can exactly claim that a certain percentage of growth is attributable to inheritance and a certain other percentage to environment. Parents and educationists need rather be concerned with the nature and conditions of nurture from year to year. Awareness of the extent of individual differences and of the variability of growth should serve as a stimulus to greater willingness for investigation; and this knowledge would further help in the discovery of methods of treatment suited to the requirements of each growing child.

Summary

1. Most noticeable aspect of the child's total growth is the change that takes place in his physical size including both height and weight.

2. Growth in height and weight both is very rapid in the early life as the child multiplies several thousand times during the first nine month's period.

3. Growth continues at a rapid rate during infancy. After that it is alternatively rapid and slow; and gradually tapers in the middle teens in the case of girls and a few years later in the case of boys. This conclusion is about the average child but the fact is that each child individually has a unique pattern of growth which may differ significantly from the average of the group.

4. Baldwin (1921) and a few others hold a view that growth in height is comparatively uniform for each child. But, there is considerable evidence to show that the growth is not smooth and continuous and that it goes by spurts.

5. Olson and Hughes (1942) give the concept of "organismic age" which is a composite of the child's height, weight, dental, carpal, mental, grip and reading age and which is considered a more stable index of growth.

6. Growth patterns of boys and girls differ in a number of important ways. Boys are taller and heavier and their final status is of greater height and weight.

7. Girls reach their final status (physical and physiological maturity) eighteen months earlier than boys.

8. Girls are on the average both taller and heavier than boys during the period from 11 to 14. They are, generally, taller and heavier than boys throughout their period of growth.

9. Growth is also related to socioeconomic and cultural status. Upper class children tend to be taller than children of middle or lower class.

10. Physical growth is more dependent upon heredity than is any of the other aspects of growth.

11. It is generally agreed that such things as the illness that befall growing children have only a temporary effect upon their growth and do not affect their final status appreciably.

12. Endocrine imbalance (hereditary or environmental) can effect a considerable departure from normality both in the rate of maturing and in the final status.

13. Wide variations exist in the physical size of children of any given age.

14. During the preadolescent period there is rapid growth which tapers off with the advent of puberty.-It may, however, occur upto three years before and (in some ten percent of the cases) upto three years after the attainment of sexual maturity as described by Dearborn and Rothney (1941).

15. Many physical and physiological changes of preadolescent period are connected with the growth spurt of this period. For example, different parts of the body grow rapidly at different times. Boys' feet may grow temporarily out of all proportions resulting in awkwardness which may cause some embarrassment to the adolescent. In the same way glandular changes may result in his face breaking out in a rash of acne.

16. Attainment of sexual maturity and a need for reorganization of the self-concept and social consciousness are the most important characteristics of preadolescent period as these are bound to have psychological repercussions.

17. Keliher (1941) has shown that puberty takes place any time from ages 10 to 17 and from 11 to 18 in the case of girls and boys respectively. The late or early emergence of puberty may create many kinds of developmental problems.

QUESTIONS

1. Discuss geographical foundation of the development.
2. Discuss biological foundation of the development.

21

Evolution of Sentiments

Emotional development is the most pervasive of all aspects of growth and development of children. Emotions set the pattern and the tone of life. They greatly influence the physical, intellectual and social growth and development of children. They are also related to learning and adjustment. They, largely, control human behaviour. If not handled porperly they give rise to many kinds of problems which may upset the whole balance of life. They constitute an integral part of human personality. Hence, an understanding of child's emotional development is of utmost importance for both the parents as well as the teachers.

Emotions are said to be the "stirred-up states" of the human organism. They involve varying degrees of feelings, vast viscaral changes such as increased heart beat and increased circulation of blood, and certain impulses such as urge to runaway when afraid of something. But, the feeling aspect of an emotion is its most vital aspect. In fact, feelings define an emotion.

As a child grows his basic emotional reactions are modified in two ways. In the first place the stimuli capable of arousing emotions change and, thus, the emotional responses are controlled. The child learns that some of his childish fears like fear of loud noises and strange objects are groundless. But, now, there are many other things to be afraid of like germs, ghosts, and sin. He anticipates many dangers and develop low-grade chronic emotions. Secondly, child's emotional reactions are controlled by the culture as the cultural demands and traditions do not allow certain emotional expressions while they support and encourage learning of certain emotional responses. The growing child consistently learn from adults and other children how his emotions ought to be expressed. Truly, there are some emotional expressions that are innate and need not be learned such as smiling, laughing, crying, etc., but there are many others which the child develops as he grows. How emotional development occurs sequentially is described in detail in the following pages.

Growing Peace

Spitz (1970) writing about emotional development in infancy said that the first emotion visible at birth is a state of diffuse excitation in the nature of displeasure and no pleasurable emotion is observable as its counterpart. It is only a state of quiescence. A variety of emotions develop from this beginning in the course of the first year of life. It is not clear, however, what emotion the child is trying to express. But, it is seen by most psychologists as child's essentially non-adaptive behaviour. To James (1890) infancy is a period of "great blooming, buzzing confusion". The infant is, generally, described to have no clearly differentiated emotions. The reason given is the inadequacy of physical development required for expressing emotions. It is, generally agreed that at this stage the hypothalamus and cerebral cortex which are involved in the expression of emotions are not sufficiently developed.

Distinguished Sentiments

Spitz (1970) summarizes several years' studies of early emotional development. A more comprehensive investigation is presented by Bridges (1932). He has shown that the first stage in the development of emotions is that of general excitment or agitation. More specific emotions gradually evolve from this state of development. According to him emotions of distress and delight are the first in the sequence to develop about the age of three months. By the age of six months distress is differentiated into fear, disgust and anger. At about 12th month elation and affection develop out of excitement. At 18th month anxiety and jealousy evolve out of anger and distress while affection for adults and affection for children spring out of affection. When the child is two years old he is capable of expressing emotions of fear, disgust, anger, jealousy, distress, excitements, delight, joy, elation, affection for adults and affection for children. Individual differences and variations over the ages have also been noted by Bridges.

Spitz has also described child's progressive development of specific emotions in relation to ages. According to him two distinct emotional responses are differentiated during the first two months of life: These are pleasure and displeasure which appear in reaction to physical stimulation. The emotion of pleasure is visible in the third month when the infant smiles in response to a human partner's face. Displeasure is also manifested in child's reaction to physical and psychological stimulation, particularly when the child is left alone when its human partner goes away. He found that negative emotions such as anxiety differentiated from displeasure also appears after sixth month indicating minimum of ego involvement. In his description jealousy appears in the ninth and tenth month. Between the tenth and twelfth months disappointment, anger, love sympathy, friendliness, joy; and a positive sense of property become observable. Spitz also says that age levels mentioned should not be considered as definite limits. They designate approximate ages at which these emotions appear. Age levels may vary widely both according to individuals and circumstances. Spitz also stated that during the whole of the first year emotional discrimination is manifested approximately two months earlier than any other form of perception. He emphasized that the regularity in the emergence of emotional response depends, largely, on adequate mother-child relationship.

Underplaying Statements

Watson (1929) had theorized that every human being is born with three emotions, namely, love, fear and anger. He thought that these emotions were inherited by people. Inheritance of emotions is not however, a widely accepted, psychological fact. A generally accepted view is that what is inherited are the physical and physiological apparatuses which operate in emotional expressions, not the emotions.

As the child advances in age his physical and mental maturation and the environment affect the expression of his emotions. Two kinds of changes are registered eventually—(1) decrease in overt expression of emotions, and (2) change in emotional sensitivity. Throughout the period of childhood and till adulthood these changes continue for various reasons.

The reasons of decrease in overt expression of emotions are (1) decrease in the intensity of the feeling tone, (ii) changes taking place in the visceral and the central nervous system which are involved in the emotion, (ii) increased learning and enhanced capacity to adjust and adapt to the social reality, (iv) acquisition of other means of expressing feelings, (v) gradual development of self-concepts i.e., "I am a big boy now" consciousness. Considerable differences have, however, been found in emotional expressions of children of various cultural groups, socio-economic levels and age groups.

The growing age is found linked with a change in the stimuli which lead to emotional reactions. Certain situations and factors which earlier evoked emotional reactions are of no significance now; for example, mother's leaving the child at home when he is three years old does not irritate the child while at age-2, perhaps, it would do so violently. Several situations, objects and things which were a cause of fear earlier remain no more at such an advanced age. These changes are, by and large, due to child's increased ability to better understand his relationship with the environment around, the realization of what is desirable and what is undesirable, his growing experience and increased control of feelings and sense of security. Child's developing self-concept and emerging value system may also be responsible for a change in his emotional sensitivity.

Developed Sentiments

Emotional maturity should be the last stage in the emotional development of the child. The study of emotional development is of use only when it helps in moving the child to grow mature gracefully. The teachers must accept this as their bounden duty. If even a grown up child in the school or in the home shows temper tantrums, undue anger, jealousy, anxiety, fear resentment, dependence and despondency, he emotionally is immature and a cause of concern. If it is desired to successfully guide the growth of the child in the area of emotional development it is necessary to fully understand the goals toward which one should strive to. And this, no doubt, is the goal of helping and guiding the child to be emotionally mature.

Emotional maturity is not a quite objectively defined concept. Yet, it is generally agreed that an emotionally mature person as described by Mouly (1967), (i) leads a rich emotional life having developed adequate integration of feelings and emotions with the rest of his behaviour, (ii) instead of repressing and suppressing his emotions is capable of channeling them into constructive directions, (iii) feels secure, (iv) has a realistic understanding of his worth, his strengths, and his limitations, (v) accepts himself, (vi) does not slavishly conform to group standards and does not unduly depend upon others, (vii) is relatively free from anxiety and can devote his energies constructively to the solution of his problems, (viii) has realistic aspirations to fit his abilities (ix) has confidence in himself, (x) has developed a mature sense of humor and a positive outlook on life.

Immature Age

Adolescence is a period of transition from childhood to adulthood. At this stage most of the adolescents begin to show signs of puberty and continue to do so until most of them are mature physically, mentally and emotionally. This period covers roughly the period from about the age of 12 to the early twenties, It is said that adolescence is an age of problems, "a period of great storm, and stress". During this period most of the adolescents achieve emotional maturity. But, there are many who fail to achieve this goal. Many fail to achieve emotional maturity. Many personal, socio-economic, cultural and psychological factors interfere with adequate emotional adjustment and they have to face many kinds of emotional problems.

Characteristics: Adolescence is a face of emotional development which many parents and teachers fear. It is considered a "terrible period". The adolescents are, by and large, emotionally unbalanced, unstable and unpredictable, often unreasonable. For that reason they are generally, regarded, "passing through a difficult phase of growth". As held by Stanley Hall adolescence is a "new birth". According to him consequent upon biological and sexual maturity marked changes take place within the individual during this period with the result that his total personality is radically changed. He described this period as one of "storm and stress" for that reason. According to him the adolescent, at this stage, is "erratic, emotionally unstable and unpredictable."

The above view of adolescence presented by Stanley Hall is not accepted as such by many other psychologists, particularly the anthropologists Margaret Mead and others who said that adolescence is not a period completely different from the rest of life. To them it is one part of a continuous growth process. They explained the "storm and stress" of the adolescence period as an artifact of culture caused by socio-economic factors rather than biological factors. They found that in some cultures like that of the Samoa Island adolescence is a "pleasant age".

Consensus of opinion, however, seems to be that adolescence presents difficult problems of emotional adjustment. Rapid physical changes and mental development, increased experiential growth, sexual maturity, emergence of new attitudes and ideas, vocational consciousness and social orientation which develop in the adolescents at this age necessitate, on the part of them, making of appropriate adjustments to life-situations. In the beginning these adjustments are not easy and, hence, cause stress in the life of the adolescent. A whole array of emotional problems may attend these adjustments. The degree of stress, however, depends on how these adjustments are emphasized in a particular culture. The more important and serious they are considered in a society, the more stressful these become for the adolescents living in that society.

An important characteristic of adolescence is that the individual at this stage experiences a strong feeling of being out of step. He feels that he is no more a child now. At the same time he also feels that he is not granted the status of adulthood. He, thus, finds himself in a "no man's land". This is generally, due to the experiences growing out of the treatment meted out to them by his parents and other members of the society. This state of affairs is central to the adolescent phase of development and is responsible for the storm and stress.

Emotional Problems of Adolescents: An emotional problem is defined as a problem that arouses emotions in the adolescent. It is a situation that makes him angry, bitter, expressed or anxious. It is a situation or condition of life that-upsets the adolescent emotionally. These problems are often accompanied by great passion and anxiety; and if they persist for a long time they are likely to upset the whole balance of adolescent's life. Persisting emotional problems may manifest themselves in the form of headaches, muscular tension, loss of keep, loss of weight, loss of appetite and "run down" state of health. In many cases, the moodiness, nervousness, instability of behaviour, temper-tanttrums, aggressiveness and hostility of adolescents may be traced back to the persisting problem.

The underlying mechanism of adolescents 'emotional problems has two main components: (a) some psychological need pressing for satisfaction, and (b) frustrating environmental situation. The need, gets thwarted and causes an emotional problem. There are several such psychological needs of adolescents which press for satisfaction, namely:-

1. The need for status, social approval and security.
2. The need for independence
3. The need for adventure
4. The need for heterosexual relations

Another source of adolescent's emotional problems includes many conditions which either belong to their body or to the society. There are numerous such conditions which worry the adolescents and make them emotionally restless. Some of these include

1. Adjustment to physical and physiological changes;
2. Adjustment to personal appearance;
3. Adherence to codes and morals;
4. Finding a Job,
5. Threat of being isolated

QUESTIONS

1. What is diffuse excitement ?
2. What is differentiation of emotion ?
3. Discuss various aspects of emotional maturity.

22

Environment as Force

The world, it seems,, is steadily drifting towards its doom by rapidly exhausting its natural resources. speaking on 'Sustainable Development of Natural Resources' at the 76th Science Congress, the well-known Indian scientist Dr. Swaminathan said, "Nature's patience is not inexhaustible and we have tested it too much already. Unless political leaders, professionals and the public worked in concert as members of a symphony orchestra, sustainable development would remain an elusive goal."

Decreasing Strength

The following statement pertaining to consumption of natural resources was included in the questionnaire for general public.

"The present generation is excessively consuming natural resources such as minerals, oils, forests, etc., which is unfair to future generation." (G-7)

Limitless Consumption

Natural resources include soil, water, air, energy, forests, flora and fauna, living aquatic resources and minerals, etc. Some of these resources such as solar energy and ocean energy are inexhaustible; forests are renewable whereas fossils and mineral resources are non-renewable.

These resources get depleted in the following ways:

Normal Utilisation: Natural resources are consumed by human beings to meet life's needs. Increasing population in the country is adding to the existing heavy load on our resources. In order to conserve resources, it would be necessary for all sections of society to control population. Government has implemented Family Planning programme to arrest the trend of fast increasing population, yet the problem of over-population stays and the burden on our resources continues.

Excessive Utilisation: The present generation seems to be over utilising the natural resources. Commercials and advertisements prompt modern man to consume more and more. Man seems to be living for this moment only, as if secretly realising that tomorrow he might die. Gandhiji said, "Earth has enough for every man's need, but not for every man's greed".

Importing material from abroad is also not a workable proposition to make up for the shortage of resources. Take the example of crude oil. According to a report, India imported 22 million tonnes of crude oil in 1987-88, which was 2296 more than the import of 1986-87. The import of crude oil touched 24 million tonnes in 1988-89 i.e., it was up by another 9 per cent in the subsequent year. Thanks to the fall in the prices of oil in 1988-89, that the burden on the country's exchequer did not increase; but even then for a country like India, with serious economic and foreign exchange limitations to pay foreign exchange to the tune of Rs. 4000 crores a year for import of crude oil is not something which should be viewed lightly. And this expenditure has been looking upwards since then. The solution, therefore, lies in exercising a strong check on consumerism.

Unscientific Utilisation: Sometimes, resources are wasted when these are not used scientifically or are. not recycled, wherever this is possible.

Pollution: Resources are wasted due to pollution also. Whereas industrialisation and mechanisation have contributed to economic prosperity, they are greatly responsible for water, air, noise, chemical and biological pollution as well as accumulation of hazardous industrial waste.

Water Pollution: Water-pollution is mainly being caused by industrial and sewage waste flowing into the rivers and the lakes. Several rivers in the country have got pollution and acquatic life-forms subsisting on these waters are in danger of getting annihilated. The dumping of nuclear waste into the oceans also poses similar dangers as well as of mutilating the species living in the oceans.

Air Pollution: Automobiles are among the biggest culprits in polluting our physical environment. It is estimated that in the cosmopolitan cities of India, the atmospheric pollution is due to gases emitted by unburnt fuel of the automobiles. The unburnt fuel emits hydro-carbons, oxides of nitrogen, carbon monoxide and carbondioxide.

Carbonmonoxide, which is colourless and odourless, is lethal when present in the air in the ratio of 4:100. Moreover haemoglobin in the blood has 240 times more affinity for absorbing carbonmonoxide as compared to absorbing oxygen. In other words, distribution of this gas in the atmosphere is like administering the people a form of slow poison.

Hydro carbons, oxides of nitrogen give rise to respiratory problems, irritation in the eyes and several other health problems. The content of these gases and subsequent hazards to our health increase manifold if automobiles emit more unburnt petrol or deisel.

In spite of these dangers, the number of automobiles is annually rising by millions in the country. If mankind is to be saved from this pollution, number of automobiles will have to be restricted by making public transport more efficient and devising other suitable measures.

Depletion of ozone-level in the atmosphere has been going on due to emission of chlorofluorocarbons (CFCs) by increasing the use of refrigerators, air-conditioners and aerosol sprays. Advanced countries of the world are more responsible for it than the developing nations. For example, America uses nearly 30 per cent of world's CFCs as against India and China which together are using about 2 per cent of CFCs.

There is also evidence that in the Arctic Region, which had been pollution free, ozone-destroying form of chlorine is hanging all over now. In the Antarctic, ozone, loss has already occurred due to man-made chlorofluorocarbons. With the loss of the ozonelayer, the ultra-violet rays of the sun would reach the earth causing skin diseases and cancer, etc.

Chemical and Biological Pollution: Use of chemical fertilizers and pesticides effects mankind in two ways. Firstly, the surface of croplands is damaged and secondly pesticides sometimes find their way into the human system. Researches have shown presence of DDT in hen eggs. Not long ago, India imported sizeable quantity of chlorodane, a highly toxic substance, from the United States. The USA banned its use in their country because it was found to cause cancer in animals but India continued to import this pesticide.

Another bizarre import was of harmful coal power plants (on hefty price) from Saarland in West Germany where these plants had been shut down, and virtually become a scrap, following protests by environmentalists and medical experts.

Burning of chemicals and suffocating materials release toxic substances (which effect blood), virus and bacteria etc.

Noise Pollution: Increasing transport and expanding industries, lead to noise pollution. Noise pollution is reported to cause many physical and psychological ailments such as headache, fatigue, hypertension, sleeplessness, deafness, and other disorders. According to WHO, 45 declibels is the safe noise limit. 'Noise' is nearly on top of the agenda in all regular meetings of the WHO. It has been estimated that the three cosmopolitan cities of India have over 90db on non festival days and much more than this on the festival days. It is said that it takes 20-50 hours of quietitude to combat the 'ill effect' of the noise caused by four hours of a rock concert. Round the clock radio and television programmes and addiction to pop and hi-fi loud music are adding further to noise pollution. This is why some commercial firms, in highly industrialised countries, have silence-rooms where the workers can retire and unwind themselves by being away from the noisy atmosphere.

Industrial Waste: This is yet another source of enviornmental pollution. The highly industrialised Western nations which have fully benefitted from the fruits of industry are now worried about the disposal of the industrial waste. These (wealthy) nations have signed contracts with ten African countries—Congo, Equatorial Guinea, Gabon, Guinea Bassau, Nigeria, Senegal, Sierra Leone, Guinea and Benin—where industrial waste would be dumped. Obviously, it is a case of rich nations criminally exploiting the poor.

There may be some divergence of views in regard to the causes of excessive dilapidation of the natural resources but there can be hardly any difference on the point that the country needs to utilise its limited natural resources wisely, otherwise the consequences would be far too serious. Industrial man has to fall in line with the environmental imperatives and redefine his strategies of progress (economic), production (of consumer goods), population (growth) and pollution (by industrial waste and otherwise).

"Lack of regard for environmental factors helped destroy the great civilisations of the Middle East, in the Tigris and Euphrates valleys, and in Jordan. Their demise is history. To the deforestation and over-grazing of the past, man today has added air pollutants at levels which inhibit photosynthesis, he has introduced oxygen using chemical agents into lakes, streams and aquifers; he has released insecticides, herbicides, end radioactions, and he has covered millions of acres of garbage, spoil and mining gangue."

Striking a note of optimism, Dr. Whitfield wrote, "We are an ingenious and adaptable species and we have the power to destroy life on our planet, we have perhaps the wisdom to save it. We are engineering the planet, whether we like it or not, so we had better do it well, controlling our own growth, limiting our greed and getting back to ways of life that can be sustained indefinitely."

Method of Instruction

Environmental education would include education from, about and for environmental sustainability. Broadly speaking, India has three ecosystems-The Himalayan Ranges, the Indo-Gangetic Plains and the Tropical Rain Forests. The content of environmental education would include some general elements for all students and some specific aspects pertaining to these three systems. Regarding general elements of environmental education, students can be educated on following lines:

Nature is a great inspirer of art and literature. The sensitive mind of Wordsworth could observe 'tongues in trees and books in running brooks'. Writers, thinkers, philosophers, saints, time and again, take refuge under nature's canopy and come out physically, intellectually and spiritually enriched. Some scholars hold that the Aryans compiled their Vedic literature in the natural environments near river Saraswati, that is why they named the goddess of learning after the name of this river. Such great is the contribution of nature to our civilisation and culture.

Learning about environment means understanding about the meaning and importance of ecological balance, role that nature plays in sustaining life, richness and diversity of replenishable and non replenishable natural resources, and so on.

Learning for environment aims at developing love and respect for things of nature—living and non-living—and protecting them from damage and pollution. It was not without meaning that trees and animals were worshipped in ancient India. Elements of nature were looked upon as gods. Thus, concern for environment is nothing new. Of course, in recent times this concern has become multi-dimensional because our problems have become more complex. Our forefathers did not pollute the Ganges and other rivers and they held them sacred; today we clean them in the name of having a pollution-free environment.

Malaysia has developed a syllabus on environment which is worked out around the following six themes. The scope and depth of these themes increases in the educational curricula from year to year.

(i) Child and his surroundings.

(ii) Interaction among man i.e., human relations.

(iii) Interaction of man with his environment.

(iv) Interaction of elements in our environments

(v) Issues related to man

(vi) Issues related to environment.

The National Council of Educational Research and Training, New Delhi, has also worked out a syllabus for environmental education.

Global Wisdom

For sometime now there has been world-wide awakening in regard to the environmental issues. The United Nations Organisation convened a conference on environment at Stockholm in 1972. It focussed attention on the dangers to human life posed by continuous degradation of the eco-system. It was followed by the Belgrade Charter of 1975; Inter-governmental meet at Tbilisi in 1977, and International Conference on Environmental Education in New Delhi.

The Globala Perium held a five-day conference in Moscow in January, 1990 to focus the attention of delegates from all over the world on 'Environment and Development for Survival'. The conference was inaugurated by the U.N. Secretary General and concluded with an address by the President of the USSR. The 1972 Stockholm Conference recommended that the Secretary General of the organisations of the United Nations System especially UNESCO should "take necessary steps to establish an international programme in environmental education (IEEP), interdisciplinary in approach, in school and out of school, encompassing all levels of education and directed towards the general public, in particular the ordinary citizen living in rural and urban areas, youths and adults alike, with a view to educating him as to the simple steps he might take, within his means, to manage and control his environment"

The Indian Parliament passed the Constitution (Forty-Second Amendment) Act, 1976 for safeguarding the environment. This legislation, which became a part of the Directive Principles of State Policy, is as follows:

Article 48A : "The state shall endeavour to protect and improve the environment and to safeguard the forests and wild life of the country".

In recent times, many countries are trying to assume world leadership in holding conferences on protection of environment. In March 1989, the Prime Ministers of France and Netherlands called a meeting of 24 countries in Hague to discuss environmental problems. America kept away from this meeting. The British Prime Minister, Ms Margaret Thatcher, convened on her own a meeting of 123 nations on measures to protect the ozone layer of the earth. This inspired America to convene another meeting to debate global environmental issues.

All nations are, today, worried over the increasing greenhouse effect such as of carbon-dioxide etc. on the environment. As a result of greenhouse gases (GHGs), the universe is experiencing changes in temperature and getting warmer, rainfall pattern is changing and sealevels are rising. Consequent to rise in sea-level, the islands of Maldives and parts of India and Bangladesh are threatened by getting submerged under water. Therefore, the world has to search for new models of development rather than following the old models. Preservation of resources and saving the atmosphere from pollution should be treated as a matter of highest concern rather than a sphere of diplomacy or a hunting-ground for leadership. The world community must choose between balanced economic growth and annihilation; between international rivalaries and cooperation; between carefully preserving the resources or wrecklessly exhausting them.

India's call at the summit meet of the Non Aligned Movement in Belgrade on September 5, 1989 had a great wisdom in it. The Indian Prime Minister sited raising of an 18 billion dollar international 'Planet Protection Fund' for saving the globe from further environmental degradation. India had proposed at the conference that each country developed or developing—should contribute 0.1 per cent of its GDP for this purpose. This fund, which should be monitored under the UN auspices,, could be used for reforestation, stemming of floods, population control, checking ozone depletion and the greenhouse effects and many other programmes which could save resources on the globe from pollution and extinction.

Though the Vanmahotsav, the Chipko Movement and the opposition generated against the Narmada Project (in Gujarat) are generating an awakening in India on environmental issues, yet a holistic and energetic approach for conservation of natural resources, compatible with the gravity of the problem, is yet to emerge. Public mind needs to be made more alive to the dangers posed by denuding of forests, pollution of water and other resources, especially the non-renewable resources. In the Union of Soviet Socialist Republic, near the city of Bratask, there is a forest where timber is estimated to last for 100 years. As and when the trees are cut in this forest, new trees are plated. By the time the existing trees are utilised, new trees would have grown in their place, as such this forest would last for ever.

If the voice of reason is not heeded to and adequate steps are not taken in time to protect natural environments, Asia would suffer for the sins of Europe, Africa for the sins of Australia, Arctic and Antartica for the sins of the United States of America and vice-versa. Lord Buddha had said, "Many a time, it is not our own sins but the sins of the others which envelop and destroy our inner repose and outer surroundings". Therefore, a coordinated and an integrated approach is called for on environmental issues by the world—community. To borrow the words of Dr. Karan Singh, Indian prince, politician and a scholar, "it is left to us if we would convert this beautiful planet into a burnt finder or will cherish her as a cradle for higher consciousness. Mankind would do well to remember the following note of wisdom and caution which he sounded at the Global forum. "We live in a shrinking world in which old traditions of conflict and competition will have to make way for the new culture of convergence and cooperation if the rich promise of the next millennium is not to evaporate in a thermonuclear inferno."

Bibliography

Addaval, S.B., *The Third India Year Book of Education Educational Research*, NCERT, New Delhi, 1968.

Buch, M.B., *A Survey of Research in Education*, Centre of Advanced Study in Education, M.S. University of Baroda, Baroda, 1974.

Citizens for Democracy, *Education, for Our People : A Policy Frame for the Development of Education* (1978-87), Allied Publishers, Bombay, 1978.

Denis, Lawton, *Education and Social Justice, Sage Publications*, London, 1977.

Don, Adams, *Education and Modernisation in Asia*, Addison Wesley Publishing Company, London, 1970.

Ehsanul, Haq, *Education and Political Culture in India*, Sterling Publishers, New Delhi, 1981.

Gandhi, M.K., *My Views on Education*, Bharatiya Vidya Bhavan, Bombay, 1970.

Ganguly, S.N., *Tradition, Modernity and Development: A Study in Contemporary Indian Society*, MacMillan Company of India, Delhi, 1977.

Ghosh, S.C., *Educational Strategies in Developing Countries*, Sterling Publishers, New Delhi, 1976.

Haragopal, G., *Administrative Leadership and Rural Development in India*, Light & Life Publishers, New Delhi, 1980.

John, W., Hanson and Cole S. Brem Beck, *Education and the Development of Nations*, Holt, Rinehart and Winston, New York, 1966.

Louis, Malassis, *The Rural World : Education and Development*, Croom Helm, London, 1976.

Mukherjee, R.K., *The Social Structure of Values*, S. Chand & Company, New Delhi, 1964.

Niblett, W.R., *Essential Education*, University of London, London,1955.

Rajagopal, M.V., *Kothari Commission on School Education: A Recapitulation and Review*, Telugu Vidyardhi Prachuranalu, Machilipatnam, 1967.

Saini, S.K., *Development of Education in India : Socio-Economic and Political Perspective*, Cosmo Publications, New Delhi, 1980.

Shrimali, K.L., *A Search for Values in Indian Education*, Vikas Publishers, Delhi, 1974.

Shukla, P.D., *Towards the New Pattern of Education in India*, Sterling Publishers, New Delhi, 1976.

Thorndike, R.L. and Hagen E., *Measurement and Evaluation in Psychology and Education*, Wiley Eastern Pvt. Ltd., New Delhi, 1969.